ACKNOWLEDGMENTS

The author would like to thank Lesly Atlas, Jennifer Arias, Kristen Azzara, Allegra Burton, Maria Dente, Leanne Coupe, Claire Alpern, Clayton Dean, Alfred Pagano, Tim Dougherty, Tommy Furuhata, David Kelley, Jacqueline Jendras, Stephanie Martin, Robert McCormack, George Miller, Matthew Reilly, Evan Schnittman, Jeff Soloway, Alex Weiner, Chris Warnasch, Tim Wheeler, and Iam Williams.

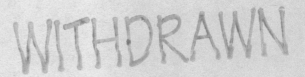

CONTENTS

PART I

Orientation

What Is the TOEIC?

The Test of English for International Communication (TOEIC) is a standardized test administered by a division (Chauncey Group International) of the Educational Testing Service (ETS), a huge, tax-exempt private company located in New Jersey. ETS is the same testing organization that administers the GRE, SAT, LSAT, and a bunch of tests in other fields, including hair styling, plumbing, and golf. The TOEIC is supposedly designed to test a non-native English speaker's proficiency in English. However, it really tests how well you take a multiple-choice exam. In any case, all the expressions, idioms, and grammar tested on the TOEIC are those most common in America, *not* in England or other English-speaking countries.

What Does the TOEIC Measure?

It is unclear exactly what the Test of English for International Communication measures. Clearly, a person fluent in English will perform better on the test than would a person only somewhat familiar with the language. However, how well you speak English is not the only factor that determines your TOEIC score. Some people get very nervous when taking a test and don't get the score they deserve. Others always do well on tests even when they don't study. Standardized tests aren't the most reliable measure of proficiency in *any* subject. So what is *really* tested by the TOEIC? Well, one might say, the TOEIC measures your performance on the TOEIC.

This book will help improve your TOEIC score by showing you how to look for shortcuts, avoid common mistakes, and practice taking the test. These skills are just as important to your TOEIC score as studying English is.

Who Takes the TOEIC and How Is It Different from TOEFL?

The TOEIC tests English used in everyday work life and in the workplace. People who might take the TOEIC include employees who use English in their daily work or who might need to take job-related courses or training classes in English, or people who want to have an internationally recognized measure of their English proficiency.

The TOEIC and TOEFL tests were developed to test different things. TOEIC tests English used in the workplace; TOEFL tests English used in academic situations. Students interested in pursuing graduate or undergraduate education in North America would take the TOEFL; employees wishing to prove their English proficiency or employers wishing to test the English proficiency of their employees would use the TOEIC.

What Does the TOEIC Test?

The TOEIC tests the kind of English used in everyday activities related to the workplace and the work world, such as corporate development, dining out, entertainment, finance and budgeting, general business, health, housing or corporate property, manufacturing, offices, personnel, purchasing, technical areas, and travel.

It does not test English used in academic situations, nor does it test factual information such as historical events. There are no math questions on the TOEIC.

How Important Is the TOEIC?

The importance of the TOEIC differs widely from employer to employer. Some employers use the TOEIC in hiring, either as a process of weighting candidates or as a cut-off score. Other companies use TOEIC scores to determine advancement within the company. Still others use TOEIC scores to help determine job placement (employees with higher scores are put in positions that require more English).

If you do not currently have a job, you may take the TOEIC in an "open administration." Your TOEIC score can be a wonderful addition to your resume, as it will demonstrate to your prospective employer that you can speak English to a degree. If your score is not as high as you'd like it to be, however, you may want to refrain from putting it on your resume until you've worked through this book and taken the TOEIC again with an improved score.

How Is the TOEIC Structured?

The TOEIC is a two-hour-long, multiple-choice test. There are two parts of the TOEIC, the Listening Comprehension section and the Reading section.

The Listening Comprehension section consists of 100 questions organized in four parts that lasts 45 minutes. There are four question types on the Listening Comprehension section:

- **Part I: 20 photograph questions.** You will see a photograph and be asked to choose the answer choice that describes what is happening in the photo. The answer choices will be read to you; they will *not* be printed in the test booklet.

- **Part II: 30 question-and-response questions.** You will hear a question and be asked to pick the correct response to the question. The question and answer choices will both be read but they will not be printed in the test booklet.

- **Part III: 30 short conversation questions.** You will hear a short conversation between two speakers. A question about the conversation and the answer choices will be printed in the test booklet.

- **Part IV: 20 short talk questions.** You will hear a short talk by one speaker. A question about the talk and the answer choices will be printed in the test booklet. There will be two to four questions about each talk.

The Reading section consists of 100 questions organized in three parts that lasts 75 minutes. There are three question types on the Reading section:

- **Part V: 40 incomplete sentence questions.** You will read a sentence with a missing word and four answer choices. You must pick the word that best fits the sentence.

- **Part VI: 20 error identification questions.** You will read a sentence with four underlined words or phrases. One of the words will be grammatically incorrect. You must find it.

- **Part VII: 40 reading comprehension questions.** You will read a passage (which can be any printed document, such as a fax, newspaper article, or memo). There will be a question about the passage with four answer choices. There will be two to five questions about each passage.

As you can see, the Listening Comprehension section moves much more quickly than the Reading section does. Since you will have to listen to spoken parts from a tape or CD on the Listening Comprehension section, you must keep up with the recording. On the Reading section, you may work at your own pace. There is no break between the sections of the test.

How Is the TOEIC Scored?

The TOEIC is scored by counting the number of correct answers marked on the answer sheet. ETS has a formula that converts the number of correct answers on each of the two main sections to a number on a scale of 5 to 495. The converted scores from the two sections are added together to get a final score of 10 to 990.

When Do I Get My Scores?

Your scores will be sent to your address several weeks after you take the test. ETS makes it clear that they will not be available any earlier. You will receive a score sheet which tells you how you scored on each of the two main sections of the test. You will also receive a certificate with your total score. Although your scores are confidential, ETS has the right to use them anonymously for any research or project it might concoct.

Where Do I Take the TOEIC?

You will probably take the TOEIC at your place of employment or your language school. If you are not employed or wish to take the TOEIC for your own reasons, you may take the test at an open administration. Many countries offer open administrations. To see if there are open administrations in your country, consult the official TOEIC website at www.toeic.com.

How Do I Register for the TOEIC Exam?

Your employer may provide you with all the paperwork you need to register for the TOEIC, especially if the test is to be administered at your place of business. If this is not the case, you will need to contact the TOEIC representative for your country. A list of the official TOEIC representatives can be found at the TOEIC website at www.toeic.com.

What Is The Princeton Review?

The Princeton Review is a test-preparation company based in New York City. We have branches in more than fifty cities across the United States and the world. We've developed the techniques found in our books and courses by analyzing actual exams and testing their effectiveness with our students. We don't want to waste your time with a lot of unnecessary information. It would be foolish for us to try to teach you every rule of English grammar or every subtlety of spoken English. Those things aren't what will raise your score.

What we will teach you is how to approach the test. Once you learn to think like the people who write the test, you'll learn what sorts of questions come up most often and what a right answer looks like. You'll learn to use your time effectively, avoid problems along the way, and find answers to questions you may be unsure of.

You need to do only two things: Trust the techniques, and *practice*.

1

The Basics

WHY PRACTICE FOR THE TOEIC?

ETS will tell you that it is not possible to learn English in a short period of time. While this is true, what you *can* learn in a short period of time is how to take an exam.

Would you rather take the test in *this* situation:

You walk into work tomorrow morning to discover that the test is being given in an hour. You rush to the testing room, unprepared, upset, and out of sorts. You arrive at the testing room nervous and unsure of what to expect. You begin the test, misread the instructions, and make time-consuming mistakes. Unfamiliar with the TOEIC, you make more silly mistakes, which continue to lower your score.

Or this one?

After preparing for the test, you arrive at the testing room on time, confident, and relaxed. You know what to bring with you. You know how long the test will take. There are no surprises. You don't waste your time or your brainpower trying to familiarize yourself with the TOEIC. You are completely used to all question types and are not intimidated by the changes ETS has made. Your score reflects your confidence.

There is no reason to panic over the TOEIC. Nothing can alleviate your stress more than knowing what to expect. Don't let your score be affected by the unknown! Prepare and get ready to improve your score.

How to Improve Your English

What this book sets out to do is to train you for the TOEIC in the most efficient way. There is not a lot of memorizing, but as with any study aid, it is best to allot a few hours of study time each day for a few weeks before the test. You'll want time to find your strengths and weaknesses. You'll want to practice the techniques and do the drills a little at a time. Do not try to finish everything in a weekend!

In addition to the information in the book, here are a couple of general pointers to help you become as familiar as possible with spoken and written English:

- **SPEAK!** Don't be intimidated by English. Try to converse with native English speakers as much as possible. If you have a friend or coworker who is an English speaker, practice with that person. Have conversations on the telephone. Learn the idiomatic expressions, feel the rhythm of the language, and get to know how Americans express themselves. Nothing can improve your English more than speaking with real people in real situations. The most important thing you can do is *speak, speak, speak!* Got it?

- **LISTEN!** Turn on the radio and television. This is a fun way to improve listening comprehension! Try to understand what is being implied in a conversation or discussion. Talk shows can be great sources of conversation, and news programs can aid your business vocabulary.

- **READ!** Buy newspapers and magazines. Get used to skimming articles to find the main ideas. Pay attention to captions under pictures. You never have to read any long passages on the TOEIC, so look for short paragraphs that are informational or conversational, and pay special attention to the business sections and advertisements.

- **BE POSITIVE!** Set reasonable goals and stick to them. Your English *will* improve if you believe it will. Eliminate your fear.

These are some of the most interesting and natural ways to practice. Make it your goal for the next few weeks to spend as much time as possible *speaking*, *listening to*, and *reading* English.

CAN I REALLY IMPROVE MY SCORE?

Yes! Yes! Yes! ETS always says that no one teaching method can help prepare someone for the TOEIC. Remember, although native speakers will do better on the TOEIC than will non-native speakers, the more familiar you are with a standardized test, the easier it will be to raise your score. Everyone can learn how to take a standardized test. The first step in doing better on the TOEIC is realizing this.

Trained Princeton Review staff, who have carefully researched and analyzed all available TOEIC material, developed these strategies and teaching methods for use on the TOEIC. Our focus is on the basic concepts that will enable you to attack the TOEIC problems, strip them down, and solve them as quickly as possible. The sooner you accept the fact that the TOEIC is not a regular test, but a standardized test with standardized "logic," the more your score will improve.

2

How to Use
This Book

THE BASICS

What do we mean, "How to use this book"? Shouldn't you just read it? Not exactly. You see, you will definitely learn just by reading through the book, but we want you to increase your score on the TOEIC. A lot. And the only way you'll really do that is by having a plan of attack for using this book to study for the test.

It may feel like a lot of extra work to you, but it's the only way to completely understand how you're doing and how to do better. It will all be worth it once you have that TOEIC certificate with the score of your dreams on it, we promise.

So now let's discuss the steps to using this book.

Read through the test-taking techniques.

The next chapter in this book is vital to your success on the TOEIC. It's called "Test-Taking Techniques," and it covers all the things you need to know to manage your time and the questions well. Read it through at least once before you move on to the specific information about the questions. Refer back to it often. When you start working the drills, you'll need to remember everything you read in this chapter so you can practice it. And practice it, again and again, until it becomes second nature.

Read each chapter, do the drills, and review.

After you've read the Test-Taking Techniques chapter and the Conversational English chapter, read the chapter on photographs questions. Make sure you understand everything you read; if you don't, go back and read the chapter again. Then do the drill. The audio portion of the photographs section and other Listening Comprehension sections is on the CDs in the back of the book. When you've done the drill, use the explanations to go over every question. Try to understand why you answered questions correctly, and why you answered them incorrectly. This step is tedious, but it's the best way to assess your performance and learn from your own work.

Once you've reviewed your work on the drill, go on to the next chapter. Do *not* read through all the chapters and then do all the drills. This is a recipe for disaster because you won't be able to examine your performance closely. Instead, read a chapter, do the drill, examine your work, and only then move on to the next chapter.

Take Practice Test 1.

Once you've finished all the chapters and their drills, take Practice Test 1. Take it as if you were in the real testing situation. Remove all distractions, like the telephone and television, and ask any friends or family not to interrupt you. Sit down at a desk or clear space in a quiet place. Put the corresponding CD in your CD player or headset and do not press PAUSE or STOP while you are taking the test. After you finish the Listening Comprehension section, do *not* take a break; instead, move directly on to the Reading section. Set a timer, alarm clock, or your watch alarm for 75 minutes and do not take any extra time. When you are done, get yourself a glass of water and relax for awhile before you score your test.

Review your performance.

Use the scoring guide at the end of the book to score your test. Now you've got your score, but your studying isn't done yet. Look at the questions you got right and wrong, and use the explanations to review exactly why you got them correct or incorrect. Make sure you understand why the correct answers are correct so that you can get similar questions right on future tests.

Also think about the other aspects of the test besides your score. Did you run out of time? Did you have time left over? Should you work faster or slower in certain sections? Did you find yourself getting nervous? Are there words you didn't know that you need to look up? Were you able to understand the speakers on the recording? Did you have enough time between the recorded conversations to read and answer the questions?

Once you answer these questions, you'll know what you need to practice. Go back and read over those chapters. Give yourself at least a day or two to think about how you can improve your test performance. Then, when you feel confident that you've adjusted your test-taking techniques, go on to Practice Test 2.

Take Practice Test 2.

Take Practice Test 2 in the same way you did Practice Test 1—as if it were the real test. And now that you've targeted your weaknesses, you have this chance to correct them.

Review your performance.

This is your last chance to evaluate the test and your performance before you take the real TOEIC. Make it count by being as picky as possible with yourself. Make sure you understand all the grammar rules and why you missed any questions you may have missed. Go back and read the transcripts of the recorded conversations so that you know what you heard.

Once you've assessed your performance on Practice Test 2, make your plan for the real TOEIC. Write down the things you want to remember, from grammar rules to the amount of time you want to spend on each error identification question. Keep reviewing your plan so that it will be easy to follow when you take the real TOEIC.

3

Test-Taking Techniques

BASICS

While it is extremely important to be prepared for the TOEIC by practicing your listening and reading skills in English, it is also vital to practice and use the test-taking techniques in this chapter. These techniques should help you manage your time and answer the questions correctly and efficiently. They should also save you stress and worry over individual questions.

This chapter contains techniques for taking the TOEIC in general, as well as techniques specific to the Listening Comprehension and Reading sections.

GENERAL TECHNIQUES

POE (PROCESS OF ELIMINATION)

Answer the following question:

What is the capital city of Madagascar?

Do you know the answer? If you don't, are there any clues in the question that can help you? Not really. Let's try the same question again.

What is the capital city of Madagascar?
(A) Paris
(B) Antananarivo
(C) Tokyo
(D) Mexico City

Now that we are given multiple-choice answers to choose from, this question is much easier. Why? Because you know that Paris is the capital of France, not Madagascar, that Tokyo is the capital of Japan, not Madagascar, and that Mexico City is the capital of Mexico, not Madagascar. Once you've eliminated those three answer choices, the only choice left, Antananarivo, must be the correct response to the question.

We've just used the Process of Elimination (POE) to answer a question. It works on the premise that, in multiple-choice questions and certain other types of questions where possible answers are provided, it's easier to find the wrong answers than it is to find the right one.

Perhaps the best thing about ETS's standardized TOEIC is that the correct answer is always in front of you. You never have to fill in a blank, or come up with the answer on your own. And because there are usually three times as many wrong answers as there are right answers, it's often easier to eliminate the wrong answers than to pick the correct one. By identifying and eliminating the incorrect answers, it is easier to find the correct answer.

Wrong answers

We like to call the incorrect answer choices "distractors." The definition of *distract* is to draw attention away from one object and focus it on another. This is exactly ETS's goal: *to draw your attention away from the correct answer and focus it on a wrong one.* This ETS strategy keeps you from earning points accidentally. Once you are able to recognize ETS's distractors, your score will improve greatly.

Improve your odds

Every time you are able to eliminate an incorrect choice on the TOEIC, you improve your chances of selecting the best answer. The more you use POE, the better your odds. Think about it. In a multiple-choice question with four possible answers, if you guess on any question, you have a one-in-four chance of getting the best answer. When you eliminate just one choice, you are down to one-in-three. Eliminate just two answers and you have a fifty-fifty chance of guessing the best answer. If you don't know the answer, you'll have to guess, so guess intelligently. This indirect way of finding the correct answer helps you avoid the traps that ETS wants you to fall in. POE is a powerful testing tool!

In the Reading section, you can skip around and answer the questions in any order you want. However, you must answer every question by the end of the Reading section. It is very important to know that you are not penalized for guessing. So use POE and make your best guess.

DON'T LEAVE BLANKS

The test is scored so that you receive one point for a correct answer and no points for either an incorrect answer or a blank. This means that there's no penalty for guessing and getting an answer wrong.

Don't leave any blanks!

Since there's no penalty for getting an answer wrong, you should fill in an answer for every single question on the TOEIC, even if you run out of time. Keep an eye on the clock, and when you have two minutes left, go through your answer sheet and fill in a bubble for any questions you skipped or didn't get to.

Of course, it's better for you if you have the time to eliminate one or two answer choices before you guess, but even if you can't do this, it is still to your advantage to guess. And when you guess, you should pick one letter, your "guessing letter," and fill in that letter for all the guesses you make on the TOEIC. It doesn't matter which letter it is, as long as you stick to the same one for all your blind guesses.

Think of it this way: You are trying to shoot a water pistol at your younger brother. If you keep moving the water pistol, and he keeps dodging the water, chances are that you may never hit him. On the other hand, if you keep the water pistol steady and your brother keeps moving, he will eventually run in front of the pistol and he'll get wet.

The TOEIC is the same way. There is a relatively even distribution of correct answer choices, so that there are approximately the same number of (A) answers, (B) answers, (C) answers, and (D) answers. This means that if you guess four times and guess the same letter all four times, statistically speaking you should get one answer right. If you pick different letters for each of your guesses, you may never hit a correct guess. Remember though, only use your letter on questions where you're guessing blindly. If you can eliminate even one of the answer choices, you should be able to make an "educated" guess.

Before you turn in your answer sheet at the end of the TOEIC, make sure you've filled in an answer for every question (and that you haven't filled in more than one answer for any question!).

LISTENING COMPREHENSION TECHNIQUES

The following techniques apply only to the Listening Comprehension section. This section is generally harder than the Reading section is, so it is doubly important to use the techniques.

Pay Attention to Photos

On some standardized tests, the photos are irrelevant to the question being asked, or, even worse, deliberately distracting. This is not the case on the TOEIC. In questions containing photographs, the photos are the keys to answering the question correctly. You should study them carefully. You should get in the habit of looking at a photograph and summarizing what is happening in the photo. For instance, if you see a photo of a woman and a man at a table containing full wine glasses and plates of food, you can assess that the people are sharing a meal (probably dinner). This may be a personal dinner or a business dinner. What are the people in the photo wearing? Where are they? These details will give you clues to what's going on in the photo.

On the other hand, you don't want to read too much into a photo. In the example in the previous paragraph, it is reasonable to assume that they are at dinner, but it is not reasonable to assume that they are necessarily a romantic couple. They could be coworkers or business partners of some sort at a meeting.

Practice assessing photographs without jumping to unwarranted conclusions, and you will improve your speed on photograph questions.

Small details may be the point

Bear in mind that the correct answer choice may be one which asks about small details in the photo that don't seem significant at first glance. For instance, the correct answer choice to the dinner photo may say something like this.

There are wine glasses on the table.

When you hear this statement, you may be tempted to eliminate it because it is so obvious and so unimportant. But remember that the goal of the photograph questions is to choose the answer choice that accurately describes the photo. You must choose the statement that reflects the reality of the photo, not your interpretation of it.

Read the Questions Ahead of Time

On the short conversation and short talk questions, it is vital that you read the question before you hear the recording. This may be tricky because of the timing of the section. The test is designed so that the recording plays the conversation, then pauses for five to eight seconds so that you can read the question, find the answer, and fill in your answer.

Instead, you should use the five to eight seconds to read the question and the answer choices, then listen to the conversation and quickly fill in the answer. It won't take you long to find the answer, because you read the question before you heard the conversation. While you were listening to the conversation, you knew exactly what information you were listening for, and once you heard it, you could choose the correct answer.

This means that you'll have to rush on the first question so that you can use the pause after the first question to read the question and answers for the second question. Then you'll be on the right schedule with time to read all the other questions before the recording plays. It's possible you may pick the wrong answer on the first question since you're rushing through it. But since you will get more questions right by reading the question first, getting the first question in the section wrong may be a sacrifice worth making in order to get a higher score overall.

Practice reading the question and answers first when you take the practice tests in this book. Then you will be completely comfortable with this technique when you take the actual TOEIC.

Be aware that the short talks (the last part of the Listening Comprehension section) are followed by two to four questions. This means that you'll have to read a few questions ahead before the recording plays. You may feel a little uneasy about this, but practice it, get used to it, and you'll find it much easier to answer questions correctly.

Practice Listening to American English

This last technique is fairly obvious, but it bears repeating. Practice listening to American English whenever possible. Although the TOEIC claims to be a test of all forms of English, the fact is that the test is made in the United States and the speakers on the recording are American. They all have standard American accents, which means they speak the way the reporters on the national television news speak. This is wonderful news, because it means that you only have to concentrate on understanding one American accent.

A great way to practice listening to the standard American accent is to listen to radio broadcasts over the Internet. This is wonderful because you can listen to them from any computer with Internet access anywhere in the world. Also, you can listen to a story as many times as you need to, and some sites have written transcripts of the stories so you can read along as you listen. While there are hundreds of websites for local American stations, the website www.npr.org is the website of National Public Radio. They have reports on all sorts of topics, so this is the mother lode of radio reports.

READING TECHNIQUES

The following techniques apply only to the Reading section. This section is generally easier than the Listening Comprehension section, but that doesn't mean that you can let down your guard. Use these techniques to increase your efficiency and help you relax on the second half of the TOEIC.

Be Methodical

It is too easy to get overconfident about your English speaking and reading ability and to approach the Reading section of the TOEIC the wrong way. Many people attempt to choose the answer choice that "sounds right" to them. Unfortunately, all the answer choices on the TOEIC are designed to sound good, so this so-called method doesn't work very well.

A better way to approach the Reading section is to be extremely methodical in reading the questions and evaluating the answer choices. There are specific details about how to answer each type of question in the chapters covering those question types. By following a series of steps and using logic and POE, you will get more questions correct and use your time more efficiently.

Use Your Time Wisely

You have almost twice as much time to answer 100 reading questions as you did to answer 100 listening comprehension questions. Don't make the mistake of becoming too relaxed with your time, though. It is important to pace yourself and allot your time wisely. The reading comprehension questions take much more time to work and answer than the sentence completion and error identification questions do. To avoid being rushed on the last section, you should budget your time so that you have half of the total 75 minutes to answer the reading comprehension questions.

Use the practice tests in this book to judge whether you are working too quickly or too slowly on any section of the test. Note when you feel rushed and whether you run out of time or finish early. Then adjust your speed so that you finish on the real test with only a few minutes left to check over your answer sheet to make sure you've filled in exactly one answer choice for each question.

If you find that you consistently finish with lots of time left, and are happy with your score, don't adjust your pacing. Instead, make notes by any questions that you're not absolutely positive about, and go back to them. Spend the remaining time using POE to be sure that you've chosen the best possible answer.

Skip Around, But Then Come Back

Skip around all you like in the Reading section of the TOEIC. There are no recordings to go with the questions in this section, so it doesn't matter if you tackle the questions out of order. If you are having a hard time with a question or just don't like it, you can skip it and move on to other questions you can answer more easily. Or, you can completely change the order of the section. For instance, you may feel really confident about reading comprehension questions and not so confident about error identification questions. If that's the case, you should do the reading comprehension questions first so that you can move on to the rest of the section with confidence and a positive attitude.

Of course, if you answer questions out of order, you must be very careful when you fill in your answers. If you aren't, you could make mistakes and hurt your score on the test.

You also need to make sure to mark any questions you've skipped so you can come back to them at the end of the section. Depending on how much time you have left, you can either work the remaining questions completely, try to eliminate an answer choice or two and guess, or just guess blindly. Whatever you do, though, don't forget to fill in an answer choice for every question!

Practice Reading American English Documents

The TOEIC is supposed to test written English of all types, but in reality it tests almost exclusively American written English. Even when the names and locations on the reading passages are not in the United States, the language is still mostly American. This certainly simplifies the idioms and expressions you have to learn.

To prepare for the TOEIC, you should read as many American materials as you can get your hands on. Start in your office with any English-language handbooks, memos, e-mail, and the like. Then try American newspapers. You can read most of them on the Internet. *The New York Times* is at www.nytimes.com (you have to register, but it doesn't cost anything). *The Washington Post* is at www.washingtonpost.com.

THE WEEK OF THE TEST

By the week of the test, you should be confident in your test-taking abilities. Keep in mind that you are not really memorizing information for this exam. By the week of the test, you should have reviewed most of the tips and drills in this book. It's a good idea to save some practice test material for the last week. When you work on this practice material during the last week, be sure to time yourself, and try to complete an entire section in one sitting. It's important to get a feel for the amount of time you will have for each section so that it will not come as a surprise to you on test day.

But don't cram too much studying into the last week. If you were running a marathon, would you run five marathons the week of the race? Of course not. That would leave you exhausted on the day of the race (or in the hospital). The same is true with test practice. You want to feel confident and prepared, not exhausted and sick of test questions. During the last week, you should try to stay well-rested and healthy, and review just enough to keep your level of confidence high.

The night before the exam, plan to eat a light meal and maybe see a movie. Don't study. All you will learn that last night is how to be nervous. You're well-prepared, so relax and get a good night's sleep.

THE DAY OF THE EXAM

Be sure to bring the following items to the test with you:

- Photo identification—This can be a passport, driver's license, military ID, or national ID.

- Confirmation number or ticket—Depending on how you registered for the TOEIC, you should have either a confirmation number or a ticket. Bring it along with you to the test.

- A watch—The proctor will write the time remaining on a blackboard or dry-erase board at the front of the room. However, it isn't a bad idea to bring your own time source, as long as it is silent.

- A positive attitude—This is perhaps your biggest advantage to cracking the TOEIC.

- Two or three pencils

You are not allowed to bring anything else into the TOEIC testing rooms. No food, drinks, tobacco, paper, beepers, cellular phones, pagers, pens, calculators, books, pamphlets, dictionaries, and so forth are allowed. There is no break between the two sections of the test. If you must go to the bathroom during the test, you will not be allowed to make up the time you miss, so try to go to the bathroom before the test starts. It is important that you eat before you start the test. Being hungry or tired in the middle of the exam will likely affect your score. Even though you cannot bring food into the room, you may want to bring a snack to eat right before the test starts.

Now relax and feel confident. You'll be well-prepared and will do your best.

THE BASICS

PART ◆ II

Listening
Comprehension

THE BASICS

The Listening Comprehension section of the TOEIC is the most difficult section of the test. Not only do you have to understand the speaker, but you also have to remember what the speaker said in order to answer the questions. On top of that, you've got only five seconds between questions, so you can't spend any extra time on a difficult question. If you fall behind, you're sunk.

It sounds tough, but don't worry. There are definite ways to improve your performance on the Listening Comprehension section of the TOEIC, and we've got a few tips to make the experience less stressful for you. Read closely, follow the examples, do the drills, and you'll be all set.

In the Listening Comprehension section of the TOEIC, you will have to answer 100 questions in 45 minutes. There are four parts in this section of the test.

- **Part I: Photographs.** In this part, you will see a photograph and hear four statements about the photograph. You will be asked to choose the statement that most accurately describes the action in the photograph. There are 20 photographs questions on the test.

- **Part II: Question and Response.** In the question-and-response part of the test, you will hear a question asked by one speaker, followed by three responses from another speaker. You will be asked to choose the response that best answers the question. There are 30 question-and-response questions on the test.

- **Part III: Short Conversations.** In this part of the test, you will hear a short conversation between two speakers. A question about what was said will be printed in your test booklet. You will be asked to choose the response that best answers the question, based on the short conversation you heard. There are 30 short conversations questions on the test.

- **Part IV: Short Talks.** In this part of the test, you will hear a short talk by one speaker. For each talk, there will be several questions followed by four answer choices printed in your test booklet. You will be asked to choose the response that best answers each question based on the short talk you heard. There are 20 short talks questions on the test.

PHOTOGRAPHS QUESTIONS

THE DIRECTIONS

The first 20 questions (numbered 1–20) in the Listening Comprehension section of the test are photographs questions. Directions for completing the photographs questions appear in a box at the beginning of the section. The directions box looks like this:

PART I

Directions: For each question, you will see a picture in your test book and you will hear four statements. The statements will be spoken just one time. They will not be printed in your test book, so you must listen carefully to understand what the speaker says.

When you hear the four statements, look at the picture in your test book and choose the statement that best describes what you see in the picture. Then, on your answer sheet, find the number of the question and mark your answer.

Sample Answer

Ⓐ ● Ⓒ Ⓓ

Now listen to the four statements.

Statement (B), "They are discussing something," best describes what you see in the picture. Therefore, you should choose answer (B).

Read these instructions now and review them ahead of time so that you won't waste any time reading them during the actual test. The only things you need to understand from them are that

- you will see a photo for each question and will hear four statements,
- the statements will not be repeated and they are not printed in your book, and
- you should pick the statement that best describes what you see in the photo.

THE QUESTIONS

Each photographs question consists of a photograph printed in your test booklet and four statements you'll hear from a tape (or CD). Look at an example:

The speaker on the tape will say:

    (A) *They are having an argument.*
    (B) *The man seems happy.*
    (C) *The man and woman are walking.*
    (D) *The weather is rainy.*

Three of the four answer choice statements are incorrect, meaning that they do not describe the photograph. Only one statement is correct.

THE TRAP

The major trap in the photographs questions is that the statements are spoken but not printed in your test booklet, so you can't hear or read them more than once. The other trap is that many, if not all, of the answer choice statements may sound like they *could* describe the photograph. This means that you have to be very organized about answering the questions in this section in order to process each statement as you hear it. Don't worry though, we'll show you how to do these questions.

QUESTION-AND-RESPONSE QUESTIONS

THE DIRECTIONS

The next 30 questions (numbered 21–50) in the Listening Comprehension section of the test are question-and-response questions. Directions for completing the question-and-response questions appear in a box at the beginning of the section. The directions box looks like this:

PART II

Directions: In this part of the test, you will hear a question or statement spoken in English, followed by three responses, also spoken in English. The question or statement and the responses will be spoken just one time. They will not be printed in your test book, so you must listen carefully to understand what the speakers say. You are to choose the best response to each question or statement.

Now listen to a sample question.

You will hear:

You will also hear:

Sample Answer

The best response to the question "Have you eaten lunch yet?" is choice (A), "I'm going to the cafeteria right now." Therefore, you should choose answer (A).

Read these instructions now and review them ahead of time so that you won't waste any time reading them during the actual test. The only things you need to understand from them are that

- you will hear one speaker asking a question and another speaker giving three possible responses to that question, and

- you have to pick the response that most logically follows the question.

THE QUESTIONS

For each question-and-response question, you will hear one speaker ask a question, and then another speaker give three responses. One of those responses makes sense as an answer to the question, while the other two do not. You are asked to choose the response that makes the most sense.

Keep in mind that there is nothing written in the test booklet for this question type. Everything is spoken on the tape or CD. Let's look at a typical TOEIC question-and-response question. The only thing printed in the test book for each question will be:

Mark your answer on your answer sheet.

The speakers on the tape might say the following:

(Woman)   *How much was the bill at the hotel?*

(Man)   (A) *I was only there for one night.*
           (B) *My credit card was charged for $100.*
           (C) *No, I already paid it.*

Two of the responses you heard do not make sense as answers to the question. Pick the one that does make sense.

THE TRAP

One major trap in the question-and-response questions is that there's nothing for you to read. The only words printed for each question are "Mark your answer on your answer sheet." Helpful, huh? So you have to be prepared to process each response as you hear it. The other major trap is that there are only three answer choices for these questions, not four answer choices as there are on every other section of the TOEIC. You could accidentally fill in answer choice (D) on your answer sheet and miss a question. When you finish the question-and-response questions, you should glance through questions 21–50 on your answer sheet to make sure that you didn't fill in any of the (D) bubbles. If you did, change the (D) to a (C).

SHORT CONVERSATIONS

THE DIRECTIONS

The next 30 questions (numbered 51–80) in the Listening Comprehension section of the test are short conversations questions. Directions for completing the short conversations questions appear in a box at the beginning of the section. The directions box looks like this:

PART III

Directions: In this part of the test, you will hear 30 short conversations between two people. The conversations will not be printed in your test book. You will hear the conversations only once, so you must listen carefully to understand what the speakers say.

In your test book, you will read a question about each conversation. The questions will be followed by four answers. You are to choose the best answer to each question and mark it on your answer sheet.

Read these instructions now and review them ahead of time so that you won't waste any time reading them during the actual test. The only things you need to understand from them are that

- you will hear a short conversation between two people,

- then read a question about that conversation in your test booklet followed by four answer choices, and

- then pick the answer choice that best answers the question.

THE QUESTIONS

For each short conversations question, you will hear a short conversation between two speakers. Then you will read a question in your test booklet based on the conversation you just heard. This question will be followed by four answer choices. You are asked to choose the answer choice that best answers the question. Let's look at a typical TOEIC short conversations question. The question will be printed in the test booklet.

> Who asked for the report?
>
> (A) Ms. Kwok
> (B) Ms. Kwok's assistant
> (C) Ms. Channing
> (D) The messenger

The speakers on the tape will say:

(Woman 1) *Ms. Channing, I called the messenger to come pick up the latest compliance report.*
(Woman 2) *Really? Where are you sending it?*
(Woman 1) *To Ms. Kwok downtown. Her assistant called me before lunch to ask me to send it over.*

Three of the answer choices do not answer the question correctly. One of them does. Pick that answer choice.

THE TRAP

The major trap in the short conversations questions is that some of the answer choices will reflect what you *thought* you heard instead of what you actually heard during the conversation. The best way to avoid this trap is to read the question *before* you hear the conversation.

SHORT TALKS QUESTIONS

THE DIRECTIONS

The last 20 questions (numbered 81–100) in the Listening Comprehension section of the test are short talks questions. Directions for completing the short talks questions appear in a box at the beginning of the section. The directions box looks like this:

PART IV

Directions: In this part of the test, you will hear several short talks. Each will be spoken just one time. They will not be printed in your test book, so you must listen carefully to understand and remember what is said.

In your test book, you will read two or more questions about each short talk. The questions will be followed by four answers. You are to choose the best answer to each question and mark it on your answer sheet.

Read these instructions now and review them ahead of time so that you won't waste any time reading them during the actual test. The only things you need to understand from them are that

- you will hear several short talks, one at a time,
- there will be several questions printed in the test booklet based on each talk followed by four answer choices for each question, and
- you have to pick the answer choice that best answers each question, based on the talk you heard.

THE QUESTIONS

For each short talks question, you will hear a short talk given by one speaker. Then there will be a pause while you read the questions based on that talk in the test booklet. There will be anywhere from two to four questions based on each talk. The talk will not be repeated. Each question will be followed by four answer choices. You are asked to choose the answer choice that best answers the question, based on the talk. Let's look at a typical TOEIC short talks question. The question will be printed in the test booklet.

> Who is speaking?
> (A) A teacher
> (B) A store manager
> (C) An auto mechanic
> (D) A chicken farmer

The speaker on the tape will say:

Attention all shoppers. There is a car parked in the parking lot with its headlights on. The car is a late-model blue Toyota Corolla, with license plate G45 HY1. If this is your car, please turn the headlights off so your battery doesn't run down. Thank you for your attention to this announcement. Don't forget that boneless skinless chicken breasts are on sale this week in the meat department, and have a nice day.

Three of the answer choices do not answer the question correctly. One of them does. Pick that answer choice.

THE TRAP

The major trap in the short talks questions is that some of the answer choices will reflect what you *thought* you heard instead of what you actually heard during the talk. This is exacerbated by the fact that there is more than one question for each talk. The best way to avoid this trap is to read the questions before you hear the talk.

WHAT DOES THE LISTENING COMPREHENSION SECTION TEST?

Before you feel too grateful for the opportunity to demonstrate your English skills, think for a minute about what this section really measures. If you wanted someone to show how well he or she could "communicate in English with others," what would you do? You would probably try to have a conversation with that person.

What you probably *wouldn't* do is make him or her sit in a room full of computers with 30 other people, listen to a tape of out-of-context sentences and answer a bunch of multiple-choice questions that have nothing to do whatsoever with anything relevant. That kind of test would measure

- how well you hear,
- your ability to comprehend non sequiturs, and
- your ability to stay calm under pressure.

But does it measure your ability to communicate in English with others? Not very well. The one thing the TOEIC Listening Comprehension section does with total accuracy is measure how well you do on the TOEIC Listening Comprehension section. Nothing more.

How to Tackle the Listening Comprehension Section

The following chapters will teach you how to use some of the weaknesses of the Listening Comprehension section to help you rather than hurt you. We'll also show you how to use the Process of Elimination (POE) to find the right answers, *even if you didn't understand what you heard.*

How Much Will Your Scores Improve?

How much your scores improve will depend on how much you practice and on your consistency when you do it. If you use these techniques, your scores will improve. But you should also practice, practice, practice listening and speaking in English. If you have planned well in advance, you may have a few months to prepare for this test. In the Conversational English chapter, we've included some suggestions for ways to work on your listening skills. Get started as soon as possible!

Scoring the Listening Comprehension Section

Half your total score on the TOEIC is determined by your performance on the Listening Comprehension section of the test. ETS converts the number of questions you answer correctly out of the 100 questions on the Listening Comprehension section to a scaled score. The Listening Comprehension section is scored on a scale from 5 to 495.

4

Conversational English

PRACTICING LISTENING TO ENGLISH

As is often said in the English language, "practice makes perfect." In other words, if you want to learn to do something well, you should do it over and over again until you have mastered it. If you wanted to, say, learn to play the piano, or help lead your basketball team to the finals, you would probably put in several hours of practice per week. The same goes for learning a new language.

Here are a few activities you can practice to help prepare you for the Listening Comprehension section of the TOEIC.

- Talk on the telephone (in English, of course). Speaking on the phone eliminates facial expressions, gestures, and any other clues as to what the person on the other end of the line is saying. The same is true for the Listening Comprehension section—you can rely only on the speakers' voices to answer the questions.

- Listen to talk shows and news reports on the radio or over the Internet. (As we mentioned in the Test-Taking Techniques chapter, you can listen to many programs in American English on www.npr.org.) Like the telephone, the radio eliminates physical clues that help you determine what the speaker is saying.

- Practice speaking English where it is difficult to hear. If you have friends with whom you can practice speaking English, go to noisy places to do it, such as restaurants or nightclubs, or even train stations.

VOICE EMPHASIS

When speaking to people face to face, visual clues help you understand not only the words they use, but also the meanings of those words. Facial expressions, hand gestures, and body posture can all help you understand what a person is saying. However, in the TOEIC Listening Comprehension section, you can't see the speaker, so you are forced to rely solely on vocal cues.

In spoken English, people place emphasis on certain words in a given sentence to convey additional meaning beyond dictionary definitions. The most common way to place emphasis on a word is by raising or lowering the pitch or volume of one's voice. This will enable that word to stand out from the rest of the sentence. One of the things that vocal emphasis can tell you is which information in the sentence the speaker considers to be the most important.

WHAT'S IMPORTANT?

In the following sentence, every word is stressed equally.

Jane's red bag is on the table.

However, when emphasis is placed on specific words in the sentence, the intention of the speaker changes slightly.

Jane's red bag is on the table.

When the sentence is spoken with emphasis placed on the word *Jane's*, that word becomes the most important in the sentence. In other words, the primary goal of the speaker is to communicate the ownership of the bag. The person the speaker is talking to probably thought the bag belonged to someone else, and the speaker wants to clear up the misunderstanding.

*Jane's **red** bag is on the table.*

When the emphasis is on *red*, the color of the bag is what's important. The other person most likely thought that a different bag was being discussed, probably of another color.

*Jane's red **bag** is on the table.*

Now the emphasis is on the actual item. The other person may have thought that something else belonging to Jane was on the table, such as a red book or a red sweater.

*Jane's red bag **is** on the table.*

The emphasis is on *where*. The other person may have just said, implied, or thought that the bag was not on the table.

*Jane's red bag is **on** the table.*

The speaker wants to make clear that the bag is on—not under, next to, in front of, or behind—the table. The other person probably misunderstood the location of the bag.

*Jane's red bag is on the **table**.*

Again, the speaker clarifies the location of the bag for the other person. In this case, the other person was probably confused about *what* the bag was on. He or she might have thought that the bag was on something else, such as the cabinet, the stairs, or the bed.

Voice emphasis drill

Directions: For the following drill, play CD #1 Track 5 of the CD that came with this book. You will hear the sentences that are printed below. Each sentence will be read several times, with emphasis on a different word each time. For each example, circle the word or words that were stressed. Then, on the line below the sentence, jot down a couple of words to express the implied meaning of what the speaker said. (You will have about ten seconds to do this, so don't worry about writing complete sentences). If the drill moves too quickly for you, you also have the option of pausing the disk between sentences. When you're done, check your answers on page 50.

1. Louis always recycles his newspapers.

   _____

2. Louis always recycles his newspapers.

   _____

3. Louis always recycles his newspapers.

   _____

4. Louis always recycles his newspapers.

   _____

5. Louis always recycles his newspapers.

   _____

6. Diane will arrive at three o'clock on Tuesday.

   _____

7. Diane will arrive at three o'clock on Tuesday.

    _____

8. Diane will arrive at three o'clock on Tuesday.

    _____

9. Diane will arrive at three o'clock on Tuesday.

    _____

10. Diane will arrive at three o'clock on Tuesday.

    _____

11. What do you want?

    _____

12. What do you want?

    _____

13. What do you want?

    _____

14. This test is pretty easy.

    _____

15. This test is pretty easy.

    _____

16. This test is pretty easy.

    _____

17. This test is pretty easy.

    _____

WHAT'S UNDERSTOOD?

In spoken English, it's sometimes acceptable to speak in ways that violate the rules of written grammar. One of the most common violations is speaking in incomplete sentences. This is possible because one speaker can use the context supplied by the other speaker, without having to repeat it. Here's an example.

There's an elephant at our front door.
***What's** at our front door?*
*An **elephant**!*
*It's **where**?*
*At the **front door**!*

*At **whose** front door?*

Ours!

If you looked at any of these "sentences" by themselves, they wouldn't make any sense. But since you know what the first speaker said, the meaning is clear.

WHAT'S IMPLIED?

Many words in English take on additional meaning when spoken aloud. You can often recognize these situations because if you took the meaning of the words literally, the sentence wouldn't seem to mean anything. Many of these expressions use exaggeration or sarcasm to make a point. Take a look at these examples.

*You **could** help me with the dishes.*

The speaker doesn't mean that the other person "has the ability" to help with the dishes. The emphasis on *could* carries with it the implication that the speaker believes the other person should help with the dishes. The speaker is being sarcastic. The other person would probably respond by apologizing and would start to help.

*It **can't** be eleven o'clock already!*

Another use for *can*. The speaker doesn't mean that it's impossible for it to be eleven o'clock. Rather, the speaker knows it is eleven o'clock and is very surprised by how quickly time has passed. Depending on the context, the speaker is either happily or unhappily surprised by the time.

*You can say **that** again.*

Here, the speaker probably doesn't want the other person to really say the same thing over again. By emphasizing *that*, the speaker shows that he or she agrees strongly with what the other person said.

Do you need a little help?

> *Help? I need a **miracle**!*

Are you hungry?

> *Hungry? I'm **starving**!*

In each case, the person answering the question uses exaggeration to mean "Yes, I certainly do!" or "I certainly am . . . but much more than you can imagine!"

Some emphasized expressions

The following are some expressions you might find on the TOEIC that have special meanings *only when they are emphasized by the speaker*.

can't

Can't is emphasized to indicate the speaker's surprise in a particular situation. The speaker means: I know that it *is* true, but I can't believe it!

*It **can't** be eight o'clock already!*

*This **can't** be my last dollar!*

*That **can't** be our bus pulling out of the station!*

can always

The speaker uses *can always* to remind you that you still have another alternative.

*If you don't like the party, you **can always** go home.*

*You **can always** change your mind.*

did/was/is

When the second speaker emphasizes the auxiliaries *did*, *was*, or *is* in response to the first speaker, the second speaker is expressing surprise.

I just got home from the concert.

*So you **did** go.*

David really enjoys his new car.

*So he **did** buy a new one.*

Professor Weiner really helped me with those math problems.

*Oh, so he **did** help you.*

Don't you love Michael's new musical arrangements?

*So, those **are** his arrangements.*

Did you see Andrew and his new girlfriend at the hockey game?

*So, they **were** there.*

We all noticed that you weren't in class on Monday.

*So, it **wasn't** cancelled.*

if only

If only means "I really wish."

__If only__ I had known before now!

__If only__ I had a million dollars!

only

The word *only*, when emphasized, answers a question enthusiastically, meaning "Yes," "Of course," or "Yes, a lot!"

Did you have fun at the dance?

*I **only** danced my feet off!*

Did you really want to spend time with me?

*I **only** drove a whole hour to see you!*

Does Sam know anything about American politics?

*He's **only** read everything that's ever been published about it!*

The speaker uses we'll "be lucky if" to indicate that something is unlikely to happen.

The speaker uses "might as well" to express that something is so unlikely or far-fetched that it is out of the realm of possibility.

We *might as well* be in Timbuktu.

We *might as well* walk to New York from Kansas!

CLICHÉS

A cliché is a phrase or expression that has become overly familiar or commonplace. All of the following are clichés that appear on the TOEIC and are used to express simple ideas. We've grouped them by meaning in order to make them easier to learn.

agreement

To say the least.

That's putting it mildly.

You can say that again.

That's for sure.

Don't I know it.

Now, that's an idea.

There you go!

Now you've said something (. . . I agree with, whereas you didn't before.)

I'll say.

I couldn't agree with you more.

Count me in.

Why not!

Do I ever!

You bet!

disagreement

I doubt it.

Probably not.

Not likely.

I wouldn't say that.

Don't bet on it.

Don't count on it.

Don't be too sure.

I don't think so.

No way.

Never.

Not in a million years.

don't do it

I wouldn't if I were you.

Oh no you don't!

Cut it out!

Not here you don't.

Better leave well enough alone.

Forget it!

Don't bother.

You can't be too careful.

I don't know

I couldn't tell you.

I wouldn't know.

I haven't the vaguest.

I haven't the foggiest.

I haven't any idea.

Who knows?

It's a mystery to me.

Don't look at me.

Don't ask me.

It's over my head.

You got me.

Beats me.

question/suggestion

How about . . . ?

Why not . . . ?

What about . . . ?

What would you say to . . . ?

What do you think about . . . ?

Would you mind if . . . ?

Shouldn't you . . . ?

surprise/disbelief

Isn't that something!

I can't believe that . . .

My goodness!

How about that!

It/He/She's too good to be true!

We made it!

You're kidding!

You're joking!

Come on!

It can't be!

Who says?

To think I . . . !

No! You don't say!

No way!

Get out!

thank you

Thanks!

I appreciate it.

Thanks a lot.

I don't know how to thank you.

You're a lifesaver.

I'll never be able to repay you.

I'm grateful.

What did you say?

Pardon me?

Excuse me?

Sorry?

What?

you're welcome

It's the least I can do.

Forget it.

Don't mention it.

Never mind.

It doesn't matter.

No problem.

HOMONYMS

Another trap you need to know about when listening is **homonyms**—words that are spelled differently, but sound alike. These are used to fool you. The following is a list of some common pairs of homonyms. This is by no means a complete list. We have not included every definition for each word—just the most common definition. Remember, when you come across a homonym, the most important thing to do is to put the word into context.

Homonyms drill

Directions: Write a short sentence or phrase after each of the following homonyms to familiarize yourself with the differences. Because your sentences will vary, ask an English speaker to check them for you to make sure that you got them right.

by: near "Her house is **by** the shopping mall."

_____

buy: to purchase "I want to **buy** a new car."

_____

banned: not allowed "Short skirts are **banned** at her school."

_____

band: a music group "The **band** at the party played only the most popular songs."

_____

cell: the smallest unit of living matter "The amoeba consists of a single **cell**."

_____

sell: to make a sale "I want to **sell** this old car and buy a new one."

_____

die: to become dead or expire "The man will likely **die** from his severe injuries."

_____

dye: used to color things "What **dye** did you use to get that interesting purple color?"

_____

fair: festival, carnival "The town **fair** is held every summer."

_____

fare: cost "The round trip **fare** by airplane is $200."

_____

flower: daisy, tulip, rose "I love to grow **flowers** in my garden."

_____

flour: ingredient in baking "I need two cups of **flour** for the cake."

_____

here: this place "Come **here** right now!"

_____

hear: listen "Did you **hear** what I said?"

_____

hire: to employ someone "I need to **hire** a tutor to help me with my studies."

_____

higher: more elevated "Put the books on a **higher** shelf."

_____

hole: an empty space "Last week, I dug a big **hole** to plant those seeds."

_____

whole: entire "He ate the **whole** pie before anyone else could even have a piece."

_____

hour: a sixty-minute time period "This class is one **hour** long."

_____

our: possessive form of we "We like **our** new teacher."

_____

I: me, myself "**I** am taking a vacation next month."

_____

eye: what you see with "My **eyes** are bothered by cigarette smoke."

_____

jeans: denim pants "**Jeans** are really comfortable to wear."

_____

genes: biological units of inheritance "He inherited blue eyes from his mother's **genes**."

_____

maid: someone who cleans "The **maid** will clean your room."

_____

made: past tense of *make* "I **made** the bed myself."

---

new: not used "I bought this **new** dress today with the money I earned."

---

knew: past tense of *know* "I **knew** that you were going to show up at the party!"

---

pale: light in color "Jane is **pale**—she hasn't been to the beach."

---

pail: a container "She carried a **pail** of milk from the barn."

---

plain: simple, unadorned "This dress is too **plain**—there are no designs on it."

---

plane: airplane, for flying "We flew to Europe in that new **plane**."

---

principal: the head of a school "**Principal** Jones supervises the whole school."

---

principle: belief "Stand by your **principles**."

---

red: the color "Stop at a **red** light."

---

read: past tense of *read* "I **read** a whole book last night."

---

reflex: unconscious movement "I pulled my hand out of the water in a **reflex**."

---

reflects: casts back an image "The lake **reflects** the trees perfectly."

---

sail: on a boat "The **sail** catches wind and pushes the boat."

---

sale: a discount, bargain "I bought this coat on **sale** and saved a lot of money."

_____

sea: ocean "We swam in the **sea** today."

_____

see: to view, use your eyes "I **see** that you are wearing the sweater I gave you for your birthday."

_____

scene: where something takes place "That **scene** in the movie was filmed in New York City."

_____

seen: past tense of _see_ "I've **seen** that movie three times!"

_____

sense: as in common sense "That advice makes good **sense**."

_____

cents: pennies, money "The phone call cost twenty-five **cents**."

_____

sew: use a needle and thread "I want to **sew** the rip on these jeans."

_____

so: who cares? "**So** what? I really have no interest in what you are saying."

_____

son: male child "She has one **son** and two daughters."

_____

sun: the Earth revolves around it "The **sun** is very hot today!"

_____

soul: spirit "Buddhists believe that the **soul** is reincarnated."

_____

sole: only "He was the **sole** survivor of the train accident."

_____

tale: story "That was some **tale** Jack told us."

_____

tail: at the end of an animal "Don't pull the cat's **tail**!"

_____

wait: to pause, stop "**Wait** for me—I'll be right there."

_____

weight: heaviness "The **weight** of this package is three pounds."

_____

way: direction "Which **way** should we go?"

_____

weigh: to figure out how heavy something is "Did you **weigh** these vegetables?"

_____

weather: atmospheric conditions, what it's like outside "The **weather** report calls for rain."

_____

whether: if "I need to know **whether** you will go."

_____

won: defeated an opponent "We **won** the game by 2 to 1."

_____

one: the number 1, or alone "There is only **one** girl on the softball team."

_____

wood: material from a tree "The furniture is made out of **wood**."

_____

would: form of _will_ "I **would** like a new table."

_____

worn: past tense of _wear_ "Have you **worn** those shoes yet?"

_____

warn: to caution "I **warn** you—he's a tough teacher."

_____

IDIOMS

Idioms are words or phrases that do not translate literally. For example, "break down" may not mean to break something in a downward motion, but to lose control. The TOEIC does not test idioms frequently, but it does test them occasionally. Try the following drills to test your knowledge of idioms. If you do not do as well as you'd like to, you should study idioms. In the Appendix at the back of this book, you'll find lists of two types of idioms. They aren't exhaustive lists of all American English idioms in existence, but they are a good start.

Idiom drill 1

Directions: Choose the answer choice that best answers each question. Then check your answers on page 51.

1. (Woman)   *I heard that the award ceremony was wonderful.*

   (Man)   *Yes, John broke down when he won the humanitarian award.*

   What does the man mean?

   (A) John's award was broken.
   (B) John got emotional when he won.
   (C) John only received one award.
   (D) The award was humanitarian.

2. (Man)   *Will you help me clean the kitchen?*

   (Woman)   *Sure. You clear away the dishes and I'll wash the pots.*

   What does the woman want the man to do?

   (A) Wipe off the dishes.
   (B) Take the dishes off the table.
   (C) Take the pots away.
   (D) Put the dishes away.

3. (Man)   *It's so sad that Harvey isn't feeling well.*

   (Woman)   *What a bad time for him to come down with chicken pox!*

   What does the woman mean?

   (A) Harvey was coming over with chicken.
   (B) Harvey has chicken pox.
   (C) Harvey fell down.
   (D) Harvey is having a bad time.

4. (Woman)   *When did that new movie house open?*

   (Man)   *I don't know—it seems like it went up in a week!*

   What does the man suggest?

   (A) The movie house was built quickly.
   (B) The movie house is very tall.
   (C) He doesn't understand the woman's question.
   (D) It opened a week ago.

5. (Woman)   *Have you heard about the principal's new plan to make the school day longer?*

   (Man)   *She'll never go through with it!*

   What does the man mean?

   (A) He likes the principal's plan.
   (B) The principal went through the school.
   (C) Her plan is possible.
   (D) The principal will not carry out her plan.

6. (Man)   *How long have you been working on that paper?*

   (Woman)   *Three hours—I give up!*

   What does the woman want to do?

   (A) Give the man the paper.
   (B) Stop working on the paper.
   (C) Throw the paper up in the air.
   (D) Work longer.

7. (Man)   *Did you see John's new haircut?*

   (Woman)   *I don't know if that crazy style will fit in with his conservative friends.*

   What does the woman suggest?

   (A) John's haircut is not like any of his friends' haircuts.
   (B) John's hair won't fit his head.
   (C) John's friends are too conservative.
   (D) She hasn't seen John's haircut.

8. (Woman)   *What time do you want to wake up?*

   (Man)   *Well, I'll set the alarm to go off at eight in the morning.*

   What does the man want to do?

   (A) Put off the alarm.
   (B) Eat in the morning.
   (C) Wake up at eight in the morning.
   (D) Get a new alarm.

9. (Man)   *Did you hear about that new vaccine?*

   (Woman)   *What a breakthrough for people with that sickness!*

   What does the woman mean?

   (A) It's good news for people with that sickness.
   (B) People with that sickness will get sicker.
   (C) The vaccine is broken.
   (D) Scientists are not through with their study.

10. (Man)   *What do you want to do today?*

(Woman)   *It's hot outside, let's just hang around.*

What does the woman suggest?

(A) That they do nothing.
(B) That they go home.
(C) That they walk around.
(D) That they hang pictures.

Idiom drill 2

Directions: Match the idiom with its definition. Then check your answers on page 51.

1	pushover	A	to refuse
2	pull off	B	to elapse or overlook
3	pass up	C	to bear an embarrassment
4	pass by or pass over	D	to do in spite of problems
5	over with	E	to terminate someone's employment
6	off limits	F	to stay in communication with
7	live down	G	restricted
8	laid up	H	someone easily taken advantage of
9	lay off	I	sick in bed
10	keep in touch with	J	finished

Idiom drill 3

Directions: Choose the answer choice that best completes the sentence. Then check your answers on page 51.

1. "Pick one topic and ------ it throughout your term paper."

(A) stick around
(B) step on one's toes in
(C) stick to
(D) pull out of

2. "I'm in a real rush now, but ------ later and I'll have more time to talk."

(A) stop by
(B) drop out
(C) turn over
(D) turn off

3. Jane was ------ with work and couldn't be here.

   (A) up to date
   (B) tied up
   (C) filled up
   (D) touched up

4. Smitty felt that rudeness was a real ------.

   (A) turnoff
   (B) turn down
   (C) turn over
   (D) stop up

5. Patty always sets her alarm so that she can ------ at 8:00 A.M.

   (A) think over
   (B) write down
   (C) think through
   (D) wake up

6. The beginning of the second book brings the reader ------ with what happened in the first book.

   (A) up over
   (B) up to date
   (C) up against
   (D) think over

7. At our school, no one would even think to ------ against the administration for fear of getting in trouble.

   (A) step in
   (B) sign in
   (C) speak out
   (D) step up

8. Always a quiet boy, Jose was too shy to ------ in class.

   (A) speed up
   (B) step down
   (C) speak up
   (D) step in

9. "Why don't you ------; I'm sure that Mr. Smith will be here any second."

   (A) step up
   (B) sign in
   (C) stick around
   (D) think better of

10. Americans ------ being able to buy anything they want in a large convenience store; in other countries, it is not always so easy.

   (A) think over
   (B) think through
   (C) think better of
   (D) think nothing of

Answers to the drills

Voice emphasis drill

1. *Louis*—The other person thought that someone else recycles newspapers.

2. *always*—The other person implied that Louis hadn't recycled newspapers at some time in the recent past; the speaker is surprised.

3. *recycles*—The other person thought that Louis did something else with his newspapers.

4. *his*—The other person thought that Louis recycled someone else's newspapers.

5. *newspapers*—The other person thought that Louis recycled something other than newspapers.

6. *Diane*—The other person thought that someone else was coming.

7. *will*—The other person thought or implied that Diane wasn't coming.

8. *arrive*—The other person thought that Diane would be doing something else at three o'clock—leaving, for example.

9. *three o'clock*—The other person thought that Diane would arrive at a different time.

10. *Tuesday*—The other person thought that Diane would arrive on a different day.

11. *what*—The other person asked for something unusual or something that the speaker didn't understand.

12. *you*—The other person was talking about what someone else wanted, which is not what the speaker is interested in.

13. *want*—The other person was talking about what they have to do, or what they don't want, or something else entirely.

14. *this*—The speaker wants to make it clear that while this test may be easy, she finds other tests difficult.

15. *is*—The speaker anticipated a difficult test and therefore is surprised that it turned out to be so easy.

16. *pretty*—The speaker doesn't believe that the test is as easy as the other person implied.

17. *easy*—The speaker is disagreeing with the other person who found the test more difficult than the speaker did.

Idiom drill 1	Idiom drill 2	Idiom drill 3
1. B	1. H	1. C
2. B	2. D	2. A
3. B	3. A	3. B
4. A	4. B	4. A
5. D	5. J	5. D
6. B	6. G	6. B
7. A	7. C	7. C
8. C	8. I	8. C
9. A	9. E	9. C
10. A	10. F	10. D

5

Photographs
Questions

THE BASICS

For photographs questions in the TOEIC Listening Comprehension section, your task is to look at a photograph and listen to four spoken statements. Then you must choose the statement that most accurately reflects the photo. The statements will not be repeated. In other words, you have one chance to listen and remember.

There are 20 photographs questions on the test. There are five seconds between the questions.

The photos you will see will be of everyday situations and business scenes. You will see photos of people in offices, riding the bus, eating in restaurants, and so on.

THE METHOD

THE INSTRUCTIONS

While everyone else is listening to the instructions, you should be setting up your test booklet to help you use POE successfully. Next to each question, write the letters *A*, *B*, *C*, and *D* in a vertical line, like this:

A
B
C
D

With your booklet set up this way, when you hear the statements, you can cross out letters that correspond to statements you know aren't correct (we'll describe how to figure that out in a minute).

This plan sounds really inconsequential, but it is the cornerstone for acing the photographs section of the TOEIC. You can easily get confused if you don't keep track of the statements and eliminate the ones that are incorrect. When you write down the letters, you'll be able to keep everything straight as you hear the statements. It is vitally important to approach the photographs questions this way, since the statements will *not* be repeated, and you only have five seconds between questions. That means you have to eliminate each statement as you hear it, because you won't ever hear it again. You also have to choose an answer choice and fill it in on your answer sheet within five seconds. Five seconds is not a lot of time. So you can't waste any time trying to remember what the statements were. You have to process them *as you hear them*.

There are two very different tasks you must complete for each question in order to answer it successfully. Let's explore each one in depth right now.

INTERPRET THE PHOTOGRAPH

On some standardized tests (particularly the TOEFL, which you may have taken), the photograph that accompanies a question is not important to the question, and may even be there to distract you from the question. This is absolutely not the case on the photographs section of the TOEIC. The photograph and your ability to interpret it accurately are exceedingly important to answering the question. In fact, without correctly interpreting the photograph, there is no way for you to answer the question correctly.

However, it may be possible to answer the question correctly without completely understanding all of the statements. So, in essence, this question type tests your powers of observation more than it tests your understanding of spoken American English.

In order to interpret the photo correctly, you need to consider several aspects of it, including the setting of the photo and the people or other subjects of the photo, their condition, and any action they may be taking.

Setting

Is the setting outdoors or indoors? Is it day or night? What time of year does it appear to be? Are there buildings, streets, or vehicles in the photograph? What do they look like? These are all things to observe.

Subject

Once you have examined and identified the setting of the photo, you should turn your attention to the subject. In many cases, it will be a person or a few people. In other cases, however, there will be no people in the photo. In this case, the subject will be the most prominent thing in the photo, for instance a bus, or a telephone, or a table. It should not be difficult to identify the subject, but make sure you actually look at the photo and consider everything in it.

Notice the condition of the subject(s) in the photograph. Is the subject a man or a woman? How old does the subject appear to be? What are his/her physical characteristics? How is the subject dressed? What is the subject's likely occupation? What is the subject's mood or expression? Is the subject an inanimate object? Is there anything particularly interesting or unique about the subject? Or, is it commonplace?

Pay attention to action in the photograph. What is the subject doing? Is the subject engaged in some activity, or is it merely resting? How would you describe that activity?

Let's try this assessment with an example. We'll evaluate this example using the criteria we've established.

Setting: The setting is a conference room or classroom of some sort with a big table. There is a dry-erase board, and some plants along the wall.

Subjects: The subjects are a man at the dry-erase board and several other people sitting around the table. The man at the board has a long pointer, and the people at the table have papers and notepads. The man at the board looks as if he is giving a lecture or talk of some sort, and the people around the table are listening to the talk and some are taking notes.

We have observed all we can about this photo. Let's move on to the answer choice statements.

INTERPRET THE STATEMENTS

Listen to CD #1 Track 6 to hear the answer choice statements for the photo on the previous page. As you hear each statement, listen carefully to determine whether it applies to the photo. If it doesn't, cross off the corresponding letter from the letters you wrote next to the photo before you began. On the real exam, when you hear statements that don't apply to the photo, cross out the letters you wrote in your test booklet. Be sure to cross them out physically! The letter you are left with is the correct answer.

Look out for traps

Just because there's no actual question with each photograph doesn't mean that there aren't traps you need to watch out for. As long as there are answer choices, ETS will find a way to try to trick you with them. Fortunately for you, we know how to avoid the traps. Read on to find out how.

Soundalikes

Soundalikes are answer choices that sound like something that is happening in the photo. For instance, if a woman is holding a map, the soundalike answer choice could say "The woman is *folding* a map." *Folding* and *holding* sound alike. Written on the page, this might not seem too distracting. However, if you see that the woman is "holding" a map, you might be trapped by the soundalike "folding" a map. Sneaky, huh?

Therefore, it's up to you to listen very closely to the statements and bear in mind that there will be incorrect answer choices that sound like they could be correct. Let's look at answer choice (C) in our photo question.

(C) The table is strong.

In this case, a true statement about the photo would be "the table is long." *Strong* and *long* sound very similar, so ETS is hoping you'll pick this distractor answer. If you're aware that this type of trap is on the test, you will be less likely to fall into it. Stay aware, and try to eliminate any soundalike answer choices you hear.

Misrepresentations

There are answer choices that twist what is actually happening in the photograph to make a statement that isn't true but that contains elements in the photo. For instance, the photo might show a woman getting on an elevator. The misrepresentation answer choice could say "The woman is getting off the elevator." While the photo does indeed contain both a woman and an elevator, the statement does not reflect the actual action of the photo. This may be the most common type of trap answer on the TOEIC, so make sure you are ready to identify and eliminate misrepresentations. Let's look at answer choice (B) from the photo question.

(B) The students are giving a lecture to the professor.

First of all, this statement introduces a new idea—that the standing man is a professor and the people sitting around the table are students. This may or may not be the case. Putting that aside, however, the statement is also a major misrepresentation. In the photo, it looks as if the man is showing or teaching something to the people at the table, not the other way around. This answer choice is designed specifically to trap you by mentioning elements in the photo, but claiming that they are doing something they are not. Cross out letter *B* which you wrote in the test booklet.

Now that you know that plenty of wrong answer choices contain elements that are in the photo, you shouldn't fall into the trap anymore. As soon as you hear a statement that misrepresents the action in the photo, eliminate it.

Exaggerations

Exaggerations are close cousins of the misrepresentation. Exaggeration answer choices take what's actually in the photo and just go a little too far. For instance, the photo might show two people talking. The exaggeration answer choice could say something like "The man and woman are married."

Here's the problem: You don't know that the man and woman *aren't* married. This makes it really tempting to choose that choice, or at least not to eliminate it right away (especially if the other two answer choices are *definitely* wrong). This is the trap of the exaggeration answer choice. You can be tempted to choose it simply because you don't feel that you can eliminate it for sure. Let's look at answer choice (A) from the photo question.

(A) The people are in a marketing meeting.

The people in the photo *could* be in a marketing meeting. There's nothing to indicate that they aren't. But there's nothing that tells us for sure that it's a meeting about marketing, or even that it's a meeting at all. It could be a class or support group or sales pitch. You should eliminate this answer choice. However, we understand that it might be difficult for you to eliminate a choice that you can't determine to be definitely false. Don't worry. If you read on, you'll see how to get to the correct answer choice without immediately eliminating anything you're not sure about.

What must be true?

Even if you understand all four statements perfectly, there may not be one clear-cut winner among the statements. In fact, two or even three of the statements might make you stop and consider them. If you don't completely understand one or more of the statements, it will be even more difficult to decide which one is the best one.

Don't underestimate the effects of the way the statements are worded to deliberately distract you from the real answer. ETS writes them this way on purpose to prevent you from answering all the questions correctly.

There is an unspoken question for each photo. This question is: *What can you infer from the photo?* To answer this question correctly, you need to understand the definition of *inference* on a standardized test.

Imagine that you are a detective who has arrived at a crime scene to find a dead man lying on the floor. After searching the room completely, you find nothing out of the ordinary but several strands of long, blonde hair. What can you infer from this information?

In real life, you could infer many different things. You could infer that the man had a blonde girlfriend. Or that the murderer had blonde hair. Or that the murderer was wearing a blonde wig. Any of these inferences are reasonable.

On a standardized test, however, you cannot make any of these inferences. The only thing you can infer from the information is that at some point, someone with long, blonde hair was in the room.

Think about that. This kind of "inference" does not leave any room for deduction or thought, only for the rewording of information you already have. In other words, you are not supposed to fill in any gaps in information with your own thoughts. You are only supposed to go by the information that is already there. You are not allowed to consider things that can be true, only things that *must* be true.

You must approach all the photo questions the same way, by being as strict and minimal as possible in your thinking. If the photo doesn't show it, you cannot assume it, even if it makes complete sense in the natural world.

For each statement, you are looking for the answer to the question: "What can you infer from the photo?" But remember that you are only looking for the statement that *must* be true based on the photo. For each statement, ask yourself, "Does this have to be true, based on the photo?" If the answer is "no," eliminate that answer choice. You will only be able to answer "yes" about one answer choice. Pick that choice.

Let's listen to the answer choices again. Play CD #1 Track 6. (There's a written transcript of the answer choice statements at the end of this chapter, before the drill.)

Answer choice (A) says, "The people are in a marketing meeting." Does this *have to be true?* No. Eliminate it.

Answer choice (B) says, "The students are giving a lecture to the professor." Does this *have to be true?* No. Cross it off.

Answer choice (C) says, "The table is strong." Does this *have to be true?* No. (It doesn't even really make sense.) Eliminate it.

Answer choice (D) says, "The man is talking to the people." Does this *have to be true?* Yes. Fill in (D) on your answer sheet and start studying the next photo.

But what if you don't understand everything?

If you don't completely understand all four statements, you are not automatically doomed to crash and burn on that question. Instead, you should use the "What *must* be true?" concept to help you narrow down the choices. There is, of course, no guarantee that you'll choose the correct answer, but you can definitely increase your chances by using this technique.

To start, you should interpret the photograph as usual. Then listen to the four statements, assessing each one as you hear it. If there are any that you can eliminate immediately, cross them off. Remember that anything you can eliminate for sure will increase your odds of answering the question correctly. For any statements you can't immediately eliminate, jot down the main concept of the statement. You don't have time to write much, so write only a few words. For instance, for answer choice (C) in the photo we've been working with, you could write "table strong."

Let's pretend that you eliminated answer choices (A) and (B) in the example, and are left with statements (C) and (D). You didn't understand all of statement (D). This is what you have written in your test booklet:

~~A~~
~~B~~
C table strong
D man ?

Here's where the technique comes in. There is *no way* for you to know if statement (D) *must* be true, because you don't know what it says. However, you can assess statement (C). If statement (C) *must* be true, then eliminate (D) and pick (C). If statement (C) doesn't have to be true, then eliminate (C) and pick (D). Even if you don't understand (D), if you know that (A), (B), and (C) are not correct, then (D) has to be correct. Let's try it.

Does the table *have to be* strong, based on the photo? No. Eliminate (C). That means (D) must be the answer.

Getting the hang of it

Now that you're a master of using the "What *must* be true?" concept, combined with POE, to answer photographs questions correctly, don't lose points by losing steam. Be sure you're filling in the correct bubble on the answer sheet. Then, as soon as your pencil leaves the answer sheet, start studying the next photograph. That way you'll be able to give all your attention to the spoken statements as you hear them, instead of splitting your attention between the photo and the statements.

Remember: Do not leave any blanks. If you cannot answer a question for any reason, fill in the bubble for that question with the letter you picked to be your "guessing letter."

Transcript of the example answer choices

> (A) *The people are in a marketing meeting.*
> (B) *The students are giving a lecture to the professor.*
> (C) *The table is strong.*
> (D) *The man is talking to the people.*

Photographs drill

Play CD #1 Track 7 to hear the statements, and answer the following questions.

1.

2.

3.

4.

5.

6.

7.

8.

9.

10.

Answers to the photographs drill

1. B
2. A
3. D
4. B
5. C
6. B
7. D
8. A
9. C
10. C

Explanations

1. **B** Answer choice (A) is a soundalike: "Sells clothes" instead of "is closed." Eliminate it. Answer choice (B) *must* be true: "Not open" means "closed." Answer choice (C) is an exaggeration: There is no indication of when the store will open. Cross it off. Answer choice (D) is just wrong—there is no woman in the photo. Get rid of it.

2. **A** Answer choice A *must* be true: A sign saying EXIT with an arrow indicates that you can leave in that direction. Answer choice (B) is a misrepresentation. Cross it off. Answer choice (C) has nothing to do with the photo. Eliminate it. Answer choice (D) is not correct—the photo is not about a hallway. Eliminate it.

3. **D** Answer choice (A) is an exaggeration: We don't know for sure what the woman is saying. Eliminate it. Answer choice (B) is an exaggeration: We don't know what she is doing. Get rid of it. Answer choice (C) is an exaggeration: The woman could be the head of the company, but we don't know for sure. Cross this one off too. Answer choice (D) **must** be true—she is wearing a suit.

4. **B** Answer choice (A) is a misrepresentation: The bus is in service, not out of service. Get rid of it. Answer choice (B) must be true—the bus is on the street. Answer choice (C) is a misrepresentation: The only person visible on the bus is the driver. Eliminate it. Answer choice (D) is an exaggeration: The driver could be a woman, but this isn't obvious from the photo. Eliminate this one.

5. **C** Answer choice (A) is wrong—there is no man in the photo. Eliminate it. Answer choice (B) is a misrepresentation: The store also sells chains. Cross this one off. Answer choice (C) *must* be true: There are many watches in the photo. Answer choice (D) is a soundalike: The word *watch* is used here as a verb instead of a noun. Get rid of it.

6. **B** Answer choice (A) is an exaggeration: The people could be eating lunch, but there's no indication that they all are. Cross it off. Answer choice (B) *must* be true: There are many people sitting in the room in the photo. Answer choice (C) is a misrepresentation: The lights are on, not off. Eliminate this one. Answer choice (D) is wrong—there's no information about the menu in the photo. Eliminate it.

7. **D** Answer choice (A) is a soundalike: "Sell one" sounds like "cell phone." Eliminate it. Answer choice (B) is an exaggeration: The seats may be comfortable, but we don't know for sure. Cross it off. Answer choice (C) is an exaggeration: We don't know whether the woman will fasten her seat belt or not. Get rid of this one too. Answer choice (D) *must* be true—the woman has a mobile phone.

8. **A** Answer choice (A) *must* be true—the woman in the photo is smiling. Answer choice (B) is an exaggeration: We don't know for sure what they are discussing. Eliminate it. Answer choice (C) is an exaggeration: We don't know if they're in a class, or if that class is hard. Eliminate it too. Answer choice (D) is an exaggeration: We don't know if the bending man is a team leader. Cross it off.

9. **C** Answer choice (A) is a misrepresentation—he's not on the phone. Eliminate this one. Answer choice (B) is an exaggeration: He may be about to leave, but we can't tell for sure. Get rid of it. Answer choice (C) *must* be true: The man is looking at his computer. Answer choice (D) is an exaggeration: He may be analyzing a report on his computer, but we don't know for sure. Cross this one off.

10. **C** Answer choice (A) is an exaggeration: We don't know where the taxi is going to go. Eliminate it. Answer choice (B) is a misrepresentation: The man is getting into or out of the taxi, not paying the driver. Cross it off. Answer choice (C) *must* be true—the door of the taxi is open. Answer choice (D) is an exaggeration: It may be true, but we don't know for sure. Eliminate it.

Photographs drill transcript

1.
   (A) *The store sells clothes.*
   (B) *The store is not open.*
   (C) *The store will open at 8.*
   (D) *She will call later.*

2.
   (A) *Follow the arrow to leave the subway.*
   (B) *There is no exit from this door.*
   (C) *If you have a question, please ask it now.*
   (D) *The hallway is empty.*

3.
   (A) *She is explaining an idea.*
   (B) *She is conducting a sales meeting.*
   (C) *She is the head of the company.*
   (D) *She is wearing a suit.*

4. (A) The bus is out of service.
    (B) The bus is on the street.
    (C) The man is getting off the bus.
    (D) The bus driver is a woman.

5. (A) The man is buying a watch.
    (B) The store sells only watches.
    (C) There are many watches on display.
    (D) Watch out for the broken stairway.

6. (A) Many people are eating lunch.
    (B) There are lots of people sitting in the room.
    (C) The lights are off.
    (D) The menu is very extensive.

7. (A) The woman is trying to sell one.
    (B) The seats are comfortable.
    (C) The woman will not fasten her seatbelt.
    (D) The woman has a telephone.

8. (A) The woman is smiling.
    (B) They are discussing strategy.
    (C) The class must be hard.
    (D) The team leader is giving feedback.

9. (A) He's on the telephone.
    (B) He's about to go home.
    (C) He's looking at his computer.
    (D) He's analyzing a report.

10. (A) The taxi is going to the airport.
    (B) The man is paying the taxi driver.
    (C) The door is open.
    (D) The driver has been working all day.

6

Question-and-Response Questions

THE BASICS

In the question-and-response part of the TOEIC Listening Comprehension section, your task is to listen to a question asked by one speaker, and choose the correct response out of three choices spoken by another speaker. The question and answer choices will not be repeated. In other words, you have one chance to listen and answer.

There are 30 question-and-response questions on the test. The speakers may be a man and a woman, two women, or two men.

The trickiest thing about question-and-response questions is that there is nothing written in the test booklet to help you answer them. Neither the question nor the answer choices are written down. There isn't even a photo to help you get an idea of the context of the question. This makes it very difficult to get your bearings before the question and all three answer choices have gone by.

THE METHOD

THE INSTRUCTIONS

While everyone else is listening to the instructions, you should be setting up your test booklet to help you use POE successfully. Next to each question, write the letters A, B, and C (there are only three responses in this section) in a vertical line, like this:

A
B
C

With your booklet set up this way, when you hear the statements, you can cross out letters that correspond to statements you know aren't correct (we'll describe how to figure that out in a minute).

This setup is just as important on the question-and-response section of the TOEIC as it is on the photographs section. Writing down the letters and physically crossing them off in the test booklet enables you to keep track of the answer choices. When it planned this section, ETS was counting on the fact that you would not be able to keep all the answer choices straight in your head. Keeping track of them on paper gives you a huge advantage over anyone else taking the test. Don't get lazy and forget to write down the letters, as this wastes the best opportunity you have to beat the test makers at their own game.

What does this have to DO with anything?

As we said earlier, the real problem with this section is that there's no context for the questions and responses. You have no idea who the two speakers are. They could be coworkers, friends, store clerk and customer, train conductor and passenger, or any other individuals. This makes it very difficult to understand enough of the question to focus on which answer choice is the best response. The only ways to increase your odds on this section are to listen actively and eliminate as you listen.

LISTEN ACTIVELY

The question is the only "context" you'll get to help you choose the best response, so you can't afford not to listen closely. Focus on it to determine the purpose of the question. What is being asked for? The best way to determine purpose is to listen for words that *always* ask questions. Pay close attention to these question words. Commonly used question words are *who, what, why, when, where,* and *how.*

Know what type of answer each question word should get. For instance, the question "who" should be answered with the name of a person.

Here's a chart to help you keep track.

Question Word	Answer Must Be
who	a person
what	a thing
why	a reason or explanation
when	a day, time, or other time reference
where	a location
how	a process

The phrase "how come" means "why." It is casual, so you will probably not hear it on the TOEIC.

Any question that does not begin with a question word must be answered either affirmatively or negatively. (In the United States we call these questions "yes/no questions.") Unfortunately, the correct answer choice does not actually have to contain the word "yes" or the word "no." There's more about that in the next section of this chapter, though.

As you do the drill in this chapter and the two practice tests, pay special attention to the question words you hear and practice predicting what type of answer you need to hear. Once you get good at this you'll find that incorrect answer choices begin to stand out more. Once they stand out, you'll be able to eliminate them more easily.

Let's practice listening now. Listen to CD #1 Track 8 on the CD that came with this book. (The transcript of this conversation is at the end of this chapter, right before the drill.) Listen carefully to hear the question and answer choices. Focus on the purpose of the question.

ELIMINATE AS YOU LISTEN

As you listen, you should be able to determine that some of the answer choices are not correct. Eliminate them immediately by crossing out the letters you wrote down in your test booklet. There are some special incorrect answer choices that you will see over and over again on the question-and-response questions.

Soundalikes

Soundalikes are responses that contain words that sound like words in the question. In other words, the question might ask, "How far did she drive?" but the soundalike answer choice would say, "The music was live." The words "drive" and "live" sound similar, so anyone not listening to hear exactly what the question asks could be tricked into picking this answer choice. Let's look at answer choice (A) in our example question.

(A) Yes, the leaves at the airport have turned brown.

The word *leaves* sounds like *leave* and the word *airport* is in both the question and the answer choice. The question doesn't ask anything about leaves, though. Eliminate this answer choice.

The correct response will hardly ever contain a word from the question. So if you hear a word that sounds like a key word from the question, eliminate it. Remember that this section is supposed to simulate the language of real questions and answers. When people answer a question in conversation, they usually do not repeat the question. For example, if someone asks you, "How are you feeling?" you would not be likely to answer, "I'm feeling fine." You would probably just say, "Fine."

Yes/no

There are many yes/no questions in the question-and-response section. And there are many responses beginning with the words *yes* or *no*. Unfortunately, the yes/no questions don't always correspond to the yes/no answer choices. In fact, many times the correct answer to a yes/no question will not start with *yes* or *no*.

For example, the question might be, "Do you want to go to lunch with us?" This is a yes/no question. The correct response, however, may be, "I can't right now. I have to finish this report." What this means is that you may or may not *want* to go to lunch, but you *can't* go to lunch. The response doesn't contain the word *no*, though.

Don't automatically assume that an answer choice beginning with *yes* or *no* is the correct response to a yes/no question. On the other hand, the correct response to a yes/no question could easily begin with *yes* or *no*. Just stay alert and be prepared for either possibility.

Let's look at answer choice (B) from the example question.

(B) No, I haven't traveled by air this year.

The question is a yes/no question, and this answer choice begins with the word *no*. However, it doesn't actually answer the question. The question asks if the woman will leave *now* or *in the future* for the airport. This answer choice talks about the past. Get rid of it.

LISTEN FOR THE CORRECT ANSWER

If you've predicted what type of response you need to hear to the question, you should be able to pick out the correct answer as you listen to the choices. The question asks if the woman will be leaving now. Answer choice (C) gives the answer.

(C) Actually, I'm going in two hours.

Fill in the answer quickly

Remember that time is important in the Listening Comprehension section, so you'll have to keep moving. Once you've identified the correct answer, fill it in on the answer sheet as quickly as you can. You can avoid wasting time looking for the correct line on the answer sheet by aligning the answer sheet underneath your test booklet so the bottom line showing is the one for the next question. Double-check that you're filling in the right bubble for the right question number. With 30 questions in this section, it can be easy to get off track. Check after every five questions to make sure that you're still on the right number.

Also, don't forget that there are only three answer choices on the question-and-response section. If you fill in any bubbles for answer choice (D), you will get that question wrong. Make sure you haven't filled in any (D) bubbles. (If you go back over your answer sheet and find that you *have* filled in a (D) in numbers 21–50, change it to (C), since that's probably what you meant.)

Listen for the next question

This section is a lot like a tennis match. You don't know what's going to happen next, so the only thing you can do is stay on your toes and focus on your opponent. Even when you answer one question correctly, you still have to pay attention to the next one. Listen to the question and try to predict what kind of answer you need to hear. Then eliminate bad answer choices as you hear them.

Remember: Do not leave any blanks. If you cannot answer a question for any reason, fill in the bubble for that question with the letter you picked to be your "guessing letter."

Transcript of the question-and-response example

(Man)   *Are you leaving for the airport soon?*

(Woman)   (A) *Yes, the leaves at the airport have turned brown.*

                   (B) *No, I haven't traveled by air this year.*

                   (C) *Actually, I'm going in two hours.*

Question-and-response drill

Play CD #1 Track 9 to hear the questions and responses.

1. Mark your answer on your answer sheet.

2. Mark your answer on your answer sheet.

3. Mark your answer on your answer sheet.

4. Mark your answer on your answer sheet.

5. Mark your answer on your answer sheet.

6. Mark your answer on your answer sheet.

7. Mark your answer on your answer sheet.

8. Mark your answer on your answer sheet.

9. Mark your answer on your answer sheet.

10. Mark your answer on your answer sheet.

Answers to the question-and-response drill

1. C
2. A
3. B
4. C
5. A
6. B
7. C
8. A
9. B
10. C

Explanations

1. **C** The question word *when* needs an answer containing a time reference. Eliminate answer choice (B). A question word can't have a *yes* or *no* answer. Cross off (A). Answer choice (C) tells when the train was supposed to come.

2. **A** Answer choice (B) refers to visual "sight" instead of a location "site" referred to in the question. Get rid of it. Answer choice (C) uses *sooner* to reference the word *late*, not the word *lately* in the question. Eliminate it. Answer choice (A) answers the question.

3. **B** Answer choices (A) and (C) answer different questions about the taxi than the one being asked. Eliminate them. Answer choice (B) gives the number.

4. **C** Answer choice (A) answers *when*, not *where*. Cross it off. Answer choice (B) uses soundalikes: "Herald Pass" for "her password." Eliminate it. Answer choice (C) tells where the note is.

5. **A** Answer choice (B) does not say anything about Mr. Ramos. Eliminate it. Answer choice (C) mentions "papers," which are not in the question. Cross it off too. Answer choice (A) tells where Mr. Ramos works.

6. **B** Answer choice (A) discusses the Woman's form, not The Man's. Eliminate it. Answer choice (C) mentions Seoul, which wasn't mentioned in the question. Get rid of it. Answer choice (B) tells where the form is.

7. **C** Answer choice (A) answers the question *who*, not *what* time. Cross it off. Answer choice (B) tells when the party ends. Eliminate this one too. Answer choice (C) tells when the party will begin.

8. **A** Answer choice (B) mentions "it," not the CEO. Eliminate it. Answer choice (C) mentions Man 1's wife. Get rid of this one. Answer choice (A) says that Man 2 hasn't heard the news yet.

9. **B** Answer choice (A) mentions a package. Cross it off. Answer choice (C) talks about the past, but the question asks about the present. Get rid of this one. Answer choice (B) answers the question.

10. **C** Answer choice (A) answers the question *where*, not *when*. Eliminate it. Answer choice (B) answers the question "with whom is she working." Cross it off too. Answer choice (C) tells when the report will be done.

Question-and-response drill transcript

1. (Woman) *When was the train supposed to arrive?*
   (Man)   (A) *No, not until 5:30.*
            (B) *I didn't bring an umbrella today.*
            (C) *Half an hour ago.*

2. (Man)   *Have you been to the construction site lately?*
   (Woman) (A) *Yes, it's really coming along.*
            (B) *Yes, my vision is much better since the surgery.*
            (C) *No, we expected it sooner.*

3. (Man)   *What's the number you called to get a taxi?*
   (Woman) (A) *Yes, that's the one I use all the time.*
            (B) *It's easy—777-7777.*
            (C) *I can't drive my own car because it's being repaired.*

4. (Man 1) *Where did Elaine write down her password?*
   (Man 2) (A) *Right before she went on vacation.*
            (B) *No, you should turn left down Herald Pass.*
            (C) *It's on a note on her computer.*

5. (Woman) *Does Mr. Ramos work in the Houston office or the Austin office?*
   (Man)   (A) *He used to work in the Austin office, but he was transferred last month.*
            (B) *No, there is no opening in the building.*
            (C) *Yes, his papers are in order.*

6. (Man)   *Where did you leave my expense form?*
   (Woman) (A) *I filled out my expense form last week.*
            (B) *I dropped it in your in-box.*
            (C) *You don't have all your receipts from the Seoul trip.*

7. (Man)   *What time is the party starting?*
   (Woman) (A) *The whole department is invited.*
            (B) *It should end at 10.*
            (C) *Right after the board meeting is over.*

8. (Man 1)   Haven't you heard about the CEO?
   (Man 2)   (A) No, what happened to him?
             (B) Yes, I bought it yesterday.
             (C) Your wife is on the phone.

9. (Woman)   Can you send the shipping department an e-mail for me?
   (Man)   (A) Yes, the package will arrive.
             (B) Yes, as soon as I find the address.
             (C) No, I haven't done it yet.

10. (Man)   When did she say the report would be finished?
   (Woman)   (A) Through the mail.
             (B) She is working with her assistant.
             (C) At the end of the week.

Short Conversations Questions

THE BASICS

In the short conversations part of the TOEIC Listening Comprehension section, your task is to listen to short conversations and answer questions based on what is either stated or implied. The conversations will not be repeated. In other words, you have one chance to listen and remember.

There are 30 short conversations questions on the test.

The good news is that the questions are all very straightforward. There are no tricks; instead, you will be asked about details from the conversation. What makes them difficult is that (a) you may not understand everything the speakers say in English, (b) you will only hear the conversation once, and (c) you have to remember everything you heard while you also evaluate the answer choices to eliminate them.

Fortunately, we have ways for you to get around these problems.

YOU MIGHT NOT UNDERSTAND

Say what?

Somewhere in the short conversations section, you'll hear a statement that sounds something like this:

"Question number sixty-six. Hey, that's the *blah over blah blah bee blah!*"

In other words, you have no idea what the speaker said. Now, while you're trying to remember when in your English studies you ever heard *"blah blah bee"* (or was it *"bee blah blah"*?), you hear ". . . *blah blah,* don't you think?"

You panic. You only heard part of what the speakers said and now you have just a few words on which to base your answer choice.

No context

The short conversations that ETS gives you do not accurately depict real conversations. As we've already pointed out, in real, face-to-face conversations, you rely on many visual factors, such as facial expressions and hand gestures, to help you understand what the other person is saying. Also, knowing something about the person or the topic gives additional meaning to the words used. Furthermore, if he or she uses some words or expressions that you're not familiar with, you can use the context of the rest of the conversation to help figure out what they mean.

None of these cues are available in the short conversations questions. The largest hurdle to get over in order to do well on this section is the lack of context. For these questions, the information presented is completely isolated. The questions can be about anything. However, there is some good news. The questions can be about anything, but the answers are all right in front of your eyes.

The good news

Although there are some problems with the TOEIC, one of the test's weaknesses can make your job much easier. To help you understand how this works, we're going to explain some of the reasons why the TOEIC is constructed the way it is.

Most tests you take in school are not multiple-choice. The primary reason for this is that teachers don't like them. Teachers don't like multiple-choice tests because they don't do what tests are supposed to do—provide some meaningful indication of how much a student has learned. Here's why. Complete the following sentence:

When I haven't had time to prepare for an exam, I would have the best luck if my teacher asked me to
- ○ write an essay
- ○ answer questions orally
- ○ write short answers to pointed questions
- ○ choose the best answer from among four options

Most people would pick "Choose the best answer from among four options." Why? Because on a multiple-choice test, you don't necessarily have to *know* the right answer; you can eliminate some answer choices, and then guess! Remember that the correct answer is *always* in front of you on the computer screen.

ETS's DILEMMA

Let's say that two people are taking the TOEIC. One of them speaks English almost fluently. The other hardly speaks English at all. The one who hardly speaks English has a lot of trouble understanding the words on the recording and hears something like this:

Question number 76.

(Man)	*Blah blah blah* Mary.
(Woman)	Will Mary *blah bee blah blah* Sunday?
(Man)	Sunday *blah bee blah* Mary's *blah blah*.
(Narrator)	What does the man mean?

Now look at the answer choices. Remember, the only words this person understood were *Sunday* and *Mary*.

(A) School is in session nine months out of the year.
(B) Hats are not usually worn during dinner.
(C) Mary rarely works on Sunday.
(D) The operation was very expensive.

So which answer would he choose? "Mary rarely works on Sunday," of course, because it contains the words he recognized from the question. "Mary rarely works on Sunday" is also the right answer, so this person who hardly understands English just answered the question correctly.

This presents ETS with a problem. Of course the person whose English is very good is also going to answer the question correctly. He will understand the question word for word. According to this particular question, both test takers now have the same level of English proficiency. If this happens on too many questions, it is a disaster for ETS. It means that the test is a failure. If the test is a failure, companies will no longer use it to assess the proficiency of their employees, so no one will buy the test anymore.

So ETS had to come up with a way to keep people from guessing correctly on too many of its questions. Now look at the same question with different answer choices:

Question number 76.

(Man)	*Blah blah blah* Mary.
(Woman)	Will Mary *blah bee blah blah* Sunday?
(Man)	Sunday *blah bee blah* Mary's *blah blah*.
(Narrator)	What does the man mean?

(A) Sunday is a day Mary often works.
(B) Mary rarely works on Sunday.
(C) Some days Mary's work is awful.
(D) Mary has had a terrible cough since Sunday.

If this was all you understood of the short conversation, would you be able to tell which is the right answer? Probably not. Now, most of the answer choices contain those same two words that you could hear in the conversation, so it would be hard to choose among them. Although the statement remained the same, this question just became much harder. Nothing has changed but the answer choices.

The first example was much too easy to have ever appeared on an actual TOEIC. Too many people would correctly guess the answer. To fix this, ETS had to change the answer choices so that the wrong answers don't seem so wrong. In fact, ETS tries to make the wrong answers sometimes look *better* than the right answers. In other words, ETS creates distractors to divert your attention from the correct answer. Let's look at how they do it.

A BRIEF LESSON IN QUESTION WRITING

First ETS comes up with the short conversation:

(Man)	*I just talked to Mary.*
(Woman)	*Will Mary be in on Sunday?*
(Man)	*Sunday is usually Mary's day off.*
(Narrator)	What does the man mean?

and the right answer:

    (B) Mary rarely works on Sunday.

Now comes the hard part for ETS. It has to come up with three wrong distractors that don't *seem* wrong. On many questions, ETS will phrase an answer choice so that it's very close to the right answer but means just the opposite.

    (A) Sunday is a day Mary often works.

This wrong answer will attract thousands of test takers who *almost* understood the conversation. If you see two answer choices that are opposites, chances are, one of them is the correct one. Make your best guess and fill it in.

ETS will also include answer choices that contain some of the same sounds and words as the conversation.

    (C) Some days Mary's work is awful.
    (D) Mary has had a terrible cough since Sunday.

Some days sounds like *Sunday*, and *awful* and *cough* sound like *off*. These answers will attract those who were able to pick out the sounds of the statement, but didn't understand the sense of it. If answer choices contain these types of soundalikes, you can bet they are wrong.

Now take a look at the answer choices again.

    (A) Sunday is a day Mary often works.
    (B) Mary rarely works on Sunday.
    (C) Some days Mary's work is awful.
    (D) Mary has had a terrible cough since Sunday.

Three out of four of them mention Sunday, three out of four of them mention work, and they all include Mary. In order to make it harder for you to guess, ETS regularly includes words from the conversation in both correct and incorrect answer choices. So don't be fooled into thinking you can select the correct answer just by looking for words from the conversation.

IT ALL GOES BY SO FAST

The remaining two problems, that you only hear the conversations once and that you have to remember everything you heard while you evaluate the answer choices to eliminate them, are essentially problems of timing. Guess what? You can manipulate this timing problem simply by switching the order in which you approach the question. By reading the question and answer choices *before* you hear the conversation, you'll be able to listen for exactly the information you need. This puts the odds of answering the question correctly in your favor.

READ THE QUESTION FIRST

At the beginning of the short conversations section, there is a set of instructions. The speaker on the tape will read through the instructions, asking you to follow along as he reads. Since you've already read the instructions in this book and understand exactly how to work the questions, you don't need to listen and pay attention to this part. What you *should* do during this time is read the first question (number 51). This serves two major purposes. First of all, it gives you an enormous hint as to what the conversation will be about. Let's take a look at a question and decide what the conversation must be about.

> What is wrong with the pipes in the man's room?
>
> (A) They are leaking water.
> (B) They are making a loud sound.
> (C) They don't have any insulation.
> (D) The maintenance man has taken them to room 345.

In this question, the conversation is about a problem with some pipes. You know that the setting will be a hotel or some other place in which a person would have a room, not an office or restaurant or transportation setting. Since the question talks about "the man's room," you also know that at least one of the speakers will be a man. That's actually a lot of information to know about a conversation you haven't even heard yet.

The other purpose of reading the question ahead of time is to let you know what to listen for. In this question, you should get your ears and brain ready to process the information about the specific problem with the pipes.

Now, here's the real kicker: If you read the answer choices ahead of time, too, you can just wait for the correct answer to drift past your actively listening ears. Instead of a mad scramble to remember what you heard, frantically eliminate, and then fill in the answer, answering the question becomes an orderly and structured process. You know what the conversation's going to be about, and you know what the answer choices are, so you only have to pay close attention until you hear the correct answer choice.

LISTEN CAREFULLY

The simplicity and clarity of the "read ahead" method should not lure you into complacency. The unfortunate truth is that *you still have to listen to the conversation*. If you don't understand what the speaker is saying at all, having read the question ahead of time won't make much difference to you. If you find that you do not understand the conversations when you do the drill at the end of this chapter, you should go back to Chapter 4 and review the techniques for understanding conversational English.

This doesn't mean that you have to understand every word. As long as you have a pretty good idea of the message and flow of the conversation, you should be able to eliminate wrong answers effectively.

Let's practice listening now. Listen to CD #2 Track 5 that came with this book. (The transcript of this conversation is at the end of this chapter, right before the drill.) Listen carefully to hear what the problem is with the pipes in the man's room.

ELIMINATE AS YOU LISTEN

As you listen, you should be able to determine that some of the answer choices are not correct. Eliminate them immediately by crossing them out physically in your test booklet. There are some special incorrect answer choices that you will see over and over again in the short conversations questions.

Answer choices that are too predictable

Some answer choices are there because they are too predictable. They are the answer choices that you'd pick before you even hear the conversation. The problem is that, many times, the conversation isn't about the predictable situation. For example, let's look at answer choice (A) in our question about the problem pipes.

> (A) They are leaking water.

This answer choice is supremely predictable. If someone you know said that they had been having problems with their pipes, you would probably just automatically assume that the problem was that they were leaking water. After all, the whole job of a pipe is to carry water, so any disruption in that would be a big problem.

In this conversation, however, the pipes aren't leaking. As soon as you hear the man talking about a noise, you know that the problem with the pipes isn't the predictable one. Eliminate the predictable answer choice.

Soundalikes

Soundalikes are a truly dirty trick on the part of ETS. These are distractor answer choices put there because they sound like something in the conversation, but they aren't the real answers. In other words, the conversation might say, "I just bought a new car" but the soundalike answer choice would say, "I got lost when I drove too far." The words "new car" and "too far" sound similar, so anyone not listening to hear exactly what the answer choices say could be tricked into picking this answer choice. Let's look at answer choice (C) in our pipe question.

> (C) They don't have any insulation.

The word *insulation* in the answer choices sounds like the word *presentation* in the conversation. There is nothing about insulation in the conversation.

Bear in mind that it is okay for words in the conversation to be in the correct answer choice. Sometimes they have to be, particularly if the question asks about a name, for instance. But don't pick an answer choice *just because* you hear a word from the answer choice in the conversation.

Sometimes you can eliminate a soundalike answer choice as you're listening to the actual conversation. If you're particularly aware of the soundalike phenomenon, you could hear "presentation" in the conversation and think, *Aha! "Insulation" sounds a lot like "presentation." I bet it's a soundalike—I'll cross it off.* This is a level of POE mastery to aspire to, but don't worry if you don't get there. You'll still have a good chance of picking the correct answer choice.

Misrepresentations

The most devious trap answer choices are the ones that are misrepresentations of what was said in the conversation. The words and concepts from the conversation are in the answer choice, but the choice twists them to be wrong. It is much easier to fall into this trap if you don't read the question and answer choices before you listen to the conversation. If you don't, you have to rely on your memory of what was said as you're reading the answer choices, so you are more vulnerable to misrepresentations. Reading the question ahead of time helps with that. But if you aren't paying careful attention to the conversation, you could pick a misrepresentation of what the conversation is *actually* saying. Let's look at answer choice (D) from the pipe question.

> (D) The maintenance man has taken them to room 345.

This answer choice is extremely tempting, because the words *maintenance man* and *room 345* are in the conversation. However, the maintenance man hasn't done anything yet with the pipes, and they're already in room 345. This answer choice is a classic misrepresentation. Cross it out in the test booklet.

LISTEN FOR THE CORRECT ANSWER

As you listen to the conversation, you should be able to pick out the correct answer. In the pipe conversation, you hear, "The pipes in my bathroom have started making a loud banging noise." This is answer choice (B).

> (B) They are making a loud sound.

Fill in the answer quickly

Remember that time is important in the Listening Comprehension section, so you'll have to keep moving. Once you've identified the correct answer, fill it in on the answer sheet as quickly as you can. You can avoid wasting time looking for the correct line on the answer sheet by aligning the answer sheet underneath your test booklet so the bottom line showing is the one for the next question. Double-check that you're filling in the right bubble for the right question number.

Read the next question

You've successfully conquered one short conversations question, but there are still 29 others. In order to work the next one well, you'll need time to read the question and answer choices *before* the conversation plays on the tape. As soon as you've filled in an answer choice, go immediately to the next question and answer choices and read them quickly. Then follow the same steps to eliminate choices while you're listening to the short conversation.

Remember: Do not leave any blanks. If you cannot answer a question for any reason, fill in the bubble for that question with the letter you picked to be your "guessing letter."

Transcript of the short conversation example

> (Man) *Front desk? The pipes in my bathroom have started making a loud banging noise that's getting progressively louder.*
>
> (Woman) *That doesn't sound good! You're in room 345? I'll send a maintenance man up right away.*
>
> (Man) *Thank you. I'm working on a presentation for a client and I can't concentrate with all this noise.*

If you follow the plan we've just outlined, you should be able to answer the short conversations questions much more effectively and without as much anxiety and confusion. If you're ready to test your skills, work through the drill that follows.

Short conversations drill

Play CD #2 Track 6 to hear the conversations, and answer the following questions. Answers can be found on page 85.

1. What is the woman doing?

   (A) Paying for a purchase at a store.
   (B) Making a withdrawal at a bank.
   (C) Sending a greeting card.
   (D) Asking directions on a bus.

2. What will the man do when Mr. Herrod calls?

   (A) Ask him to call again at 3.
   (B) Interrupt the woman in her meeting.
   (C) Invite him to a meeting.
   (D) Begin the marketing meeting.

3. Where was the iron?

   (A) In the closet of room 302.
   (B) At the front desk.
   (C) Behind the wall.
   (D) On a lower floor.

4. What does the woman want the man to do?

   (A) Help her find her desk.
   (B) Figure out what's wrong with her computer.
   (C) Catch a mouse in her office.
   (D) Check the telephone connection.

5. Why is the woman asking about the leave policy?

   (A) She is pregnant.
   (B) She has already taken time off.
   (C) She is planning ahead.
   (D) She wants to buy some furniture.

6. What does the woman advise the man to do?

   (A) Sleep with a bag over his head.
   (B) Leave on Saturday instead of Friday.
   (C) Turn on a light during the trip.
   (D) Take a nap on the airplane.

7. What is going to happen in a few minutes?

   (A) There will be a meeting upstairs.
   (B) The ship will leave from the port.
   (C) Everyone will help with the report.
   (D) No one will do anything.

8. What will be different about the office?

   (A) It will become greater.
   (B) Yuko won't work there anymore.
   (C) It will become a school.
   (D) Mr. Masters will go to school.

9. Where does this conversation take place?

   (A) The post office.
   (B) A computer store.
   (C) A restaurant.
   (D) A bookstore.

10. When will the flight come in?

    (A) Early.
    (B) Late.
    (C) Today.
    (D) Tomorrow.

Answers to the short conversations drill

1. A
2. B
3. A
4. B
5. C
6. D
7. A
8. B
9. C
10. D

Explanations

1. What is the woman doing?

(A) Paying for a purchase at a store.
(B) Making a withdrawal at a bank.
(C) Sending a greeting card.
(D) Asking directions on a bus.

1. **A** The question "cash or charge?" is commonly used in English to ask how a person wants to pay for a purchase at a store, so answer choice (A) is right. A debit card is another way to pay for a purchase, so the mention of the debit card does not indicate that she wants to make a withdrawal from a bank (the predictable answer choice (B)). There is no indication that she is sending a greeting card (C) or asking directions (D).

2. What will the man do when Mr. Herrod calls?

(A) Ask him to call again at 3.
(B) Interrupt the woman in her meeting.
(C) Invite him to a meeting.
(D) Begin the marketing meeting.

2. **B** The woman says, "Please come get me when he calls" to indicate that the man should interrupt her in the meeting. Answer choices (A), (C), and (D) are all misrepresentations of the conversation, since they contain words from the conversation but do not tell what was actually said.

3. Where was the iron?

    (A) In the closet of room 302.
    (B) At the front desk.
    (C) Behind the wall.
    (D) On a lower floor.

3. A The second man says, "There should be one in your closet," and the first man replies, "Ah, here it is!" This indicates that the iron was in the closet, answer choice (A). Answer choices (B) and (C) are misrepresentations, since the front desk and wall were both mentioned. Answer choice (D) is a soundalike—*lower floor* sounds like *I didn't see it before*.

4. What does the woman want the man to do?

    (A) Help her find her desk.
    (B) Figure out what's wrong with her computer.
    (C) Catch a mouse in her office.
    (D) Check the telephone connection.

4. B The woman says, "My computer seems to be stuck" and then asks, "Can you come down here to have a look at it?" This indicates that she wants the man to fix her computer, answer choice (B). Answer choice (A) is a soundalike—*Help Desk* is a name for the department in a company that helps the employees use their computers. Answer choices (C) and (D) are misrepresentations. Both *mouse* and *connection* refer to the computer, not to a rodent and a telephone.

5. Why is the woman asking about the leave policy?

    (A) She is pregnant.
    (B) She has already taken time off.
    (C) She is planning ahead.
    (D) She wants to buy some furniture.

5. C The woman says, "I'm just trying to get some information so we can make plans for the future." She is planning ahead, answer choice (C). Answer choice (A) is a misrepresentation. Answer choice (B) is just wrong. Answer choice (D) is a soundalike—*furniture* for *future*.

6. What does the woman advise the man to do?

    (A) Sleep with a bag over his head.
    (B) Leave on Saturday instead of Friday.
    (C) Turn on a light during the trip.
    (D) Take a nap on the airplane.

6. D The woman says, "If you sleep on the flight," which means that she is suggesting that they take a nap on the flight, answer choice (D). Answer choices (A) and (C) are soundalikes—*bag* for *jet lag* and *light* for *flight*. Answer choice (B) is a misrepresentation.

7. What is going to happen in a few minutes?

(A) There will be a meeting upstairs.
(B) The ship will leave from the port.
(C) Everyone will help with the report.
(D) No one will do anything.

7. **A** When the first man asks, "See you upstairs in a few minutes?" the second man replies about "the meeting," answer choice (A). Answer choice (B) is a soundalike—*ship* for *shipping* and *port* for *report*. Answer choices (C) and (D) are misrepresentations.

8. What will be different about the office?

(A) It will become greater.
(B) Yuko won't work there anymore.
(C) It will become a school.
(D) Mr. Masters will go to school.

8. **B** The woman says, "Yuko's leaving the company." She will not work there anymore, answer choice (B). Answer choice (A) is a soundalike—*greater* instead of *great for her*. Answer choices (C) and (D) are misrepresentations.

9. Where does this conversation take place?

(A) The post office.
(B) A computer store.
(C) A restaurant.
(D) A bookstore.

9. **C** The man says he is a "server" and the woman asks for a beer. This conversation must be taking place in a restaurant, answer choice (C). Answer choices (A) and (D) are just wrong. Answer choice (B) is a trap because the word *server* can also be a piece of computer equipment.

10. When will the flight come in?

(A) Early.
(B) Late.
(C) Today.
(D) Tomorrow.

10. **D** The man asks, "What time does Ms. Olmos' flight come in tomorrow?" Answer choice (D) is correct. Answer choice (A) is a misrepresentation. Answer choices (B) and (C) are just wrong.

Short conversations drill transcript

1. (Man)   *Will that be cash or charge?*

   (Woman)   *Can I use my debit card?*

   (Man)   *Of course. The funds will be debited directly from your bank account.*

2. (Woman)   *I'm going into that marketing meeting now, Ken. I won't be out again until 3.*

   (Man)   *Mr. Herrod hasn't called yet. Should I let you know if he calls while you're in the meeting?*

   (Woman)   *Oh, I'd forgotten about that! Yes, please come get me when he calls.*

3. (Man 1)   *Hello. Do you have an iron I could borrow, and an ironing   board? I'm in room 302.*

   (Man 2)   *There should be one in your closet, sir. On the left side, near the wall.*

   (Man 1)   *Ah, here it is! I didn't see it before. Thank you very much.*

4. (Woman)   *Is this the Help Desk? My computer seems to be stuck. I've been jiggling the mouse, but I can't find the cursor on the screen.*

   (Man)   *Have you checked the cord to make sure the mouse is plugged in completely?*

   (Woman)   *That's the first thing I checked. The connection's fine. Can you come down here to have a look at it?*

5. (Woman)   *I'd like to ask about the maternity leave policy. How much time off is usually given?*

   (Man)   *Oh, are you pregnant? Congratulations.*

   (Woman)   *Actually, I'm not pregnant yet. I'm just trying to get some information so we can make plans for the future.*

6. (Woman)   *So when do you leave on vacation?*

   (Man)   *We're leaving late Friday night, so we'll get there on Saturday morning.*

   (Woman)   *If you sleep on the flight, the jet lag won't be so bad.*

7. (Man 1)   *See you upstairs in a few minutes?*

   (Man 2)   *Oh, no! I completely forgot about the meeting. I'm not done with the shipping report.*

   (Man 1)   *Can I help with anything? I'm not doing anything right now.*

8. (Woman)   I just found out that Yuko's leaving the company.
   (Man)   Yes. She's decided to go back to school to get a Master's degree.
   (Woman)   That's great for her, but the office won't be the same without her.

9. (Man)   My name is Christopher, and I'll be your server this evening. May I bring you a drink?
   (Woman)   I'd love a beer. What do you have on tap?
   (Man)   Budweiser, Heineken, Guinness, and a local beer called Narragansett.

10. (Man)   What time does Ms. Olmos' flight come in tomorrow?
    (Woman) Let me check. [Pause.] Her e-mail said 5 P.M.
    (Man)   I guess I'll have to leave the office early to go pick her up.

8

Short Talks
Questions

THE BASICS

On short talks questions in the TOEIC Listening Comprehension section, your task is to listen to short talks and answer two to four questions based on what is either stated or implied. The talks will not be repeated. In other words, you have one chance to listen and remember enough to answer two to four questions.

There will be 20 questions on this section, and approximately eight talks.

The good news is that the questions are all very straightforward. There are no tricks; instead, they ask about details from the talks. What makes them difficult is that (a) you may not understand everything the speakers say in English, (b) you will only hear the talk once, and (c) you have to remember everything you heard in the talk while you try to answer two, three, or four questions based on that one talk.

Of all the parts of the Listening Comprehension section of the TOEIC, this one is probably the most challenging. By the time you finish with these questions, you will probably be very tired of listening to and remembering information from recordings.

THE METHOD

You should approach the short talks section in a way similar to the way you approached the short conversations section. The major difference is that you have to be able to answer multiple questions dealing with the same talk. That adds a whole new level of challenge. We'll be repeating some of the basic techniques from the Short Conversations chapter. Be sure to read through this chapter carefully, though; although some parts are repeated, others are new, and we'll be walking you through short talks examples. Besides, it won't hurt you to read through the techniques one more time.

IT ALL GOES BY SO FAST

The same timing problems exist on the short talks section as on the short conversations section. There is no effective way to listen to the talk first and then jump into the questions. The talk goes by quickly and you only get to hear it once. Then you have to remember it in order to answer the questions correctly.

You can *still* manipulate this timing problem simply by switching the order in which you approach the question. By reading the questions and answer choices *before* you hear the talk, you'll be able to listen for exactly the information you need. This puts the odds of answering the questions correctly in your favor.

READ THE QUESTION FIRST

As in other parts of the test, you will get a set of instructions at the beginning of the short talks. The speaker on the tape will read through the instructions, asking you to follow along as he reads. Since you've already read the instructions in this book and understand exactly how to work the questions, you don't need to listen and pay attention to this part. Use this time to read the first several questions. How many should you read? This is the difficult thing to figure out. You could be asked two, three, or four questions on any given talk.

Since you don't have the ability to predict how many questions belong to a given talk, you should split the difference in the number of questions you could be asked. Read the next three questions in the section and assume that they all belong to the next talk. This way, if the talk has three questions, you're all set. If the talk only has two questions, you can ignore the third one you read (but you'll still probably remember a little bit of it for the next talk). If the talk has four questions, you'll have to read the fourth one after you've answered the first three. This way of splitting the difference isn't perfect, but it's the only way to work ahead without making yourself crazy.

You will be told which questions belong to each talk *before* the talk starts. At the beginning of each talk, the speaker will say something like, "Questions 81–83 refer to the following notice." So, you will know which questions belong to each talk before you hear it. However, you won't know when you're reading ahead. Remember, you should be reading the questions during the instructions portion (and then later during the silent intervals between the talks), so split the difference and read ahead three questions.

A note about question order: While it would make sense to assume that the questions are asked in the order in which they are found in the talk, this is not the case. The questions are not in chronological order. This means that you may hear the answer to the second question on a talk before you hear the answer to the first question on a talk. As long as you actively eliminate wrong answers by crossing them out in the test booklet, you should be able to keep track of the questions and answer choices.

So let's assume that while the speaker is reading the instructions for the short talks section, you're busy reading the first three questions (numbers 81–83). This serves two major purposes. First of all, it gives you an enormous hint as to what the talk will be about. Let's take a look at three questions and decide what the talk must be about.

Where would this announcement most likely be heard?
What should the passengers do?
Where is the destination of the flight?

Based on these questions, the talk will probably be some sort of announcement on an airplane (indicated by the words *announcement* in the first question, *passengers* in the second, and *flight* in the third).

The other purpose of reading the questions ahead of time is to let you know what to listen for. In this question, you should get your ears and brain ready to process the information about the announcement. You have specific information to listen for, and you can ignore everything else. This simplifies your task considerably.

Now, here's the real kicker: If you read the answer choices ahead of time, too, you can just wait for the correct answers to drift past your actively listening ears. Instead of a mad scramble to remember what you heard, frantically eliminate, and then fill in the answer, answering the questions becomes an orderly and structured process. You know what the talk's going to be about, and you know what the answer choices are, so you only have to pay close attention until you hear the correct answer choices.

In the next sections of this chapter we'll practice using this question:

What should the passengers do?

(A) Sit down.
(B) Unbuckle their seat belts.
(C) Use the restroom.
(D) Make an announcement.

LISTEN CAREFULLY

The simplicity and clarity of the "read ahead" method should not lure you into complacency. The unfortunate truth is that *you still have to listen to the talk*. If you don't understand what the speaker is saying, having read the questions ahead of time won't make much difference to you. If you find that you do not understand the talks when you do the drill at the end of this chapter, you should go back to Chapter 4 and review the techniques for understanding conversational English.

This doesn't mean that you have to understand every word. As long as you have a pretty good idea of the message and flow of the talk, you should be able to eliminate answers effectively.

Let's practice listening now. Listen to CD #2 Track 7 that came with this book. (The transcript of this talk is at the end of this chapter, right before the drill.) Listen carefully to hear where the announcement would be heard.

Eliminate As You Listen

As you listen, you should be able to determine that some of the answer choices are not correct. Eliminate them immediately by crossing them out physically in your test booklet. There are not very many trap answers on the short talks section. This is because this section is difficult enough simply because of the multiple-question-per-talk format—introducing too many trap answers would make this section much too difficult. There are only a few consistent distractors.

Answer choices that are too predictable

Some answer choices are there because they are too predictable. They are the answer choices that you'd pick before you even hear the talk. The problem is that, many times, the talk is more complicated than that. If any of the answer choices leap out at you before you've even heard the talk, listen carefully, since they may not be the correct answer.

Wrong place

The most common distractor answer choices are those that are actually in the talk, but not in the part that the question asks about. For example, the question might ask about how long a meeting is going to be. The beginning of the talk might say that the meeting will be at 2, and later say that the meeting is expected to last an hour. The correct answer to the question of how long the meeting will last is "one hour." However, a distractor answer will be two hours. Since you heard the word *two* in the talk, you may be tempted to choose that answer choice.

The presence of answer choices from the wrong place in the talk means that you have to pay special attention to the talk. Of course you're paying attention anyway, but be sure to listen to details like numbers, places, names, and the like. These are most often the subjects of wrong-place distractor answer choices.

Let's look at answer choice (D) from the example question.

(D) Make an announcement.

This answer choice is tempting, because the word *announcement* is in the talk. However, the talk does not say that the passengers will make an announcement; it says that the captain will make another announcement later on. This answer choice is an example of something that is in the wrong place in the talk. Cross it out in the test booklet.

Listen for the Correct Answer

As you listen to the talk, you should be able to pick out the correct answer to each question. In the talk you hear, "I'd like everyone to return to their seats." This is answer choice (A).

(A) Sit down.

Fill in the answer quickly

Remember that time is important in the Listening Comprehension section, so you've got to keep moving. Once you've identified the correct answers, fill them in on the answer sheet as quickly as you can. You can avoid wasting time looking for the correct line on the answer sheet by aligning the answer sheet underneath your test booklet so the bottom line showing is the one for the next question. Double-check that you're filling in the right bubble for the right question number. You can fill in each answer as you find it, but that wastes time going back and forth. Plus, if you're filling in the answer on the answer sheet while the talk is still going, you can't listen and eliminate answer choices on the following question. Instead, circle the correct answer choice for each question, and transfer the answers for all of the questions belonging to one talk to the answer sheet at once.

Read the next three questions

You've successfully conquered the first few short talks questions, but there are still seven other talks. In order to work the next one well, you'll need time to read the question and answer choices *before* the talk plays on the tape. As soon as you've filled in the answer choices, go to the next three questions and answer choices and read them quickly. Then follow the same steps to eliminate and answer the questions.

Remember: Do not leave any blanks. If you cannot answer a question for any reason, fill in the bubble for that question with the letter you picked to be your "guessing letter."

Transcript of the short talk example

Questions 81 through 83 refer to the following announcement.

This is your captain again from the flight deck. It looks like we're about to hit some turbulence, so I'd like everyone to return to their seats and put on their seat belts. It should probably last for about 20 minutes or so, until we start our descent. We'll do our best to get you back down to the ground without any major inconvenience, but it's safer for everyone if we're all buckled in. I'll make another announcement when we know which gate we'll be coming into at the Denver airport.

If you follow the plan we've just outlined, you should be able to answer the short talks questions much more effectively and without as much anxiety and confusion. If you're ready to test your skills, work through the drill that follows.

Short talks drill

Play CD #2 Track 8 to hear the talks, and answer the following questions. Answers can be found on page 97.

1. Where is the destination of the flight?

   (A) The West Coast.
   (B) Denver.
   (C) New York.
   (D) The Midwest.

2. Who is making the announcement?

   (A) The pilot.
   (B) The flight attendant.
   (C) The booking agent.
   (D) A passenger.

3. How long will the turbulence last?

   (A) Until the seat belt sign goes on.
   (B) Until they land.
   (C) A few hours.
   (D) About 20 minutes.

4. How long will the tour be?

   (A) About $3\frac{3}{4}$ hours.
   (B) About 30 minutes.
   (C) About 45 minutes.
   (D) About $4\frac{1}{2}$ hours.

5. Which tour will be given at 4:30?

   (A) Sculpture of the Andes.
   (B) Permanent exhibits.
   (C) We Call It Maize.
   (D) Andrea's tour.

6. How many main floors does the museum have?

(A) One.

(B) Two.

(C) Only a sculpture garden.

(D) $4\frac{1}{2}$.

7. Who is the talk directed to?

(A) Clothing representatives.
(B) Potential salespeople.
(C) The company's competitors.
(D) Maya Dicioffi.

8. What kind of job does the woman have?

(A) Loan officer.
(B) Family counselor.
(C) Art teacher.
(D) Skin care salesperson.

9. Where does this talk take place?

(A) A private house.
(B) A computer store.
(C) An airplane.
(D) A day-care center.

10. What would cost less than $200?

(A) Buying products from Alesse Skin Care.
(B) Starting a company like Alesse Skin Care.
(C) Starting a business selling Alesse Skin Care.
(D) Teaching a beauty class for Alesse Skin Care.

Answers to the short talks drill

1. B
2. A
3. D
4. C
5. A
6. B
7. B
8. D
9. A
10. C

Explanations

1. Where is the destination of the flight?

(A) The West Coast.
(B) Denver.
(C) New York.
(D) The Midwest.

1. **B** The talk says, "I'll make another announcement when we know which gate we'll be coming into at the Denver airport."

2. Who is making the announcement?

(A) The pilot.
(B) The flight attendant.
(C) The booking agent.
(D) A passenger.

2. **A** The talk says, "This is your captain again from the flight deck." The captain of the flight deck is the pilot.

3. How long will the turbulence last?

(A) Until the seat belt sign goes on.
(B) Until they land.
(C) A few hours.
(D) About 20 minutes.

3. **D** The talk says, "It should probably last for about 20 minutes or so."

4. How long will the tour be?

(A) About $3\frac{3}{4}$ hours.

(B) About 30 minutes.

(C) About 45 minutes.

(D) About $4\frac{1}{2}$ hours.

4. **C** The talk says, "This tour will last about 45 minutes."

5. Which tour will be given at 4:30?

(A) Sculpture of the Andes.
(B) Permanent exhibits.
(C) We Call It Maize.
(D) Andrea's tour.

5. **A** The talk says, "'We Call It Maize' is on the mezzanine, and 'Sculpture of the Andes' is in the sculpture garden. Tours for those two exhibits leave at 3:45 and 4:30 respectively." In this context, "respectively" means "in that order," so the Maize tour (mentioned first) is at 3:45 (mentioned first) and the Sculpture tour (mentioned second) is at 4:30 (mentioned second).

6. How many main floors does the museum have?

(A) One.
(B) Two.
(C) Only a sculpture garden.
(D) 4 1/2.

6. **B** The talk says, "We will see all the major exhibits on the two main floors of the museum."

7. Who is the talk directed to?

(A) Clothing representatives.
(B) Potential salespeople.
(C) The company's competitors.
(D) Maya Dicioffi.

7. **B** The talk says, "If you think you might be interested in joining the Alesse family, let me know at the end of the class and we can schedule a one-on-one chat to discuss the Alesse opportunity." This is a way of saying that Maya Dicioffi would like you to become an Alesse beauty "instructor," or salesperson.

8. What kind of job does the woman have?

(A) Loan officer.
(B) Family counselor.
(C) Art teacher.
(D) Skin care salesperson.

8. **D** The talk says, "I'm an independent beauty instructor with Alesse Skin Care." She is in the business of selling skin care products by teaching people how to use them.

9. Where does this talk take place?

(A) A private house.
(B) A computer store.
(C) An airplane.
(D) A day-care center.

9. **A** This talk would not be appropriate in a computer store, on an airplane, or in a day-care center, but it would be fine in a private house.

10. What would cost less than $200?

(A) Buying products from Alesse Skin Care.
(B) Starting a company like Alesse Skin Care.
(C) Starting a business selling Alesse Skin Care.
(D) Teaching a beauty class for Alesse Skin Care.

10. **C** The talk says, "Alesse Skin Care provides women with the opportunity to own their own businesses for an initial investment of less than $200." This means that they would be working selling Alesse products, not starting a business similar to Alesse or buying Alesse products. Teaching classes is part of the Alesse business, but after the initial investment the person would be teaching many classes, not just one.

Short talks drill transcript

Questions 1 through 3 refer to the following announcement.

This is your captain again from the flight deck. It looks like we're about to hit some turbulence, so I'd like everyone to return to their seats and put on their seat belts. It should probably last for about 20 minutes or so, until we start our descent. We'll do our best to get you back down to the ground without any major inconvenience, but it's safer for everyone if we're all buckled in. I'll make another announcement when we know which gate we'll be coming into at the Denver airport.

Questions 4 through 6 refer to the following announcement.

If you could all gather around me tightly, we'll all be able to hear. My name is Andrea, and I'm a tour guide here at the Anthropology Museum. This tour will last about 45 minutes, during which time we will see all the major exhibits on the two main floors of the museum. I'll be pointing out the most significant works and displays we have here at the museum, and answering any questions you may have. If you find that you want to know more, we also have two excellent visiting exhibits. "We Call It Maize" is on the mezzanine, and "Sculpture of the Andes" is in the sculpture garden. Tours for those two exhibits leave at 3:45 and 4:30 respectively.

Questions 7 through 10 refer to the following short talk.

Good afternoon and welcome to our beauty class. My name is Maya Dicioffi and I'm an independent beauty instructor with Alesse Skin Care. Tonight I'm going to lead you through a truly transformative experience. First you'll give yourself a rejuvenating facial, and then I'll consult with each of you individually to choose a makeup palette that maximizes your features. Alesse Skin Care provides women with the opportunity to own their own businesses for an initial investment of less than $200. If you think you might be interested in joining the Alesse family, let me know at the end of the class and we can schedule a one-on-one chat to discuss the Alesse opportunity.

PART III

Reading: Grammar-Based Questions

THE BASICS

Now that you've tackled the more challenging listening questions, let's move on to the Reading section and the grammar-based question types: sentence completion and error identification. These questions are inherently less challenging than the listening questions, because the element of time pressure is diminished. While you have a set amount of time (75 minutes) to finish the last 100 questions of the test (which include the grammar-based questions and the reading comprehension questions), you aren't pressured by the tape to finish any one question in a set amount of time. This means that you can spend more time on the questions that you find harder, and less time on the questions that are easier for you.

If you have taken any kind of U.S. standardized test (such as the SAT, TOEFL, or GMAT) in the past, you will probably recognize the basic format of the sentence completion and error identification questions. But just because the questions look familiar doesn't mean you should go with your instincts and answer them without a specific plan. They contain plenty of traps, as we'll discuss later.

SENTENCE COMPLETION QUESTIONS

THE DIRECTIONS

The first 40 questions (numbered 101–140) in the Reading section of the test are sentence completion questions. Directions for completing the sentence completion questions appear in a box at the beginning of the section. The directions box looks like this:

YOU WILL HAVE ONE HOUR AND FIFTEEN MINUTES TO COMPLETE PARTS V, VI, AND VII OF THE TEST.

READING

In this section of the test, you will have a chance to show how well you understand written English. There are three parts to this section, with special directions for each part.

PART V

Directions: Questions 101–140 are incomplete sentences. Four words or phrases, marked (A), (B), (C), (D), are given beneath each sentence. You are to choose the one word or phrase that best completes the sentence. Then, on your answer sheet, find the number of the question and mark your answer.

The third-quarter ---------- in sales caused an adjustment in the company's earnings projections.

(A) decreasing
(B) decreased
(C) decrease
(D) decreases

Sample Answer

Ⓐ Ⓑ ● Ⓓ

The sentence should read, "The third-quarter decrease in sales caused an adjustment in the company's earnings projections." Therefore, you should choose answer (C).

Read these instructions now and review them before the test, so that you won't waste any time reading them during the actual test. The only things you need to understand from them are that

- you have one hour and fifteen minutes to answer the last 100 questions of the test, and
- you should pick the best word to fill in the blank in the sentence.

THE QUESTIONS

Each sentence completion question consists of a sentence with a word or short phrase missing, and four answer choices—labeled (A), (B), (C), and (D)—under the sentence. Look at the following example:

According to the terms of the -------, each household could only receive one free software disc.

(A) promoting
(B) promotion
(C) promoted
(D) promote

Three of the above four answer choices are incorrect, meaning if they were inserted in the blank, the sentence would *not* make sense in accordance with the standard rules of English grammar.

THE TRAP

The major trap in the sentence completion questions is that many, if not all, of the answer choices may "sound good" in the sentence. If you rush to answer the questions and try to pick the correct answer by choosing the answer choice that sounds the best, you will probably miss many points. The way to score better is to know the grammar rules and apply them strictly to each question in order to eliminate incorrect answer choices.

ERROR IDENTIFICATION QUESTIONS

THE DIRECTIONS

The next 20 questions (numbered 141–160) in the Reading section of the test are error identification questions. Directions for completing the error identification questions appear in a box at the beginning of the section. The directions box looks like this:

We missed the last <u>shipment</u> of the day, and were <u>forced</u> to send the package <u>over</u> courier.
                A   B   C   D

Sample Answer

Ⓐ Ⓑ Ⓒ ●

The underlined word "over" is not correct in this sentence. This sentence should read, "We missed the last shipment of the day, and were forced to send the package by courier." Therefore, you should choose answer (D).

PART VI

Directions: In **Questions 141–160,** each sentence has four words or phrases underlined. The four underlined parts of the sentence are marked (A), (B), (C), (D). You are to identify the **one** underlined word or phrase that should be corrected or rewritten. Then, on your answer sheet, find the number of the question and mark your answer.

Read these instructions now and review them before the test, so that you won't waste any time reading them during the actual test. The only things you need to understand from them are that

- one of the four underlined words or phrases is grammatically incorrect, and

- you have to pick it.

THE QUESTIONS

The second type of grammar-based question you will encounter is the error identification question. You will see sentences in which four words or phrases are underlined. One of these words or phrases is incorrect and makes the entire sentence grammatically incorrect. The good news in this section is that you are not asked to correct or name the error; you only have to *identify* it. This means that it doesn't really matter if you are not completely sure why a particular word or phrase is wrong. Recognizing that it is incorrect is all you need to do. You will not have to supply the correct word or phrase.

One of the most obvious things to keep in mind regarding error identification questions on the TOEIC is that the parts of the sentence that are *not* underlined are *correct* as written. You can usually look to the non-underlined parts, the parts you know are correct, and use them to guide you. Articles and adjectives can tell you whether nouns are plural or singular. Pronouns replace nouns. *So pay attention to all parts of the sentence when you are looking at error identification questions.* Look at the following typical TOEIC error identification question.

New <u>employees</u> must attend an <u>orientation</u> session within <u>their</u> first week <u>to</u> work.
      A   B   C   D

Three of the above four answer choices are correct, so in other words, *they are grammatically correct.* You want to choose the answer choice that is *grammatically incorrect* in accordance with the standard rules of English grammar.

THE TRAP

The major trap in the error identification questions is that you're looking for the one incorrect answer instead of the correct answer. While it doesn't sound like a complicated concept, it can be disorienting during the actual test. Again, knowledge of the rules of English grammar can help you stay on course and pick the odd answer out.

WHAT DOES THE READING SECTION TEST?

ETS says that the Reading section as a whole measures your ability to recognize language that is appropriate for standard written English. The key word here is "recognize." You never have to come up with the answer yourself; you simply have to recognize the best answer. Think about it this way. Every day, you go to the same grocery store where you see the same manager. Although you don't know the name of the manager, his face is familiar. If you see that same manager in the subway, at the library, or in the park, you still don't know his name or anything else about him, but you will be able to recognize him and know that he works at the grocery store. The grammar-based questions of the TOEIC work the same way. They test the same grammar rules over and over again.

ETS is not that creative with its questions. Once you recognize the limited grammar rules that ETS tests, recognizing the best answer is simple. Since ETS uses multiple-choice testing, you must simply choose one of four possible choices that you recognize. Once you memorize and practice the different question types, your score will improve significantly. So, the grammar-based questions of the TOEIC simply test how well you can recognize grammar mistakes.

Process of Elimination (POE)

As you learned in the Listening Comprehension section, sometimes you aren't quite sure which answer you should choose. By eliminating the answer choices you know are wrong, you can greatly increase your chances of choosing the best answer—even if you guess. Guessing and choosing an answer from two choices makes your odds of getting the right answer much greater than guessing from four choices.

How Much Will My Scores Improve?

This depends on how much you practice. If you use these techniques, your scores will improve. But you should also practice, practice, practice reading English.

Scoring

Half your total score on the TOEIC is determined by your performance on the Reading section of the test. Sixty of the 100 questions in the Reading section are grammar-based questions. So the sentence completion and error identification questions count for 30 percent of your total TOEIC score. That's almost one-third of your score, so doing well on these questions is crucial. In order to do well, you need to remember and understand the standard rules of English grammar. The next chapter is a comprehensive grammar review designed to review everything you need to know for the TOEIC.

9

Grammar Review

WHY REVIEW GRAMMAR?

Whether or not you speak English every day for your job, you probably haven't studied the actual rules of grammar in a long time. Since success on the TOEIC has nothing to do with your ability to speak English and everything to do with your ability to spot grammatical errors, it's a good idea to brush up on the rules.

We're going to start at a basic level. If you think you're past the basics, just humor us. Read along and pay attention, and you may just pick up a tip or two along the way. If you're feeling really rusty, or you never had a good foundation in grammar rules in the first place, make sure you understand each section before you go on to the next.

PARTS OF SPEECH

The sentences in the sentence completion and error identification questions, as well as every other sentence in the English language are made up of certain **parts of speech**, which are the basic units of English. This section will cover the following parts of speech: nouns, pronouns, verbs, adjectives, adverbs, prepositions, articles, and conjunctions.

NOUNS

Words that refer to people, places, things, or ideas are called **nouns**.

Examples of nouns are

People: Martin, firefighter, Janelle, worker

Places: Ohio, country, Lake Huron, street

Things: terrier, cantaloupe

Ideas: grief, bravery

Nouns can be singular or plural. A singular noun refers to one person, place, thing, or idea. A plural noun refers to more than one person, place, thing, or idea. So, both *cantaloupe* and *cantaloupes* are nouns. The only difference is that one is singular and one is plural. They represent different quantities.

Proper nouns and common nouns

Proper nouns name specific people, places, things, or ideas. Proper nouns must be capitalized.
Common nouns are more general. They do not name specific people, places, things, or ideas. They are not capitalized unless they begin a sentence.

Proper nouns and common nouns

	Proper Nouns	Common Nouns
Person:	Tom Cruise	actor
Place:	Stockholm, Sweden	city
Thing:	The Great Depression	event
Idea:	Existentialism	courage

Collective nouns

Nouns that refer to groups of people, places, or things are called **collective nouns**. A collective noun is almost aways singular, even though the word itself refers to more than one thing (or person or place).

Examples of collective nouns are

> group
>
> collection
>
> family
>
> bunch
>
> committee

Countable vs. noncountable nouns

Another distinction between nouns is whether they refer to things that can be counted or not. A noun that refers to things that can be counted, such as hamburgers, spaceships, or magazines (or children, tables, or fish), is called a **countable noun**. A noun that refers to something intangible (like love or pollution) is called a **noncountable noun**. Noncountable nouns can also refer to things that are tangible, but can't be separated out to be counted.

Examples of noncountable nouns:

coffee	grits
air	water
wheat	equipment
money	gold
petroleum	literature
chemistry	weather
editing	grass

The distinction can be small sometimes. For example, *coffee* is noncountable, while *cups of coffee* are countable. Also, *money* is noncountable, while *dollars* (or *yen* or *euros*) are countable. Many nouns refer to abstract ideas instead of concrete things or people.

Examples of abstract nouns that are rarely countable:

beauty	courage
fear	wealth
determination	blindness
charity	grace
equality	hate

Knowing whether a noun is countable or noncountable is important because that affects the words (adjectives, articles, verbs) that can be used to modify or describe that noun.

PRONOUNS

A word that takes the place of a noun is called a **pronoun.** It stands for a person, place, thing, or idea.

There are many types of pronouns, but we're going to talk about subject pronouns, object pronouns, and possessive pronouns. Then we'll discuss pronoun agreement, and when to use **who** vs. **whom.**

Subject pronouns are words that stand in for a noun that is the subject of the sentence. (A subject is the noun that performs the action of the sentence, as we'll explain later on in this section.)

Object pronouns are words that stand in for a noun that is the object of the sentence. (An object is the noun that receives the action of the sentence, as we'll explain later on in this section.)

Possessive pronouns are words that show that one thing belongs to another person, group of people, or thing. Possessive pronouns can be subject pronouns or object pronouns.

The following chart gives examples of pronouns that are likely to be tested on the TOEIC exam.

Subject Pronouns	Object Pronouns	Subject Possessive Pronouns	Object Possessive Pronouns
I	me	my	mine
you	you	yours	yours
he	him	his	his
she	her	her	hers
it	it	its	its
we	us	our	ours
they	them	their	theirs
that	that		
those	those		
there	there		

Pronoun agreement

There's another group of pronouns that take the place of nouns, and it's important that these "other pronouns" agree with the verbs in the sentence. Is the verb singular or plural? Is the pronoun singular or plural? Do they match? You can often tell whether a pronoun is plural or not by adding the word *one* to the sentence immediately after the pronoun. Let's try it.

Each of the children was eating a cracker.

The verb *was* is singular. Is *each* singular? If you add *one* after *each*, the sentence still makes sense:

Each one of the children was eating a cracker.

Therefore, the singular pronoun *(each)* matches the singular verb *(was).*

Examples of singular pronouns include:

every

either

neither

who vs. whom

Both *who* and *whom* indicate that the identity of a specific person is unknown. In a way, they are both place-holders for specific people. Knowing when to use *who* and when to use *whom* causes trouble for some people, but it's actually a simple distinction. *Who* is a subject pronoun, and *whom* is an object pronoun. Use *who* when the unknown person is performing an action.

Who left a pair of dirty socks in the hallway?

Use *whom* when the unknown person is receiving the action.

With **whom** did you go out last night?

One way to remember when to use *who* and when to use *whom* is to answer the question. If the answer to the question is *he* or *she* (subject pronouns), use *who.* If the answer is *him* or *her* (object pronouns), use *whom.* If the sentence is a statement and not a question, just substitute *he/she* for *who* or *him/her* for *whom* in the sentence.

Who left a pair of dirty socks in the hallway?
She did.

With **whom** did you go out last night?
With **him**.

Verbs

Words that describe mental or physical actions, states of being, or conditions are called **verbs. Action verbs** express action. **Linking verbs** do not show action, but connect the subject with the predicate of the sentence. Some verbs can be used as action or linking verbs. **Helping verbs,** also known as auxiliary verbs, are used in verb phrases to help express the tense or condition of the main verb.

Examples of verbs

Action Verbs	Linking Verbs	Helping Verbs
accelerate	appear	do
give	be	have
go	feel	is
review	look	look
toss	seem	might
think		will

Verb tenses

Verbs change form to reflect time (past, present, future). The **tense** of a verb expresses the time in which the action occurs.

Tenses can be divided into the following categories:

infinitive

present

past

future

perfect

Verbs can consist of more than one word. The **principal parts** of any verb include the present, past, past participle, and the present participle of the verb. In order to recognize time in conjugated verbs, you should be familiar with these parts of verbs. The past participle is formed by adding -ed, -t, or -n to the main verb. The present participle is formed by adding -ing to the main verb. The past and the past participle parts of a verb are often the same.

Principal parts of a verb

Present	Past	Past Particle	Present Particle
work	worked	worked	working
grow	grew	grown	growing

Infinitives and gerunds

The **infinitive** form of a verb is the verb in its purest state, before it has been *conjugated*, or changed, to indicate a time (past, present, or future) in which the action occurred. The infinitive can be used as it is. Let's use the infinitive *to go* as an example.

They want **to go** away.
I would like **to eat** before I go to my office.

The infinitive can also be used as the basis for other tenses by removing the *to* and replacing it with a helping verb (also called an *auxiliary verb*).

I **will meet** him at the restaurant.

When the *-ing* ending is added to a verb to make it function as a noun, it is called a **gerund.** A gerund represents the performance of the verb in noun form.

Reading plays an important part in **learning** new skills.

Present tenses

> I *go* we *go*
>
> you *go* you *go*
>
> he/she/it *goes* they *go*

The **simple present** tense expresses action that happens currently, habitually, or repeatedly. It can also be used to describe a condition or general truth.

> I **hear** a noise outside my window. (currently)
> She **drives** by the park every Saturday. (habitually or repeatedly)
> I **love** borscht. (condition)
> January 1 **is** the beginning of the calendar year. (general truth)

The simple present tense isn't the only present tense, however. The **present progressive** tense also expresses present time. Specifically, it expresses an action that is taking place at the moment. The present progressive tense is formed by combining the simple present tense of the verb *to be* with the present participle of the verb expressing the action.

Here's an example of a sentence written in the present progressive tense.

> We **are driving** to school.

Are is the simple present form of *to be*, and *driving* is the present participle of *to drive*.

The difference between the simple present tense and the present progressive tense is definite. The simple present tense is used to describe a condition or habitual action.

> We **like** Ike.
> I **eat** breakfast at the Gramercy Café every Thursday morning.

The present progressive tense describes an action that is in progress.

> I **am wearing** a new watch.
> She **is learning** to speak Japanese.

In many languages, the simple present tense is used both to describe a condition *and* to express an action that is in progress. This is not true in English.

The simple present and present progressive tenses are active tenses. There is another present tense, the **present passive** tense. It is constructed by combining the present tense of the verb *to be* with the past participle of the verb expressing the action.

> Breakfast **is served** every day by the hotel staff.
> The athletes **are admired** by the students.

As you can see, the passive tense sometimes sounds a little awkward. The active tense is generally preferred over passive tense in business writing. The sentences above have been restated in the active tense below.

> The hotel staff **serves** breakfast every day.
> The students **admire** the athletes.

Past tenses

I *went*	we *went*
you *went*	you *went*
she/he/it *went*	they *went*

The **simple past** tense expresses an action or condition that is completed.

I **woke** up yesterday morning to the smell of pancakes.
She **was** eager to finish the project at work.

The **past progressive** tense is another past tense. It is formed by combining the simple past form of the verb *to be* with the present participle of the verb expressing the action. The past progressive tense expresses action that took place over a long time.

We **were auditing** the firm's financial statements for 14 months.

It also expresses an action that was in progress when another action occurred.

I **was walking** to work when the heel fell off my shoe.

The difference between the simple past and past progressive tenses is that the simple past expresses an action that happened once and was completed, while the past progressive expresses an action that continued over a period of time or was interrupted in the past.

The simple past and past progressive tenses are active tenses. There is another past tense, the **past passive** tense. It is constructed by combining the past tense of *to be* with the past participle of the verb expressing the action.

His allegations **were proven** to be false.
The rules **were discussed** at the last meeting of the club.
I **was taught** that 1 is not a prime number.

Both the present and past passive tenses are used when the person or thing receiving the action is more important than the person performing the action. For example, it doesn't really matter who proved that the allegations were false, just that it happened. It also doesn't matter who taught me that 1 isn't prime, just that I learned it.

Future tenses

There are two ways to form the future tense. The first is to combine the word *will* (or *won't*) with the present form of the verb. This way of forming the future tense expresses an action or condition that will (or won't) happen in the future.

I **will get** my car washed before I visit my mother.
She **won't eat** lunch with us tomorrow because she **will be** at a meeting.

The other way to form the future tense is probably more common in spoken English, but less common in written English. It expresses something that is going to happen in the future, contrasted with what is happening in the present time. It is formed by combining the conjugated form of the verb *to be* with the word *going* and the infinitive form of the verb expressing the action. Some examples are below.

I **am going to buy** a house in this neighborhood.
You **are going to get caught** in the rain this afternoon.
He **is going to apply** for a job in Indonesia.
They **are not going to be** happy about the new budget cuts.

Perfect tenses

Perfect tenses are used to express more complicated times in which the action of a sentence takes place. There are four perfect tenses: present perfect, present perfect progressive, past perfect, and future perfect.

The **present perfect** tense expresses an action that began in the past and continues into the present. It is formed by combining the helping verbs *have* or *has* with the past participle of the verb expressing the action of the sentence.

I **have eaten** more cake today than ever before.
Dr. Engelke **has taught** a popular course in Music History at the university for 14 years.
They **have forgotten** to reset the security codes in the research lab's main entrance.

The **present perfect progressive** tense expresses an action that began in the past, continues into the present, and may continue into the future. It is formed by combining the helping verbs *have been* or *has been* with the present participle of the verb expressing the action of the sentence.

I **have been editing** the users' manual for the past six months.
She **has been trying** to hire a new assistant for several months.

The **past perfect** tense expresses an action that happened before another action took place. The second action must be mentioned in the same sentence. It is formed by combining the helping verb *had* with the past participle of the verb expressing the action of the sentence.

I **had eaten** the entire tub of popcorn before the movie started.
They **had bought** a new car the week before the accident.

The **future perfect** tense expresses an action that will be completed on or by a specific time in the future. It is formed by combining the helping verbs *will* (or *won't*) *have* with the past participle of the verb expressing the action of the sentence.

I **won't have finished** the report by the annual meeting on Monday.
They **will have aired** our commercial for several weeks before we can ship the product to stores.

ADJECTIVES

Modifiers are words which give more information about, or modify, another word or phrase. Words that give more information about, or modify, nouns are called **adjectives**. A noun can be modified by more than one adjective at a time.

Regular adjectives

Regular adjectives give more detail within a sentence by describing the elements in that sentence. For example, which of the following sentences is more descriptive?

Michael saw a dog.
Michael saw a **large, gray** dog.

The second sentence gives the reader more information because it contains two adjectives, *large* and *gray*, that describe the dog.

Comparative adjectives

Comparative adjectives are also descriptive, but they're used a bit differently. Instead of providing mere description, comparative adjectives describe one noun in reference to another noun, either by adding *-er* or by preceding the adjective with *more* or *less* and adding the word *than.* For example,

regular adjective: Marvin has a **large** house.
comparative adjective: Marvin's house is **larger** than my house.

regular adjective: Penelope has always been **selfish**.
comparative adjective: Penelope has always been ***more* selfish *than*** her sister, Sarah.

Note that this second pair of sentences offers an example of a comparative adjective that does not take the *-er* ending. In other words, it is improper English to say, "Elizabeth is *selfisher* than Sarah," because *selfisher* is not a word.

Superlative adjectives

Superlative adjectives are like comparative adjectives, but they take comparisons to the next level by comparing the noun they modify to other nouns. They either end in *-est*, or have the words *most* or *least* attached to them. Let's revisit the examples we just looked at above.

regular adjective: Marvin has a **large** house.
comparative adjective: Marvin's house is **larger** than my house.
superlative adjective: Marvin's house is the **largest** house on the street.

regular adjective: Penelope has always been **selfish**.
comparative adjective: Penelope has always been ***more* selfish *than*** her sister, Sarah.
superlative adjective: Penelope is the ***most* selfish** person I've ever met.

Comparatives, superlatives, and quantity

There is another crucial difference between comparative and superlative adjectives—they are used in different situations, depending on the number of nouns being compared. If two things are being compared, a comparative adjective is used; when you're comparing three or more items, use a superlative adjective.

comparative adjective: Donatella is **taller** than her cousin, George. (2 items)
superlative adjective: Donatella is the **tallest** of the seven sisters in her family. (3 or more items)

Proper adjectives

Proper adjectives are a lot like proper nouns since they are formed with a specific person's name or a specific place. Since all proper nouns are capitalized, all proper adjectives must be capitalized as well.

French toast
English textbook
Miltonian economics
Chinese food
Spanish armada
Hawaiian punch

ADVERBS

Remember, modifiers are words that give more information about, or modify, another word or phrase. **Adverbs** are special modifiers that are added to provide a description of verbs, adjectives, and other adverbs. They may answer the questions *how, when, where*, or *to what extent*. Some examples of adverbs are below.

> After his cold finally cleared up, he was able to breathe **deeply**. (how?)
> I think the works of Anne Rice are **really** interesting. (how?)
> The director went **immediately** to the stage. (when?)
> Department heads met **there**. (where?)
> The meeting ran **long**. (to what extent?)

You can transform an adjective into an adverb (as you might have noticed) by adding some form of *-ly* to the adjective. (The form of *-ly* depends on the verb.)

> sad → sadly
> happy → happily
> phonetic → phonetically

PREPOSITIONS

Prepositions are important connectors between nouns and descriptive phrases in sentences. Some examples are below.

> The money is **on** the desk.
> The coat is **in** the closet.
> I got my hair cut **before** I went on the interview.
> Jerome walked **across** the room.
> The comb fell **behind** the dresser.
> She sent us a present **for** our anniversary.
> She arrived just **as** I was leaving.

Prepositional phrases

Prepositions can be placed in short phrases, such as "*in* the closet," "*across* the room," and "*behind* the dresser." These **prepositional phrases** function like adjectives, because they provide greater detail to the overall sentence.

> Alicia drove.   becomes   Alicia drove **to the store**.

In the prepositional phrase "to the store," *to* is the preposition, and *store* is the object of the preposition. You can go a step further in a prepositional phrase and add an adjective.

> Alicia drove **to the *grocery* store**.

The word *grocery* adds description; now we know what type of store it is.

It's possible to string two or more prepositional phrases together. The more phrases you use, the greater detail you provide.

> Alicia drove [*across town*] [*to the grocery store*] [*by the ramp*] [*at the end*] [*of the expressway*].

Now we know a lot more about Alicia's trip!

Phrasal prepositions

The prepositions we have mentioned up until now are single-word prepositions such as *on*, *in*, *around*, *behind*, and *after*. **Phrasal prepositions** have two or more words and are as descriptive as their single-word cousins. Some examples are below.

> She fell off of her bike **because of** my carelessness.
> New Mexico became a state **as of** 1912.
> I keep all of my money **in between** my mattress and box spring.

Prepositions as parts of verb phrases

Verb phrases are created when a verb and a preposition are put together. Sometimes, they are referred to as "idioms." There's a list of common idioms in the Appendix at the end of this book, but it does not contain every idiom in English. You may want to start your own list of idioms you read or hear. Here are some examples of verb phrase idioms.

> When it started raining, the umpires **called off** the baseball game.
> The children nagged so much that their mother **gave in**.
> After she graduated from college, my sister **kept in touch with** her roommate.
> Ross and Chu worked all night on the presentation, but nothing **came of** it.
> After our conversation I **hung up** the phone.
> The teacher does not **put up with** unfinished homework.

ARTICLES

Words that modify nouns by indicating whether they are definite or indefinite are called **articles**. The article that indicates that a noun is definite is *the.* The articles that indicate that a noun is indefinite are *a* and *an*.

To study the use of articles, let's use the noun *computers* as an example. First, imagine all the computers in the world. If you are referring to the *entire group* of computers, you do *not* need an article. For example, look at this sentence.

> **Computers** cost less than they did ten years ago.

You are talking about computers *in general*, not a specific computer. If you are talking about a specific group of computers, not computers in general, use the definite article with the plural noun.

> **The** computers on the third floor were damaged in the fire.

You are talking about a *specific* group of computers, not computers in general.

If you are referring to any *single* computer from this entire group, but not any one in particular, use the indefinite article. Indefinite articles *must* precede a singular noun.

> I want to buy **a** computer for my sister. I don't care what kind.

You are simply talking about any computer, not a specific one. If you are referring to a *specific* computer, use the definite article.

> **The** computer in front of me isn't working.

Now you are talking about a specific computer, not one in general.

The only question remaining about articles is when to use *a* vs. *an*. In general, you use *a* when the word following it begins with a consonant. You use *an* when the word following it begins with a vowel. There are a few exceptions to this rule (only because in spoken English, some words that begin with consonants are pronounced as if they begin with vowels), but they will not be tested on the TOEIC.

CONJUNCTIONS

Words that express a relationship between ideas are called **conjunctions**. They connect words and phrases of the same type with each other. In other words, they connect nouns with nouns, or phrases with phrases, or verbs with verbs, etc.

There are two basic types of conjunctions: those that show *agreement* between ideas, and those that show *disagreement* between ideas. Conjunctions that show agreement give additional information that agrees with or further explains the idea in the main sentence. For example, look at this sentence.

Benjamin Franklin was a successful inventor **as well as** a politician and statesman.

In the above sentence, the conjunction *as well as* provides additional information that agrees with what is already stated or implied in the main sentence. Conjunctions that show disagreement between ideas contrast the idea in the main sentence. For example, look at this sentence.

Although petroleum is refined into industrial products such as plastic and synthetic fibers, it is primarily prized for its ability to combust.

In the above sentence, the conjunction *although* contradicts the idea that is stated or implied in the main sentence. The following is a common list of conjunctions that show agreement and disagreement between ideas. Try to incorporate them into your vocabulary by practicing a few each day.

You should also be familiar with conjunction patterns. Conjunction patterns are fixed expressions that need to include all the words in the pattern in order to be correct. Look at several types of conjunction patterns typically found on the TOEIC.

either ... or
> Paleontology, which deals with prehistoric life forms, can be treated as **either** a part of geology **or** a part of biology.

neither ... nor
> Virus particles can **neither** function as living cells **nor** survive for extended periods of time outside a host.

both ... and
> **Both** earthquakes **and** volcanoes require specific geological conditions.

not only ... but also
> In order to ensure ample food supplies, **not only** do some species of fish attack intruders in their hunting territories, **but** they **also** kill their own offspring.

such ... as
> Early types of gunpowder were created with **such** materials **as** sulfur, saltpeter, and carbon in the form of charcoal.

PARTS OF A SENTENCE

The units that create a sentence are called **parts of a sentence**. Parts of a sentence can be one word or a group of words, and can be one part of speech or a combination of parts of speech. We've already covered some parts of a sentence in the process of talking about parts of speech, but we need to talk about a few more, specifically subjects and objects.

SUBJECTS

The **subject** is the part of the sentence about which something is being said. The **complete subject** consists of all the words that make up the "thing" that is being talked about in the sentence. The subject answers the question *who* or *what*. It usually appears first in a sentence, but doesn't have to.

The subject of every sentence must include a noun or a pronoun. Remember: A noun is a word that names something and a pronoun is a word that takes the place of a noun. Nouns that act as subjects can take on many forms. The subject can be a single noun, a noun phrase, multiple noun phrases, a pronoun, or a gerund.

nouns:	**Astrologers** divide the hemisphere into twelve parts.
noun phrases:	**The fluffy gray kitten** jumped onto the bed.
multiple noun phrases:	**The locket my mother gave me** is on a chain around my neck.
	Everyone who ate at the head table had stomach cramps and nausea the next day.
pronouns:	**It** was Robert Goddard who successfully fired the world's first liquid-fuel rocket.
	She used e-mail to contact the directors at corporate headquarters.
gerunds:	**Exercising** is recommended by all health-care professionals.

It's a common mistake to think that a subject can't contain a verb.

The locket my mother gave me is still on a chain around my neck.

In this example, the verb *gave* isn't the verb that describes the action of the sentence. Instead, it's just part of a clause that gives us more information about the locket. The verb that describes the action of the sentence is *is*.

Everyone who ate at the head table had stomach cramps and nausea the next day.

In the same way, the verb *ate* is part of a clause that gives us more information about *everyone*. The verb that describes the action of the sentence is *had*.

Every sentence *must* have a **main subject** (a noun or pronoun) and a main verb. On the TOEIC, it will often be helpful to find and isolate the main subject and the main verb. This will greatly increase your chances of using POE to eliminate the incorrect answer choices and select the best answer.

Compound subjects

A sentence can have one subject or many. A *simple subject* is a subject that consists of one subject. A *compound subject* is a subject that consists of more than one subject.

Robert fell asleep during the movie. (simple subject)
Robert, Madeleine, Elena, Kent, and Tina's son fell asleep during the movie. (compound subject)

Subjects on the TOEIC

The majority of subject questions on the TOEIC is found in the sentence completion part of the test. Error identification questions don't test subjects as often.

The most common way the TOEIC tests your basic knowledge of subjects is by having you identify the noun functioning as the subject. Sometimes the subject is a gerund—a form of a verb, ending in *-ing*, which acts as a noun—but usually the subject is just a regular noun. In other cases, the subject may be hidden behind a modifying phrase in the sentence. And, you may be given answer choices that include the main verb.

When you read sentence completion questions, always determine whether they contain a main subject and main verb. If a main subject or a main verb is not present, they both will likely be in the answer choices, and you will have to choose the one that fills in the missing part (either a subject or a verb).

THE PREDICATE

The second component of the sentence, which usually contains the verb and the objects, is often referred to as the **predicate**, or verb phrase. The predicate is the part of the sentence that tells something about the subject. It answers the question *what* or *what happened*. The **complete predicate** contains all of the words that say something about the subject. The **simple predicate** is the verb in the sentence.

Robert **fell asleep**. (simple predicate)
Robert **fell asleep during the movie**. (complete predicate)

You can have a compound predicate, just as you can have a compound subject. A **compound predicate** consists of two or more connected verbs.

Robert **fell asleep during the movie, drooled on his shirt, and got kicked out for snoring**.

OBJECTS

Subject nouns perform the action of a sentence, and object nouns receive it. Subject nouns "do"; **object nouns** are the items to which "something is done."

Anna took off her **coat**. (the coat was *taken off*)

There can also be many objects in one sentence.

Anna took off her **coat**, **shoes**, and **headphones**. (the coat, shoes, and headphones were *taken off*)

The objects in boldface in the previous sentences are all called **direct objects**. They are direct because they receive the action of the verb before them.

Indirect objects aren't the objects of the action of the verb, but they usually tell who or what received the object. For example, look at this sentence.

Anna gave **me** her old sweatshirt.

In this sentence, *sweatshirt* is the direct object, because it receives the action of the verb *give*. *Me* is the indirect object. It answers the question, "To whom was the sweatshirt given?"

WHAT'S NEXT

Although it is very tempting to go on to the next chapter to start learning specific techniques to work the sentence completion questions, this is counterproductive until you understand and remember the grammar rules. If this chapter confused you, and you need a more thorough grammar review from the bottom up, please read the book *Grammar Smart*, also published by The Princeton Review. It contains a clear, step-by-step review of English grammar, along with lots of exercises to test your comprehension.

You can practice your grammar skills on your own by reading English-language documents and identifying the parts of speech and parts of a sentence in them. If any of your coworkers are studying for the TOEIC too, you can trade work and check each other's answers. This is a great way to stay motivated to review grammar.

10

Sentence Completion
Questions

START HERE

Now that you've reviewed the rules of grammar (if you haven't reviewed them, go back and review them before reading this chapter), we'll put that knowledge to good use by practicing sentence completion questions.

Sentence completion questions are the questions that look like this.

> The guidelines were ------ to accommodate several different divisions of the company.
> (A) written
> (B) explained
> (C) forgotten
> (D) diverged

Your task is to pick the answer choice that best fits into the blank in the sentence.

THE STRATEGY FOR SENTENCE COMPLETION QUESTIONS

First, remember the most important tips to scoring well on the TOEIC—(1) use Process of Elimination (POE), and (2) don't leave any blanks. These techniques apply to all question types on the TOEIC. See Chapter 3 if you need a review.

Now let's focus on specific strategies for doing well on sentence completion questions. All sentence completion questions can be approached in the same way, no matter what the individual differences in the questions are. (We'll get to advice on answering specific types of questions later.)

Steps in the process

Cover the answer choices when you read the question.

Look at the answer choices and decide whether you are choosing between different words or different forms of the same word.

Come up with your own answer for the blanks.

Use the information in the sentence to help you decide which word or part of speech should go in the blank.

Match your answer to the answer choice that most closely resembles it.

Don't worry about words you don't know.

Cover the answer choices when you read the question.

The TOEIC is designed to trick you into using your ear to pick the answer that sounds the best in the sentence. Unfortunately, many times all the answer choices sound good in the sentence, so this strategy won't work. Other times, the word that sounds the best isn't the correct answer, so this strategy is even worse!

The best way to avoid the trap of picking a word based on the way it sounds is to stick to the strict plan of attack we're laying out for you now. This first step asks you to cover the answer choices with your hand while you read the question. It sounds like something a grade-school student would do, but you'd be amazed at how well it helps you focus in on the sentence itself. If you can't see the answer choices, you can't be distracted by them before you're ready to look at them objectively.

Look at the answer choices and decide whether you are choosing between different words or different forms of the same word.

Now that you've read the question, you probably have a vague idea of what sort of word should go in the blank. There are two general types of sentence completion questions. One type gives you four completely different words as answer choices to choose from. The other type gives you four different forms of the same word as answer choices to choose from. You *must* know which type of question you are dealing with! The only way to tell which type of question you are dealing with is to look at the answer choices themselves. Do this now. Let's look at the difference between these two questions.

1. The guidelines were ------ to accommodate several different divisions of the company.
   - (A) written
   - (B) explained
   - (C) forgotten
   - (D) diverged

2. The guidelines were ------ to accommodate several different divisions of the company.
   - (A) written
   - (B) writing
   - (C) write
   - (D) wrote

In question 1, the answer choices are *written, explained, forgotten,* and *diverged.* These words are very different. This means that we need to focus on differences in meaning among the words. In question 2, on the other hand, the answer choices are *written, writing, write,* and *wrote.* These words are different forms of the same word. This means that we need to focus on what part of speech fits into the blank. As you can see, the sentence itself is identical in question 1 and question 2. It is the answer choices which determine what type of question it is. We'll discuss more about the two types of questions later on in this chapter.

Come up with your own answer for the blanks.

Now that you know what type of question you're dealing with, you know how to answer it. If the answer choices are different words, you should try to come up with your own word to put in the blank. If you can't think of a word in English that fits, you can even use a word in your own language that fits the meaning of the sentence. Write that word down above the blank in the sentence or next to the answer choices.

If the answer choices are different forms of the same word, you should figure out what part of speech the word in the blank needs to be. If you can tell from the clues in the sentence which part of speech you need, great. If not, one way to do this is to come up with your own word for the blank. Then determine what part of speech that word is. Write down the part of speech you're looking for next to the answer choices.

Use the information in the sentence to help you decide which word or part of speech should go in the blank.

Sometimes you can think of a word to fill in the blank right away. That's great. But sometimes you may have a little more trouble coming up with something appropriate. Fortunately, there are always clues in the sentence that tell you what word should go in the blank.

If the answer choices are different words, you should fill in a specific word for the blank. Look at the sentence and ask yourself which of the words in the sentence the blank refers to. Then ask yourself what else you know about those words from the sentence. That tells you what goes in the blank. Sound confusing? Let's try it on our sample sentence.

1. The guidelines were ------ to accommodate several different divisions of the company.

   (A) written
   (B) explained
   (C) forgotten
   (D) diverged

We know that since the answer choice words are different, we're concerned with meaning, not parts of speech. What words in the sentence does the blank refer to? *The guidelines*. What else do we know about *the guidelines* based on the sentence? That they were used to accommodate the different divisions. A good word to put in the blank would be *used* or *made*.

When the answer choice words are different forms of the same word, figure out what part of speech goes in the blank. Look at the other words around the blank to see if they give you any clues. Are there any helping verbs or time words like *yesterday* or *tomorrow*?

If you can't figure out directly what part of speech should go in the blank, fill in the blank with a word that makes sense in the sentence. Then determine what part of speech your word is. Now you know what part of speech goes in the blank. Let's try it with our second example from earlier.

2. The guidelines were ------ to accommodate several different divisions of the company.

   (A) written
   (B) writing
   (C) write
   (D) wrote

We know that since the answer choice words are different forms of the same word, we're concerned with what part of speech goes in the blank, not with meaning.

Are there any clues in the sentence that tell you what part of speech goes in the blank? Yes. The word *were* right before the blank is a verb that can be followed by a noun or an adjective. It can also be used as a helping verb in the past passive tense when followed by the past participle of another verb.

Match your answer to the answer choice that most closely resembles it.

Now we're going to use POE to eliminate any answer choices that don't match your word, so that we'll only have one answer choice left—the one that matches the word you filled in for the blank. This step is where you win the TOEIC sentence completion race—instead of picking randomly from the answer choices, you're using methodical precision to eliminate all but the one correct answer choice. Let's go back to our two examples and show how all the work we've done finally pays off in eliminating all but the correct answer.

1. The guidelines were ------ to accommodate several different divisions of the company.

   (A) written
   (B) explained
   (C) forgotten
   (D) diverged

When we last left this question, we had decided that an appropriate word to put in the blank was *used* or *made*. (We decided this by asking what the blank referred to and what else we knew about that thing. The blank refers to the *guidelines*, and we know that they were used to accommodate different divisions.)

Now we simply go through the answer choices, one by one, and eliminate any that don't match our words. Answer choice (A), *written*, could match. Writing is the way you make guidelines, so *written* is close to *made*. Leave this answer choice in. Answer choice (B), *explained*, doesn't match either of our words. Eliminate it. Answer choice (C), *forgotten*, doesn't match either of our words. In fact, *forgotten* almost means the opposite of *used*. Get rid of it. Answer choice (D), *diverged*, doesn't match either of our words. Cross it off too.

The only answer choice left is (A), which matches the word we put in the blank. It is the correct answer. So you would fill it in on your answer sheet and move on to the next question.

2. The guidelines were ------ to accommodate several different divisions of
    the company.
    (A) written
    (B) writing
    (C) write
    (D) wrote

When we last left this question, we had decided that, based on the word *were* in the sentence, we were looking for a noun, adjective, or past participle for the blank. Let's go through the answer choices one by one to see if we can find one of these parts of speech.

Answer choice (A), *written*, is a past participle. Keep it in. Answer choice (B), *writing*, is a gerund/present participle. Get rid of it. Answer choice (C), *write*, is a present tense verb. Cross it off. Answer choice (D), *wrote*, is a simple past tense verb. Eliminate it. The only choice left is (A), the past participle. It must be the correct answer. So you would fill it in on your answer sheet and move on to the next question.

"But wait!," you say. "I had no idea how to figure out all that stuff about *were* and the past participle." Don't worry. There's another perfectly logical way to find the answer. Instead of figuring out what part of speech goes in the blank, just put your own word in the blank. Then eliminate any answer choices that aren't the same part of speech as the word you filled in. Here's how it works.

2. The guidelines were ------ to accommodate several different divisions of
    the company.
    (A) written
    (B) writing
    (C) write
    (D) wrote

Use the same steps you would use if the answer choices were completely different words to come up with a word to put in the blank. Since we've (pretty conveniently) already done this with this sentence, let's just use the word we came up with, *made*.

Now let's go to the answer choices. *Made* is some type of verb, but so are all the answer choices, so that doesn't help us. However, *made* has something to do with the past tense, so that should help.

Answer choice (A), *written*, also has something to do with the past tense. Leave it in. Answer choice (B), *writing*, is not a past tense verb at all. Eliminate it. Answer choice (C), *write*, is the present tense of the verb. Cross it off. Answer choice (D), *wrote*, is the simple past tense of the verb. Leave it in.

Now we're left with two answer choices to choose from, (A) and (D). You could stop and guess at this point and have a 50 percent chance of getting the correct answer. Or you could try to decide which one is least likely to be the answer.

Since we know that (D) is the simple past tense, let's start here. The simple past tense only uses one word, without any helper words. Look back at the sentence. The word *were* is right before the blank, which means that *were* is a helping verb in this sentence. *Were made* is not the simple past tense. So you could eliminate answer choice (D).

Remember, it doesn't matter if you know exactly why an answer choice is correct, as long as you can find the correct answer! That's what's so great about a multiple choice test. You only have to pick the correct answer, you don't have to explain it.

Don't worry about words you don't know.

Occasionally you may run into a word you don't know in the sentence or answer choices. Don't allow this to stress you out, since there are ways to work around this without missing any points.

If the word you don't know is in the sentence, you can probably use the other words to decipher its approximate meaning. In fact, you can use the same process you used to come up with a word to put in the blank to figure out what the unknown word means. Let's try it on this sentence.

Instead of skimming for the facts as he ------ did, Mr. Jenkins decided to peruse the paper for details of the situation.

Assume that we don't know the meaning of the word *peruse*. What does the word *peruse* refer to? It's something he does to *the newspaper*. What else do we know about the newspaper? That Mr. Jenkins usually skims it. Skim means to read through quickly, looking for the main idea. The sentence also contains the word *instead*, which indicates that there are two contrasting ideas. Since *skimming* means reading through quickly, *peruse* must mean the opposite—to read through slowly for meaning. In fact, the sentence says that he will *peruse* it *for details*. We figured out the meaning exactly.

If the word you don't know is in the answer choices, you don't have as many clues to its meaning. In fact, the only thing you may know for sure is what part of speech it is. If the answer choice words are all different, they are all the same part of speech.

It doesn't really matter if you know what one of the answer choice words means, however, as long as you know whether it's the correct answer or not. And you can figure that out without knowing the meaning, as long as you know the meanings of the other three answer choices. Let's try it.

The situation became ------ once our competitor announced that they were breaking the noncompete agreement we'd signed.

(A) untenable
(B) believable
(C) reliable
(D) unknowable

We see that the answer choices are different words, and that we don't know what answer choice (A), *untenable*, means. Now let's read the sentence and put in a word for the blank.

What does the blank refer to? (*The situation.*) What else do we know about the situation? That the competitor broke an agreement. A good word to put in the blank would be *difficult*.

Now we go through the answer choices one by one. Since we don't know what answer choice (A) means, we need to focus on the other three. If one of the other three means *difficult*, we should choose it and eliminate answer choice (A) (since we know it's wrong anyway). If none of the other three mean *difficult*, we should choose answer choice (A), since it must mean *difficult*.

Answer choice (B), *believable*, does not mean *difficult*. Cross it off. Answer choice (C), *reliable*, does not mean *difficult*. Get rid of it. Answer choice (D), *unknowable*, does not mean difficult. Eliminate it. Answer choice (A) must be the correct answer. In fact, *untenable* means *cannot be maintained because of its difficulty*.

THE TYPES OF QUESTIONS

Now that we've gone over the basic method for answering any sentence completion question, we can talk about specific types of questions. As we discussed earlier, there are two general categories of sentence completion questions: ones with answer choices that are completely different words, and ones with answer choices that are different forms of the same word. Within these two categories, there are even more distinctions, and we'll discuss those now.

DIFFERENT WORDS

There seem to be a few more questions on the TOEIC in which the answer choices are completely different from each other than there are questions in which the answer choices are just different forms of the same word. To help you approach these questions, we've studied the questions to find out what the differences are based on. There are five different categories we've discovered. Being able to recognize which category a question falls into can help simplify the process of finding the answer and will make you more comfortable as you're working through the question.

Modifiers

Modifiers are words that give information about another word. The most common modifiers are adverbs and adjectives. Adverbs describe verbs and adjectives, while adjectives describe nouns. It is generally fairly simple to deal with questions in which the answer choices are modifiers. First, figure out what word the blank is modifying. Then, read the rest of the sentence to see what you already know about that word. That should tell you exactly what you're looking for. Write down your own word for the blank and eliminate the answer choices that don't match it.

It is important to note that you don't have to choose between adverbs and adjectives if the answer choices are all different words. If the answers are all different words, you are looking for distinctions in meaning. Let's try one.

> The Internet, with all its advanced technology, relies ------ on infrastructure built over a generation ago.
>
> (A) heavily
> (B) newly
> (C) constantly
> (D) poorly

The blank modifies the word *relies*, so it tells us how the Internet relies on old infrastructure. The sentence also tells us that the Internet has advanced technology, but this is contrasted with the degree to which it relies on the old infrastructure, so we can deduce that it relies *strongly*. Write the word *strongly* next to the blank, and let's eliminate the answer choices that don't match it.

Answer choice (A), *heavily*, means *strongly*, so leave it in. Answer choice (B), *newly*, does not mean *strongly*. Eliminate it. Answer choice (C), *constantly*, does not mean *strongly*. You could argue that the Internet constantly needs this old infrastructure, but that isn't really the point of the sentence, since we can assume that the infrastructure is constant. Cross it off. Answer choice (D), *poorly*, does not mean *strongly*. Eliminate it.

Prepositions

Prepositions questions are some of the most difficult questions you will encounter in the sentence completion section. This is because prepositions are illogical and vary from case to case. The only real way to be sure of them is to memorize an exhaustive list, or to speak English with native speakers who will correct you when you use prepositions incorrectly. (Don't feel bad—it's hard to learn prepositions in any language, so native English speakers have problems learning prepositions in other languages, too.) At the end of this book is a list of common idioms that contain prepositions. It is by no means a complete list of all the idiomatic uses of prepositions in the English language, but it's a start.

The bad news about this is that it won't really help to put your own word in the blank when the answer choices are all prepositions. Instead, you should look carefully at the answer choices one by one and try to eliminate any whose meaning does not match the meaning of the sentence. Once you've eliminated all the answer choices you can, guess from the ones you have left. Here's an example.

> When his company's stock began to climb in value, Mr. Kobarcik decided to cash ------ his stock options.
>
> (A) through
> (B) in
> (C) around
> (D) up

When you look at the answer choices and see that they are all prepositions, you know that you are being tested on an idiomatic expression. In this case, the idiom goes with the word *climb*. If you are familiar with this idiom and know which preposition goes with *climb*, then this question will be easy for you. If not, you'll have to do your best to eliminate answer choices that don't make sense.

Answer choice (A), *through*, doesn't make much sense in this context because there is nothing to move through in the sentence, either physically or in time. Eliminate it. Answer choice (B), *in*, could be the answer. Leave it in. Answer choice (C), *around*, doesn't make much sense in this context. Around gives the idea of circling something, and Mr. Kobarcik wants to do something directly by selling his stock options. Get rid of it. Answer choice (D), *up*, could be the answer. Leave it in.

Now we're left with two answer choices, (B) and (D). If you don't know which one to choose, just take a guess and move on. The correct idiomatic expression is *cash in*, so the correct answer is (B).

Conjunctions

Conjunctions express a relationship between two ideas. They can show either agreement or disagreement between the ideas.

Some conjunctions that show agreement between the ideas

and

such as

as well as

because

also

since

in addition to

as

Some conjunctions that show disagreement between the two ideas

but

however

despite

although

in spite of

whereas

The best way to approach questions in which the answer choices are conjunctions is to identify the two ideas that have a relationship. Then decide whether that relationship is agreement or disagreement. Eliminate any answer choices that express the wrong relationship. If you have any answer choices left, examine their meanings carefully to determine which one best fits the relationship between the two ideas in the sentence.

Let's try a conjunction question.

------ the consumption of tobacco has dramatically decreased, smoking continues to be a widespread and costly health problem.

(A) Despite
(B) Although
(C) Since
(D) Neither

In this example, the first idea states that "the consumption of tobacco has dramatically decreased." The second idea states that "smoking continues to be a widespread and costly health problem." The disagreement of ideas between the main sentence and the dependent clause needs a conjunction of disagreement. Let's go through the answer choices one by one and eliminate anything that isn't a conjunction of disagreement.

Answer choice (A), *despite*, indicates disagreement. However, *despite* has to be followed by a phrase that doesn't contain a verb. The phrase before the comma does contain a verb, *has decreased*, so *despite* doesn't work. Eliminate it. Answer choice (B), *although*, indicates disagreement. Keep it. Answer choice (C), *since*, indicates agreement. Cross it off. Answer choice (D), *neither*, must be paired with the word *nor. Nor* isn't in the sentence, so *neither* can't be either. Eliminate it, and you have your answer.

Pronouns

Pronouns take the place of nouns that have already been mentioned in the sentence. There are two typical pronoun traps on sentence completion questions. The first is to give an answer choice pronoun that doesn't agree with the noun it's supposed to take the place of. For example, the noun may be plural, but the answer choice is singular.

The second trap is to give an answer choice pronoun that doesn't clearly refer to any one noun in the sentence. For example, there may be two plural nouns in the sentence, and the answer choice is *they*. If there are two plural nouns, how can you be sure which one the *they* refers to?

The best way to approach this question is to fill in your own pronoun for the blank. Use the same steps we've outlined before to identify what noun the blank takes the place of. Then decide what pronoun makes sense to take the place of that noun. Chances are that the pronoun you filled in will be one of the answer choices. Let's try one.

> Aluminum's extreme malleability, durability, and conductivity make ------
> useful for high-tension electrical power transmission.
>
> (A) them
> (B) they
> (C) which
> (D) it

We can see that all the answer choices are pronouns, so we need to determine which noun the blank takes the place of. In this sentence, the only noun the missing pronoun can modify is *aluminum*. So the answer needs to be a singular pronoun referring to *aluminum*.

Answer choice (A), *them*, is a plural pronoun. Eliminate it. Answer choice (B), *they*, is a plural pronoun. Cross it off. Answer choice (C), *which*, can only be used when it is necessary to distinguish a noun from another. This is not necessary in this sentence, so get rid of this one too. Answer choice (D), *it*, is a simple singular pronoun which refers directly to *aluminum*. Leave it in.

Similar words

There's another answer choice pattern worth mentioning. Sometimes ETS will give you words which all begin with the same letter or prefix, or end with the same suffix. The problem is that you have to pay attention even more on this type of question than on some of the others. It's easy to misread the answer choices if you're going too quickly.

To beat these questions, just go through the process as carefully as you can. Put in your own word for the blank, based on the meaning of the sentence. Then go through the answer choices carefully and eliminate the ones that don't match your word. Don't get daunted or confused by the similarities of the answer choices. Let's try one.

> As a result of the steep drop in the stock market, the pension plan
> suffered ------ losses.
>
> (A) colonial
> (B) collectable
> (C) collegial
> (D) colossal

These answer choices are so similar that we shouldn't even bother to look at them until we put in our own word for the blank, lest we get distracted by them. The blank describes the kind of losses the pension plan had. The sentence tells us that the plan *suffered,* which sounds pretty serious, and that the stock market had a *steep* drop. A good word to put in the blank would be *big.* Let's eliminate any answer choices that don't mean *big.*

Answer choice (A), *colonial*, does not mean *big*. Get rid of it. Answer choice (B), *collectable*, does not mean *big*. Eliminate it. Answer choice (C), *collegial*, does not mean *big*. Eliminate this one too. Answer choice (D), *colossal*, means *big*. Leave it in.

DIFFERENT FORMS

There are fewer questions on the TOEIC in which the answer choices are different forms of the same word than there are questions in which the answer choices are completely different words. That doesn't mean that these questions are less difficult, however. In fact, these questions can be much more challenging because you really need to understand grammatically how the missing word fits into the rest of the sentence. You can't rely on meaning to help you out.

There are two types of word-form questions: ones in which the answer choices are all different verb forms, and ones in which the answer choices are all different parts of speech. The good news is that there are very few questions on the TOEIC in which all the answer choices are verb forms. The bad news is that they are much harder than any other type of sentence completion question. Let's begin by discussing the more difficult verb forms questions.

Verb form

Verb form questions tend to be very tricky because it's hard sometimes to tell exactly which verb tense a sentence calls for. The sentence will contain clues, however, about what tense the verb should be in. They may be words indicating when the action took place, or they may be words immediately before or after the blank that restrict your options. If you have trouble answering verb form questions, go back to the chapter before this one and review all the material on verbs.

If you really can't figure out what tense the verb should be in, just put in your own word. Then eliminate the answer choices that aren't the same tense as the word you picked.

Let's try an example.

During the brief Prohibition era, the local police force ------ thousands of gallons of illegally distilled alcohol.

(A) destroyed
(B) destroys
(C) destroying
(D) to destroy

We can see that all the answer choices are different forms of the same verb. The sentence tells us that the action took place *during the brief Prohibition era*. This was in the 1920s, so the action takes place in the past. The correct answer will be a past tense verb.

Answer choice (A), *destroyed*, is a past tense verb. Leave it in. Answer choice (B), *destroys*, is a present tense verb. Eliminate it. Answer choice (C), *destroying*, is a gerund. Get rid of it. Answer choice (D), *to destroy*, is the infinitive. Eliminate this one too.

General form

General form questions are a little easier than the questions in which all the answer choices are verbs. That's because it's a lot easier to distinguish between parts of speech—like the difference between a noun and a verb—than it is to distinguish the nuances of different verb forms. Use the clues in the sentence, especially the words immediately before and after the blank, to help you determine what part of speech would work in the blank.

If you still can't decide what part of speech the blank is, put in your own word that makes sense in the blank. Then eliminate the answer choices that aren't the same part of speech. Let's try one.

The consultant knew that her only hope to restore her client's ------ position in the marketplace was to streamline its manufacturing process.

(A) competitor
(B) competition
(C) competitive
(D) compete

The missing word refers to the noun *position* immediately following it. This means that the blank can't be a verb or another noun; it has to be an adjective.

Answer choice (A), *competitor*, is a noun. Eliminate it. Answer choice (B), *competition*, is a noun. Cross it off. Answer choice (C), *competitive*, is an adjective. Leave it in. Answer choice (D), *compete*, is a verb. Eliminate this one too.

Sentence completion drill

Answers can be found on page 135.

1. The accounting error was only ------ when the company's bank account became overdrawn.

   (A) administered
   (B) rectified
   (C) discovered
   (D) prevented

2. Don't forget to ------ the form to have your expenses reimbursed.

   (A) submitting
   (B) submission
   (C) submitted
   (D) submit

3. It was simply a ------ coincidence that the project was completed in time for the new budget cycle to begin.

   (A) forgotten
   (B) unacknowledged
   (C) foreseen
   (D) lucky

4. Her new position is far ------ challenging than her old one was.

   (A) more
   (B) so
   (C) as
   (D) than

5. Mr. De la Hoz ------ his plane from Amsterdam last night because the traffic to the airport was gridlocked.

   (A) miss
   (B) missed
   (C) misses
   (D) will miss

6. The company's new family leave policy showed a strong ------ to quality-of-life issues.

   (A) committing
   (B) committed
   (C) committee
   (D) commitment

7. Improper ------ of the converter unit will void the warranty on the machine.

   (A) installation
   (B) infestation
   (C) instigation
   (D) indentation

8. The benefits committee ultimately decided not to choose ------ of the two health plans.

   (A) both
   (B) either
   (C) yet
   (D) or

9. The seventeenth child of slaves, Mary Bethune helped ------ President Roosevelt's policies on minority affairs.

   (A) developed
   (B) to develop
   (C) develops
   (D) developing

10. ------ the root and the foliage of the red beet are safe for consumption.

    (A) While
    (B) Both
    (C) Either
    (D) Though

Answers to the sentence completion drill

1. C
2. D
3. D
4. A
5. B
6. D
7. A
8. B
9. B
10. B

Explanations

1. **C** The answer choices in this question are all different words, so this question relies on meaning to find the answer. We are looking for what happened when the bank account was overdrawn. The company wouldn't have overdrawn its account if it had known about it, so a good word to fill in the blank would be "known about."

   Administered does not mean *known about*, so eliminate answer choice (A). *Rectified* does not mean *known about*, so cross off answer choice (B). You could argue that this choice makes sense in the sentence, but the sentence never indicates that the accounting error was fixed, just that the company found out about it. *Discovered* does mean *known about*, so keep answer choice (C). *Prevented* does not mean *known about*, so eliminate answer choice (D). The answer is (C).

2. **D** The answer choices in this question are all different forms of the same word, so the question relies on grammar to find the answer. The answer choices are different parts of speech. The blank is preceded by the word *to*, which indicates that the blank must be filled by a verb.

   Submitting is an adjective or a gerund, so get rid of answer choice (A). *Submission* is a noun, so eliminate answer choice (B). *Submitted* is a past-tense verb, but it can't come directly after the word *to*, so eliminate answer choice (C). *Submit* is a verb that combines with *to* to form the infinitive. Leave it in. The answer is (D).

3. **D** The answer choices in this question are all different words, so the question relies on meaning to find the answer. We are looking for a word that tells us the kind of coincidence it was that the project ended when the new budget cycle began. A good word to put in the blank would be "convenient."

   Forgotten does not mean anything like *convenient*, so cross off answer choice (A). *Unacknowledged* does not mean anything like *convenient*, so eliminate answer choice (B). *Foreseen* does not mean anything like *convenient*, so get rid of answer choice (C). *Lucky* could be similar to *convenient* in this context, so leave answer choice (D) in. The answer is (D).

4. **A** The answer choices in this question are all different words, so the question relies on meaning to find the answer. We need a word that modifies the level of challenge of her old and new positions. The missing word should provide a comparison, so the only words that could go in the bank are either *more* or *less*. *Less* is not one of the answer choice words, but *more* is. The answer is (A).

5. **B** The answer choices in this question are all different forms of the same verb, so the question relies on grammar to find the answer. The sentence gives us a big clue in the words *last night*. This means that the verb must be in the past tense.

    Miss is in the present tense, so cross off answer choice (A). *Missed* is in the past tense, so leave in answer choice (B). *Misses* is in the present tense, so eliminate answer choice (C). *Will miss* is in the future tense, so get rid of answer choice (D). The answer is (B).

6. **D** The answer choices in this question are all different forms of the same word, so the question relies on grammar to find the answer. The answer choices are different parts of speech. The blank is preceded by the word *strong*, which is an adjective. Adjectives modify nouns, so the word we're looking for must be a noun.

    Committing is a gerund, so eliminate answer choice (A). *Committed* is either a past tense verb or an adjective, so cross off answer choice (B). *Committee* is a noun, so keep answer choice (C). *Commitment* is a noun, so leave in answer choice (D).

    We have two possible answer choices, so let's look at the rest of the sentence. The word after the blank is *to*. The phrase *commitment to* is an idiomatic expression, while the phrase *committee to* is not. Eliminate answer choice (C). The answer is (D).

7. **A** The answer choices in this question are all different words, so the question relies on meaning to find the answer. We are looking for a word that tells something that must be done to the converter unit, and that can be done improperly. A good word to put in the blank would be *fixing* or something that gives the same idea.

    Installation is close to *fixing* in this context. Leave answer choice (A) in. *Infestation* does not mean *fixing*. Eliminate answer choice (B). *Instigation* does not mean *fixing*. Cross off answer choice (C). *Indentation* does not mean *fixing*. Get rid of answer choice (D). The answer is (A).

8. **B** The answer choices in this question are all different words, so the question relies on meaning to find the answer. We are looking for a conjunction that refers to the two health plans. We know that the committee didn't choose the health plans, so the correct answer must indicate that.

    Both would indicate that the committee had planned to choose the two health plans together. This doesn't make sense, so get rid of answer choice (A). *Either* indicates that the committee didn't choose one health plan or the other health plan. Leave answer choice (B) in. *Yet* is a modifier indicating time. Eliminate answer choice (C). *Or* needs *either* to make sense here. So eliminate answer choice (D) too. The answer is (B).

9. **B** The answer choices in this question are all different forms of the same verb, so the question relies on grammar to find the answer. The clue in the sentence is the word *helped* before the blank. This means that the correct answer can only be an infinitive verb, not a conjugated verb.

To develop is an infinitive, so keep answer choice (B). Eliminate the other answer choices. The answer is (B).

10. **B** The answer choices in this question are all different words, so the question relies on meaning to find the answer. We need a word that refers to the relationship between *root* and *foliage*. There is no contrast between the two, so the correct answer must be a word indicating agreement.

While does not indicate agreement, so eliminate answer choice (A). *Both* indicates agreement, so leave answer choice (B) in. In this context, *either* needs to be followed by *or* at some point in the sentence. So get rid of answer choice (C). *Though* can only begin a phrase without a verb, so eliminate answer choice (D). The answer is (B).

11

Error Identification
Questions

START HERE

The other type of grammar-based question in the Reading section of the TOEIC is the error identification question. Simply put, these questions contain four underlined words or short phrases. Three are grammatically correct, and one is incorrect.

Error identification questions are the questions that look like this:

New <u>employees</u> must attend an <u>orientation</u> session within <u>their</u> first week <u>to</u> work.
    A   B   C   D

Your task is to pick the answer choice that is grammatically incorrect.

THE STRATEGY FOR ERROR IDENTIFICATION QUESTIONS

First, remember the most important tips to scoring well on the TOEIC—(1) use Process of Elimination (POE), and, (2) don't leave any blanks. These techniques apply to all question types on the TOEIC. See Chapter 3 if you need a review.

Now let's focus on specific strategies for doing well on error identification questions. All error identification questions can be approached in the same way, no matter what the individual differences in the questions are. (We'll get to advice on answering specific types of questions later.)

Steps in the process

Focus on one underlined word at a time.

Run through the list of common errors to determine if the answer choice is okay.

Remember that the nonunderlined words in the sentence are always okay.

Don't try to rewrite the sentence.

If you're not sure about an answer choice, move on to the next one.

Don't worry about words you don't know.

Three answer choices will be okay, and only one will not. Pick that one.

Focus on one underlined word at a time.

Error identification questions are difficult for several reasons. One is that the answer choices are contained in the question itself. That can be confusing unless you've practiced enough questions to be comfortable with the format. Another, more important reason error identification questions are difficult is that they can be overwhelming. There are four different words or short phrases underlined in each sentence, and it can be daunting to sort the whole sentence out.

The best way to navigate these questions is to stay calm and focus on only one underlined word at a time. Examine each word (we'll get to that in the next step) and then decide if you want to eliminate it or keep it in as a possibly correct choice. If you decide to eliminate it, cross it off, and don't think about it again. If you decide to leave it in, move on to examine the next underlined word.

Run through the list of common errors to determine if the answer choice is okay.

The good news about the TOEIC is that it only tests certain grammar rules in the error identification questions (discussed in Chapter 9). If you learn and become familiar with these rules, you'll be able to answer almost any error identification question on the test. Once you've learned the rules, you should memorize them. Then you'll be able to go through them quickly on each question so you can see which rules apply to each answer choice.

Remember that the non-underlined words in the sentence are always okay.

Sometimes you can lose track of the fact that only one of the underlined choices can be incorrect. Do not fall into the trap of attempting to "correct" the sentence by changing the parts of the sentence that are not underlined. They are there to give you important clues to the underlined word that is used incorrectly. Use them to help you; don't fight against them.

Don't try to rewrite the sentence.

This is the worst mistake anyone can make when answering error identification questions. There is no need to determine how the sentence *should* be written. The only thing that matters is that you can figure out which underlined word is wrong. Once you've done that, fill in the correct bubble on your answer sheet and move on. There is no way to indicate a better or more grammatically correct or graceful way to write the sentence, so don't waste your time.

The error identification question is probably radically different from the kinds of questions you have encountered on other tests. Most tests ask you to find the answer that is correct. They ask that you show that you can write or speak correct English. The error identification section on the TOEIC does not. In error identification questions, you are asked to find the word or group of words that is used incorrectly. You are asked to recognize *in*correct English. The incorrect word or words is the correct answer!

Confusing?! It may be, but it makes your task much easier. Even if you aren't exactly sure why an answer choice is incorrect, as long as you have some idea what's wrong with it you can eliminate it and move on to the next question.

If you're not sure about an answer choice, move on to the next one.

There are four answer choices, so even if you can't figure out which underlined word is incorrect (and therefore the correct response), you can still probably eliminate a few answer choices. If you honestly can't tell whether an underlined word is fine or if it is grammatically incorrect, then don't worry. It's not worth wasting the time or energy stressing out about it. Instead, just move on to the next answer choice and evaluate it. If you're left with two (or more) possibly incorrect underlined words, just pick one and go on to the next question.

Don't worry about words you don't know.

Try to use the context of the sentence to help you figure out the meaning of any words you don't know. If this fails, however, don't waste time worrying about a word you don't know. Just stick to the plan, examining each answer choice separately until you find the incorrect one. If not knowing a word prevents you from eliminating three of the answer choices, just pick from among the answer choices you can't eliminate and move on to the next question.

Three answer choices will be okay, and only one will not. Pick that one.

Perhaps the trickiest aspect of error identification questions is the confusion they can induce in the test taker. After all, they are the only question type on the whole TOIEC that asks you to pick the *incorrect* answer instead of the correct answer. That's really counterintuitive and can trip you up if you're not careful.

The simplest way to combat this problem is to practice enough error identification questions before you go in to take the TOIEC so that they become routine. If you do this, you won't be distracted or confused when you take the real test. However, if there is still doubt in your mind, just pick the "odd answer out." Three answer choices will be similar (they'll be correct), while one will be different (incorrect). Pick the one that doesn't fit with the others.

THE GRAMMAR RULES TESTED ON THE READING SECTION OF THE TOEIC

Now that we've gone over the basic method for answering any error identification question, we can talk about the specific grammar rules tested in this section. As we stated earlier, you should memorize the list of rules so that you can run through it quickly for each answer choice within a question. Here's the list:

Pronouns
Verbs (tense and person)
Modifiers (adverbs or adjectives)
Conjunctions
Prepositions

Now let's talk about each rule separately.

Pronouns

Pronouns take the place of nouns. There are two typical pronoun traps on error identification questions (which are, quite predictably, the same traps that appear on sentence completion questions). The first is to give an underlined pronoun that doesn't agree with the noun it's supposed to take the place of. For example, the noun may be plural, but the underlined pronoun is singular.

The second trap is to give an answer choice pronoun that doesn't clearly refer to any one noun in the sentence. For example, there may be two plural nouns in the sentence, and the underlined word is *they*. If there are two plural nouns, how can you be sure which one the *they* refers to?

Whenever you see an underlined word that is a pronoun, find the noun it refers to. Then make sure it agrees with that noun, and that it can only refer to that one noun. If it does both those things, it's fine, and you can cross it off. If you're not sure, check out the other three underlined words before you eliminate it. If it's obviously wrong, circle it and (after you've eliminated the other three underlined words) choose it as the answer to the question. Let's try a pronoun question.

A problem with the suppliers <u>forced</u> the New York locations of NailsInc to stop payment of <u>their bills</u>
                       A   B

during the months <u>of</u> January <u>and</u> February.
                        C   D

Answer choice (A), the verb *forced*, is correct in this sentence because it expresses the simple past tense. So cross it off. Answer choice (B), the pronoun *their*, is plural. This matches with the plural noun *locations*. Unfortunately, it also matches with the plural noun *suppliers*, so the pronoun isn't specific. (B) is the incorrect answer, so you would fill it in on your answer sheet. But let's check the other answer choices to be sure. Answer choice (C), the preposition *of*, is correct in the phrase *months of January and February*. Eliminate it. Answer choice (D), the conjunction *and*, correctly connects the two ideas *January* and *February*. Eliminate it too.

Verbs

Verbs must match the subjects they belong to both in tense and in person. For example, if the subject is singular, the verb must be singular, too. But the verb must also correctly express when in time the action occurs.

A common trick on the grammar-based questions on the TOEIC (and, frankly, on any standardized test) is to separate the subject and verb by inserting prepositional and other phrases between them. If you're relying on the way the sentence "sounds" to determine which answer choice is incorrect, you can easily be fooled by these extra phrases. However, if you evaluate each underlined word individually, you will be able to spot any disagreement.

Whenever you see an underlined word or phrase that is a verb, find the subject it belongs to. Do they agree in person? Does the verb correctly express the time in which the action occurs? If you can answer "yes" to both questions, eliminate the answer choice, because it's not an error. If not, it may be the incorrect answer (but be sure to check out the other three choices before you fill it in). Let's try a verb question.

Dr. Robinson, in addition to being the leader of a group of 50 highly respected biotechnology
           <u>   </u>
            A

<u>researchers</u>, also <u>head</u> the research and development department <u>at</u> TriNoCor Pharmaceuticals.
  B   C   D

Answer choice (A), the conjunction *in addition to*, correctly connects the ideas that Dr. Robinson is the leader and that she heads the department. So eliminate it. Answer choice (B), the noun *researchers*, is correct, so get rid of it too. Answer choice (C), the verb *head,* is correct in the present tense, but here is incorrect because *Dr. Robinson* is a singular subject, while *head* is a plural verb. Answer choice (C) is the incorrect answer you're looking for. Answer choice (D), the preposition *at*, is correct. Cross it off.

Modifiers

Modifiers are words that give information about another word. The most common modifiers are adverbs and adjectives. Adverbs describe verbs and adjectives, while adjectives describe nouns. Whenever you see an underlined word or phrase that is a modifier, find the word or phrase it modifies. Then make sure they match up. For instance, if the underlined word is supposed to modify a verb, the underlined word has to be an adverb, not an adjective. If the modifier and the word it modifies match, eliminate that answer choice, because it's not an error. If not, you've found the incorrect answer (don't forget to check the other three answer choices, too). If you're not sure, check out the other three answer choices before you eliminate it. Let's try a modifier question.

Third-quarter <u>sales</u> were much <u>slow</u> than predicted, <u>possibly</u> because of the <u>unusually</u> cold autumn.
             A   B   C   D

Answer choice (A), the noun *sales,* is the subject of the sentence, and is fine. Eliminate it. Answer choice (B) is one of three underlined modifiers in this sentence (the other two are answer choices (C) and (D)). It is the adjective *slow*, which here is part of a comparison (the actual sales vs. the predicted sales). A comparison must be made with a comparative or superlative word, not just a regular adjective. *Slow* should be *slower*, so answer choice (B) is the incorrect answer you're looking for. Answer choice (C), the adverb *possibly,* correctly modifies the phrase making up the entire first half of the sentence. Cross it off. Answer choice (D), the adverb *unusually*, correctly modifies the adjective *cold.* Eliminate this one.

This question is unusual because three of the underlined words are in the same category. It shows the various ways modifiers can be used (and misused) and how to evaluate them.

Conjunctions

Conjunctions express a relationship between two ideas. They can show either agreement or disagreement between the ideas.

Conjunctions that show agreement between ideas

and	also
such as	since
as well as	in addition to
because	as

Conjunctions that show disagreement between two ideas

but	although
however	in spite of
despite	whereas

Whenever you see an underlined word or phrase that is a conjunction, find the two ideas it joins. Decide if these two ideas logically agree or disagree. Does the conjunction make the relationship clear? Check to see that the wording is not awkward, and then eliminate it, because it's probably not an error. If the underlined word doesn't make the relationship clear or makes the wording strange, it must be the incorrect answer. Let's try a conjunction question.

The CEO <u>was</u> excited <u>to launch</u> the new product until the marketing director <u>in addition to</u> the
    A   B   C

research director informed him that the company's leading competitor was planning to launch a

similar product months <u>earlier</u>.
                                   D

Answer choice (A), the verb *was*, correctly uses past tense to express the feelings of the CEO. Get rid of it. Answer choice (B), the infinitive *to launch*, is correct in this context. Eliminate it. Answer choice (C), the conjunction *in addition to*, is technically fine, but is more complicated than is necessary for this sentence. The word *and* would have been simpler while conveying the same meaning. Let's not eliminate this answer choice until we've evaluated all three of the other answer choices. Answer choice (D), the comparative modifier *earlier*, correctly modifies *to launch* (in the second part of the sentence). You can cross it off.

This question is an example of one of the most difficult error identification questions on the TOEIC. The incorrect answer isn't technically grammatically wrong, but it could be better. This, obviously, makes it more difficult to identify the incorrect answer. Once again, on the error identification questions, it's extremely important to evaluate all four answer choices before you choose one.

Prepositions

Prepositions pose the same problems in error identification questions as they do in sentence completion questions. The only real way to be sure of prepositions is to memorize an exhaustive list, or to speak English with native speakers who will correct you when you use them incorrectly. At the end of this book is a list of common idioms that contain prepositions. It is by no means a complete list of all the idiomatic uses of prepositions in the English language, but it's a start.

The bad news is that there is no secret trick that will help you know when an underlined preposition is okay or when it's incorrect. That means you'll have to work backwards. Whenever you see an underlined word that's a preposition, put a check mark or some other pencil mark by it that will remind you to go back to it. Then go through the other three answer choices. If the other words are grammatically correct, then the preposition must be incorrect, and you should choose it as your answer. If one of the other answer choices is obviously incorrect, then don't bother with the underlined preposition; just eliminate it.

So far, so good, but what if you can only eliminate two answer choices for sure, and you think there *might* be something wrong with the other one, but you aren't sure? This is when you have to make a judgment call. Read the preposition and the phrase it belongs to. If you know for sure that it's not right, choose the preposition as the incorrect answer. If you have no idea, you can either just guess between the two choices (you still have a 50 percent chance of getting it right) or wait to answer that question until the end of the section and pick the answer choice letter that gives you a more or less even distribution of letters. Let's try a preposition question.

The head partner invited <u>all</u> the employees <u>at</u> a <u>gala</u> celebration in honor of the <u>firm's</u> 30th
                             A   B   C   D

anniversary.

Answer choice (A), the adjective *all*, correctly modifies *the employees*, so cross it off. Answer choice (B), the preposition *at*, is incorrect in this case. It is not idiomatically correct to say *invite at*. Before you fill it in, check the other answer choices just to make sure. Answer choice (C), the adjective *gala*, correctly modifies the noun *celebration*, so eliminate it. Answer choice (D), the possessive *firm's*, correctly indicates that the anniversary belongs to the firm. Eliminate it too.

Even if you did not know the meaning of the word *gala*, you still had a 50 percent chance of getting this question right after eliminating answer choices (A) and (D).

Other Types of Questions

At first glance, some words won't seem to belong in any of the categories we've outlined. Don't worry. Just start digging and they'll reveal themselves to be one of the types we've already talked about. Here's an example.

<u>According to</u> developers, the purpose <u>of</u> virtual reality software is to provide the users with what
      A   B

<u>wanted</u> to explore otherwise unattainable <u>environments</u>.
  C   D

Answer choice (A), the preposition *according to*, is correct in the phrase with *developers*. Get rid of it. Answer choice (B), the preposition *of*, is idiomatically correct in the phrase *purpose of*. Eliminate it too. Answer choice (C), the verb *wanted*, is incorrect. There is no subject connected to the verb, and there is no reason for it to be in the past tense. If anything, this underlined word should contain a pronoun referring to *users* plus the present tense of the verb *want*. This is the incorrect answer you're looking for. Answer choice (D), the noun *environments*, is correct. Cross it off.

In this question, answer choice (C), *wanted*, is both a verb problem and a pronoun problem. Many error identification questions are like this in that they can be looked at from two angles. Remember that it's not really important to be able to articulate exactly *why* an answer choice is incorrect as long as you can identify *which one* is incorrect.

Error identification drill

1. Corporate espionage, the <u>act</u> of using spies <u>to obtain</u> information about a <u>competing</u> company,
   A

   <u>it is</u> generally considered inappropriate.
   D

2. Perhaps <u>as many as</u> 60 percent of all disc drives <u>installed</u> in computers in current use <u>in</u> Europe
   A

   <u>was manufactured</u> by the same factory.
   D

3. Seven out of ten <u>practicing</u> lawyers <u>in</u> New England have <u>worked</u> for <u>the</u> private firm.
   A B C D

4. <u>Although</u> synthetic nylon is mainly <u>synthesize</u> for fabric, it is also manufactured <u>to make</u> ropes,
   A B C

   insulation, fiberglass, and other common household <u>utensils</u>.
   D

5. New corporate policy states that all metal <u>containers</u> used for <u>food storage</u> must first be
   A B

   thoroughly washed and then <u>disinfection</u> to protect against <u>harmful</u> bacteria.
   C D

6. The 1979 power outage in New York City <u>caused</u> half of the city <u>to be</u> without electricity
   A B

   for several hours, crippling a <u>hundred</u> of businesses.
   C D

7. After <u>beginning</u> of any industrial revolution, the rural population <u>steadily</u> shifts <u>toward</u>
   A B C
   urban centers.
   D

8. The study of the group dynamic <u>has</u> gained <u>popularity</u> as business managers attempt <u>to find</u> the
   A B C

   optimal work environments for <u>its</u> employees.
   D

9. It was the invention <u>of</u> the <u>assembly</u> line <u>rather</u> of the increase in the average pay that increased
   A B C

   the <u>popularity</u> of the automobile.
   D

10. The Internet, <u>with</u> all <u>its</u> advanced technology, relies <u>heavy</u> on infrastructures built <u>over</u> a
    A B C D
    generation ago.

Answers to the error identification drill

1. D

2. D

3. D

4. B

5. C

6. D

7. A

8. D

9. C

10. C

Explanations

1. **D** Answer choices (A), (B), and (C) are all fine, so eliminate them. The phrase "the act of using spies to obtain information about a competing company" is a phrase describing *corporate espionage*, so you can disregard it when considering the structure of the sentence. This means that the subject of the sentence is *corporate espionage* and the verb is *is*. The word *it* in answer choice (D) is unnecessary, since it repeats the subject *corporate espionage*.

2. **D** *As many as* is correct, since it means a number that could be as large as the number that follows. So eliminate answer choice (A). *Installed* correctly tells about the condition of the disc drives, so cross off answer choice B. *In* is the correct preposition here, so get rid of answer choice (C). The subject of this sentence is *60 percent of all disc drives*, which is plural (since disc drives are countable, 60 percent would be an actual number of disc drives). Therefore, the verb should be plural also. *Was manufactured* is singular, so (D) is the incorrect answer.

3. **D** *Practicing* is fine, since it describes *lawyers*, so get rid of answer choice (A). *In* is the correct preposition, so eliminate answer choice (B). *Worked* is the correct use of the past participle with the helping verb *have*, so cross off answer choice (C). *The* is incorrect because it implies that all the lawyers work for the same firm, when the intention of the sentence is to indicate that each lawyer worked for a private firm of one type or another. (D) is the incorrect answer.

4. **B** *Although* is fine because it is a conjunction indicating that the first half of the sentence contrasts with the second half of the sentence. Eliminate answer choice (A). The verb should be in past tense, so the past participle *synthesized* should have been used in *is...synthesized*. Answer choice (B) is the incorrect answer. *To make* is the correct use of the infinitive, so answer choice (C) is fine. *Utensils* is also fine, so cross off answer choice (D).

5. **C** *Containers* and *food storage* are both fine. Eliminate answer choices (A) and (B). *Disinfection* should be *disinfected*, a verb, to go along with *washed* in the list of things that should be done according to the new corporate policy. Answer choice (C) is incorrect. *Harmful* is fine, so get rid of answer choice (D).

6. **D** *Caused* is the correct use of a singular, past-tense verb, so cross off answer choice (A). *To be* is the correct use of the infinitive, so eliminate answer choice (B). *For* is the correct preposition, so eliminate answer choice (C). It is correct to say either *hundreds* of businesses or *a hundred businesses*, depending on the meaning. The phrase *a hundred of* is incorrect, though, so answer choice (D) is incorrect.

7. **A** It is not idiomatically correct to say *after beginning of,* so answer choice (A) is incorrect. *Steadily* correctly modifies *shifts,* so eliminate answer choice (B). *Toward* is the correct preposition, so get rid of answer choice (C). *Urban centers* is fine, so eliminate answer choice (D).

8. **D** *Has* is correct as the helping verb in the present progressive tense. Eliminate answer choice (A). *Popularity* is fine, so cross off answer choice (B). *To find* is the correct use of the infinitive. Get rid of answer choice (C). *Its* is an incorrect pronoun, since it can't refer to *business managers.* Answer choice (D) is incorrect.

9. **C** *Invention* of is idiomatically correct, so eliminate answer choice (A). *Assembly* is fine as part of the compound word *assembly line.* Cross off answer choice (B). *Rather of* is idiomatically wrong, so answer choice (C) is incorrect. *Popularity* is fine, so cross off answer choice (D).

10. **C** *With* is correct as the first word in a phrase modifying the subject, so cross off answer choice (A). *Its* is a correct pronoun because it clearly refers to *the Internet.* Eliminate answer choice (B). *Heavy* is an adjective, but an adjective cannot modify a verb, in this case *relies.* So answer choice (C) is incorrect. *Over* is the correct pronoun, so eliminate answer choice (D).

PART ◆ IV

Reading Comprehension

THE BASICS

The grammar-based reading questions on the TOEIC require a solid knowledge of grammar rules. The reading comprehension questions, however, test a different set of skills. You do not need to memorize rules, but you do need to know how to read for specific information.

Sometimes reading comprehension sections on standardized tests can be truly scary, because the passages are long and dense. Luckily, the passages on the TOEIC are usually straightforward, and tend to be relatively short. They are the types of documents you see every day at work, such as e-mails and faxes, memos, advertisements, letters, and newspaper articles.

READING COMPREHENSION QUESTIONS

THE DIRECTIONS

The last 40 questions (numbered 161–200) in the Reading section of the test are reading comprehension questions. Directions for completing the reading comprehension questions appear in a box at the beginning of the section. The directions box looks like this:

PART VII

Directions: Questions 161–200 are based on a selection of reading materials, such as notices, letters, forms, newspaper and magazine articles, and advertisements. You are to choose the **one** best answer (A), (B), (C), or (D) to each question. Then, on your answer sheet, find the number of the question and mark your answer. Answer all questions following each reading selection on the basis of what is **stated** or **implied** in that selection.

Read the following example:

For your convenience, this branch will now be open on Saturdays from 10:00 A.M. to 2:00 P.M. Monday through Friday hours will remain the same, 9:00 A.M. to 4:00 P.M. The ATMs will be available 24 hours a day every day.

When will the branch close on Thursdays?

(A) 9:00 A.M.

(B) 10:00 A.M.

(C) 2:00 P.M.

(D) 5:00 P.M.

Sample Answer

Ⓐ Ⓑ Ⓒ ●

The reading selection says that the branch closes at 5:00 P.M. Monday through Friday, so on Thursday it closes at 5:00 P.M. Therefore, you should choose answer (D).

Read these instructions now and review them before the test, so that you won't waste any time reading them during the actual test. The only thing you need to understand from them is that

- you should pick the answer choice that best answers each question.

THE PASSAGES

Each reading comprehension passage is introduced with a sentence that tells how many questions follow it and what type of document it is. Then the passage itself follows that introductory sentence. It may look like this:

Questions 175–177 refer to the following memo.

To: All Employees
From: Human Resources

Please be advised that the upcoming Veteran's Day holiday is not an automatic vacation day. All employees are expected to be at work as usual at 8:30 A.M. unless they have previously arranged to take the day as a personal vacation day. The next automatic vacation day is Thanksgiving.

THE QUESTIONS

Each reading comprehension question consists of a question about the passage preceding it and four answer choices labeled (A), (B), (C), and (D). Look at an example.

On which holiday are employees expected to come to work?

(A) Human Resources Day
(B) All Employees Day
(C) Veteran's Day
(D) Thanksgiving Day

Three of the above four answer choices are incorrect, meaning that they do not match the information contained in the passage.

THE TRAP

The trap in the reading comprehension questions is that you are led to believe that you need to read the passage thoroughly and understand it completely. This is simply not true. Instead, you need to figure out the structure of the passage well enough that you can find the answers to the questions in it without having to read the whole thing. This is counterintuitive to a lot of people, but it's the best way to work through this section.

12

Reading Comprehension Questions

START HERE

Reading comprehension questions present you with a passage to read followed by two to four questions on that passage. Unlike passages on other standardized reading comprehension tests, the passages on the TOEIC are samples of writing from everyday life, such as e-mails, advertisements, and letters.

Reading comprehension questions are the questions that look like this:

Questions 175–177 refer to the following memo.

To: All Employees
From: Human Resources

Please be advised that the upcoming Veteran's Day holiday is not an automatic vacation day. All employees are expected to be at work as usual at 8:30 A.M. unless they have previously arranged to take the day as a personal vacation day. The next automatic vacation day is Thanksgiving.

On which holiday are employees expected to come to work?

(A) Human Resources Day
(B) All Employees Day
(C) Veteran's Day
(D) Thanksgiving Day

Your task is to pick the answer choice that correctly answers the question.

THE STRATEGY FOR READING COMPREHENSION QUESTIONS

First, remember the most important tips to scoring well on the TOEIC—(1) use Process of Elimination (POE), and (2) don't leave any blanks. These techniques apply to all question types on the TOEIC. See Chapter 3 if you need a review. Now let's focus on specific strategies for doing well on reading comprehension questions.

All reading comprehension questions can be approached in the same way, no matter what the individual differences in the questions are. (We'll get to advice on answering specific types of questions later.)

Steps in the process

Pace yourself.

Read the introductory sentence.

Skim through the passage.

Read the question.

Search for specific information in the passage.

Do not get lost in the passage.

Pace yourself.

The reading comprehension questions are only 40 of the 100 questions in the Reading section. However, you'll need to spend more time on the reading comprehension questions than on the other two reading question types. You may, in fact, have to spend more than half of the 75 minutes allotted for the Reading section on reading comprehension.

Don't worry about this. It is natural that it takes longer to answer questions that also have a reading passage to decipher. In fact, you should be spending enough time familiarizing yourself with the passage that it takes you very little time to answer the accompanying questions. After all, if you familiarize yourself with the layout of the passage, you should be able to go directly to the answer to any question in that passage.

Practice working reading comprehension passages using our methods until you can work through them quickly and efficiently.

Read the introductory sentence.

Before you even glance at the passage, you should read the brief introductory sentence above the passage. This sentence tells you exactly what type of document you are looking at. These are some examples of introductory sentences.

Questions 196–197 refer to the following letter.

Questions 187–188 refer to the following instructions.

Once you know what type of passage you will be reading, you can approach it in a more educated manner. For instance, if the instructions tell you that the passage is a letter, you will know exactly where to look for information such as the date, the name of the person who wrote it, and the return address of the person who wrote it.

The introductory sentence can also put the passage in context for you. You already know what type of document it is and can go on to the next step without having to orient yourself.

Skim through the passage.

Many people make the mistake of taking the words *reading comprehension* too seriously. This is a mistake that can cost you a lot of time and a lot of energy for very little payoff. You do not get any points for reading the passage, and you certainly don't get any points for comprehending the passage. You only get points for answering questions correctly.

This means that you shouldn't do any more work than is necessary to get the answer to a question. If you do, you are wasting time that you could be spending answering the other 99 questions on the Reading section.

Your main priority should be determining how the passage is arranged so that you can find specific information in it later. To do that, you should skim through the passage, looking for key words and structure.

When you skim through a passage, you should be able to answer these two questions:

1. What is this passage about in general?

2. What is the structure of this passage?

Let's try it now. Do *not* read every word and do not spend much time on this step. Spend more time thinking about and answering the two questions about the structure of the passage than you do actually reading the passage.

SmoothTrans Inc.
126 Tyler Trail
Duncan, NJ 08235
November 11, 2001

Jennifer Yakamora
Crowne Holdings
146 Avenue of the Americas
New York, NY 10014

Dear Ms. Yakamora:

This letter is a confirmation of the telephone conversation we had on November 10 regarding Crowne Holdings' new billing procedures.

Effective immediately, Crowne Holdings may bill its customers in the first half of the month for any transactions occurring in the previous month. SmoothTrans Inc. guarantees that these accounts will be posted no later than the 25th of the month in which they were billed, as long as SmoothTrans receives billing information by the 15th of that month.

We hope that this improved 10-day process time will allow Crowne Holdings to serve its customers and shareholders better. We at SmoothTrans Inc. look forward to a continuing relationship with you. If there is anything we can do to help you, please do not hesitate to call me at 973-555-1234.

Sincerely,

Lola Petrillo
Account Manager

Even though you didn't read every word of the passage, you should be able to answer the two questions.

1. What is this passage about in general?

This passage is a letter from one company to another company discussing billing dates.

2. What is the structure of this passage?

The passage is a letter with the usual addresses, date, and greeting. The first paragraph confirms that Ms. Petrillo and Ms. Yakamora talked on the phone. The second paragraph tells what they talked about. The third paragraph builds the relationship. The letter ends with a greeting and signature.

This is how you should approach every passage on the reading comprehension part of the test. Once you have an idea of where everything is in the passage, you can go on to the questions.

Read the question.

In order to answer a question, you have to read it first. For the most part, reading comprehension questions on the TOEIC are straightforward. This is good news, since it means that you can focus on finding the answer in the passage instead of unraveling layers of tricks and traps. As you read the question, think back to the passage. Don't try to remember the answer to the question; instead, try to remember where the answer to the question is in the passage.

Let's try it with the following question referring to the letter on the previous page.

When does the new billing policy go into effect?

(A) November 11
(B) November 15
(C) November 25
(D) This information is not given in the passage.

Where is this information most likely to be in the passage?

Search for specific information in the passage.

Now go back to the passage and find the answer to the question. You should have a reasonably good idea where to look for the answer since you know how the passage is arranged.

Do *not* attempt to answer the question without going back to the passage to get the information. This is how you get answers wrong. Always go back to the passage and look for the answers. Always "find the proof" in the passage.

Once you've found the answer in the passage, go back to the answer choices. Eliminate the three that don't match up with the answer you discovered in the passage. The one that matches is the correct response. Let's try it with the question we just saw.

When does the new billing policy go into effect?

(A) November 11
(B) November 15
(C) November 25
(D) This information is not given in the passage.

To answer this question, we have to go back to the passage. This information is at the beginning of the second paragraph of the letter, and in the date line.

SmoothTrans Inc.
126 Tyler Trail
Duncan, NJ 08235
November 11, 2001

Jennifer Yakamora
Crowne Holdings
146 Avenue of the Americas
New York, NY 10014

Dear Ms. Yakamora:

This letter is a confirmation of the telephone conversation we had on November 10 regarding Crowne Holdings' new billing procedures.

Effective immediately, Crowne Holdings may bill its customers in the first half of the month for any transactions occurring in the previous month. SmoothTrans Inc. guarantees that these accounts will be posted no later than the 25th of the month in which they were billed, as long as SmoothTrans receives billing information by the 15th of that month.

We hope that this improved 10-day process time will allow Crowne Holdings to serve its customers and shareholders better. We at SmoothTrans Inc. look forward to a continuing relationship with you. If there is anything we can do to help you, please do not hesitate to call me at 973-555-1234.

Sincerely,

Lola Petrillo
Account Manager

The letter says that the billing policy goes into effect *immediately.* The date on the letter is November 11, 2001, so the billing policy goes into effect on November 11. Answer choice (A) is the correct response.

Do not get lost in the passage.
It can be *really* tempting to slow down and read the passage as if you'll need to remember it. In fact, some of us can get so interested in the actual passage that we forget we're supposed to be taking a test! This, of course, is very, very bad, because it wastes a lot of time and makes us lose focus.

The best way to avoid getting lost in the passage is by focusing on *how* the passage says something instead of on *what* it says. Whenever you're reading, you should force yourself to think about how the passage is arranged instead of what the passage is really saying. You'll still pick up enough about what the passage is saying to be able to figure out where to look for the answers to the questions. And since you don't have to rely on your memory to answer the questions, it really doesn't make any sense to read the passage very well the first time through. Remember: You do not have to memorize the passage—you can refer back to it at any point

Reading comprehension drill
Answers can be found on page 162.

Questions 1–3 refer to the following e-mail.

Date: Wed. 30 Oct 2002 16:21:48 UT

From: Northeast Airlines <trip.summary@nea.com>

To: Jeanette Northrup <jnorthrup@wra.com>

Subject: Northeast Airlines Trip Summary and Receipt #7VNBLB

JEANETTE NORTHRUP

640 E 19TH ST APT 5K

NEW YORK NY 10003

Thank you for choosing Northeast Airlines.

Confirmation Number: 7KNVLB

E-Ticket Issue Date: 30OCT02

Number of Passengers: 1

YOUR RESERVATION:

Date: TUESDAY, NOVEMBER 26

Flight Number: NE0533

Departs: LAGUARDIA, NY (LGA), 26NOV at 735A

Arrives: DETROIT, MI (DTW), 26NOV at 939A

Class: V

Seats: 14B

Meal Service:

Equipment: D9S

Date: SATURDAY, NOVEMBER 30

Flight Number: NE0530

Departs: DETROIT, MI (DTW), 30NOV at 333P

Arrives: LAGUARDIA, NY (LGA), 30NOV at 524P

Class: H

Seats: UNASSIGNED

Meal Service:

Equipment: D9S

YOUR RECEIPT INFORMATION:

E-Ticket(s) Total: $268.50US Dollars

Fare: $232.56

Tax: $28.44

PFC: $7.50

Fee Detail:

Customs Fee: $0.00

Immigration Fees: $0.00

Aphis Fee: $0.00

Total New Charges: $268.50

Method of Payment: MasterCard

****

Please bring this E-Ticket Summary and Receipt with you to the Airport. Only passengers holding an E-Ticket receipt, boarding documents, or a paper ticket will be allowed to pass through the security checkpoints at the airport. All passengers must carry government issued identification at all times.

---

1. What type of document is this?

(A) A receipt for an airplane ticket.

(B) A request for a transfer from one office to another.

(C) A flight schedule for a major airline.

(D) A policy statement on airline security.

2. How long is the flight from LaGuardia to Detroit?

(A) 1 hour, 51 minutes.

(B) 2 hours.

(C) 2 hours, 4 minutes.

(D) 2 hours, 9 minutes.

3. What seat is assigned for the flight from LaGuardia to Detroit?

(A) 14B

(B) D9S

(C) 7KNVLB

(D) No seat is assigned yet.

Questions 4–7 refer to the following article.

Small Business Conference Held

Springfield—A conference honoring small businesses was held last weekend at the Sheraton Downtown. Fifty local small business representatives attended. Participants attended five seminars over the course of the weekend. The keynote speaker was Sheldon Glassman, former owner of TVs Plus, a successful audiovisual store located in Oakwood Mall. The keynote address was entitled "Staying Small in the Face of Mammoths and Multinationals." Mr. Glassman has written 12 books, the latest of which is entitled *It's Only Worth It if It's Fun*.

The next small business conference will be held January 5–7 at the Radisson Northfield. For more information or to register for the conference, please call Owners United at 315-654-1234.

---

4. Where was the conference held?

(A) Oakwood Mall
(B) Sheraton Downtown
(C) Radisson Northfield
(D) Owners United

5. How many participants attended the conference?

(A) 5
(B) 5–7
(C) 12
(D) 50

6. What does the keynote speaker do?

(A) He runs conferences.
(B) He owns an audiovisual store.
(C) He writes books.
(D) He manages a hotel.

7. The next small business conference will be held on what date in January?

(A) 5
(B) 5–7
(C) 12
(D) 50

Questions 8–10 refer to the following fax.

FAX

From: Manuel Ibarra

To: Shipping, Alben Industries

Fax Number: 213-444-7878

Date: July 23, 1999

Order:

1000 U-clamps @ $0.85 = $850.00

5000 3-inch pins @ $0.27 = $1350.00

Total order = $2200.00

Bill to:

IBC

Box 14802

Montrose, CA 98866

Ship to:

Ibarra Brothers

430 De la Huerta Avenue

Chico, CA 98756

213-555-9898

---

8. How many total parts are being ordered?

(A) 1000
(B) 2200
(C) 5000
(D) 6000

9. To what city are the parts to be shipped?

(A) Montrose
(B) Chico
(C) Ibarra
(D) De la Huerta

10. What is the total price for the U-clamps?

(A) $2200
(B) $1350
(C) $1000
(D) $850

Answers to the reading comprehension drill

1. A
2. C
3. A
4. B
5. D
6. C
7. B
8. D
9. B
10. D

Explanations

1. **A** This e-mail is a receipt for an airline ticket. This information can be found in the subject of the e-mail. Answer choice (A) is the correct response.

> Date: Wed. 30 Oct 2002 16:21:48 UT
>
> From: Northeast Airlines <trip.summary@nea.com>
>
> To: Jeanette Northrup <jnorthrup@wra.com>
>
> Subject: **Northeast Airlines** Trip Summary and **Receipt** #7VNBLB

Eliminate answer choice (B), since there is no mention of a transfer in the e-mail. Get rid of answer choice (C), since the e-mail only contains information about two flights, not the whole airline's schedule. Cross off answer choice (D), since there is very little about airline security in this e-mail.

2. **C** The flight from New York (LGA) to Michigan (DTW) is from 7:35 to 9:39 in the morning. This flight is 2 hours and 4 minutes. Eliminate answer choices (A), (B), and (D). The correct response is (C).

> Departs: **LAGUARDIA,** NY (LGA), 26NOV at **735A**
>
> Arrives: **DETROIT,** MI (DTW), 26NOV at **939A**

3. **A** 14B is the seat assigned on the flight from LaGuardia to Detroit, so answer choice (A) is the correct response. D9S is the type of plane used for the flight from LaGuardia to Detroit, so eliminate answer choice (B). 7KNVLB is the confirmation number of the reservation. Cross off answer choice (C). There is no seat assigned for the flight from Detroit to LaGuardia, not from LaGuardia to Detroit. Eliminate answer choice (D).

Date: TUESDAY, NOVEMBER 26

Flight Number: NE0533

Departs: **LAGUARDIA,** NY (LGA), 26NOV at 735A

Arrives: **DETROIT, MI** (DTW), 26NOV at 939A

Class: V

Seats: **14B**

Meal Service:

Equipment: D9S

Date: SATURDAY, NOVEMBER 30

Flight Number: NE0530

Departs: DETROIT, MI (DTW), 30NOV at 333P

Arrives: LAGUARDIA, NY (LGA), 30NOV at 524P

Class: H

Seats: UNASSIGNED

Meal Service:

Equipment: D9S

4. **B** Oakwood Mall is the location of the audiovisual store owned by Sheldon Glassman. Eliminate answer choice (A). The Sheraton Downtown is the location of this year's small business conference. Answer choice (B) is the correct response. The Radisson Northfield is the location of the upcoming small business conference in January, so cross off answer choice (C). Owners United is the name of the group giving information about the upcoming conference. Get rid of answer choice (D).

> Springfield—A conference honoring small businesses was held last weekend at the **Sheraton Downtown.** Over 50 local small business representatives attended. Participants attended five seminars over the course of the weekend. The keynote speaker was Sheldon Glassman, former owner of TVs Plus, a successful audiovisual store located in Oakwood Mall. The keynote address was entitled "Staying Small in the Face of Mammoths and Multinationals." Mr. Glassman has written 12 books, the latest of which is entitled *It's Only Worth It if It's Fun.*

5. **D** 5 is the number of seminars at the conference, so get rid of answer choice (A). 5–7 are the dates in January in which the next small business conference will be held. Eliminate answer choice (B). 12 is the number of books written by Sheldon Glassman. Cross off answer choice (C). The passage says that "Fifty" attendees were at the conference. Answer choice (D) is the correct response.

> Springfield—A conference honoring small businesses was held last weekend at the Sheraton Downtown. **Fifty local small business representatives attended.** Participants attended five seminars over the course of the weekend. The keynote speaker was Sheldon Glassman, former owner of TVs Plus, a successful audiovisual store located in Oakwood Mall. The keynote address was entitled "Staying Small in the Face of Mammoths and Multinationals." Mr. Glassman has written 12 books, the latest of which is entitled *It's Only Worth It if It's Fun.*

6. **C** The passage states that Mr. Glassman *used* to own an audiovisual store, but that he *currently* writes books. Eliminate answer choices (A), (B), and (D). The correct response is (C).

> Springfield—A conference honoring small businesses was held last weekend at the Sheraton Downtown. More than 50 local small business representatives attended. Participants attended five seminars over the course of the weekend. The keynote speaker was Sheldon Glassman, **former owner** of TVs Plus, a successful audiovisual store located in Oakwood Mall. The keynote address was entitled "Staying Small in the Face of Mammoths and Multinationals." **Mr. Glassman has written 12 books,** the latest of which is entitled *It's Only Worth it if it's Fun.*

7. **B** 5 is the number of seminars at the conference, so cross off answer choice (A). 5–7 are the dates in January in which the next small business conference will be held. Answer choice (B) is the correct response. 12 is the number of books written by Sheldon Glassman. Eliminate answer choice (C). The passage says that "more than 50" attendees were at the conference, so eliminate answer choice (D) too.

> The next small business conference will be held **January 5–7** at the Radisson Northfield. For more information or to register for the conference, please call Owners United at 315-654-1234.

8. **D** 1000 is the number of U-clamps being ordered. Eliminate answer choice (A). $2200 is the amount the total order costs, so get rid of answer choice (B). 5000 is the number of 3-inch pins being ordered. Cross off answer choice (C). 6000 is the number of U-clamps plus the number of 3-inch pins being ordered. Answer choice (D) is the correct response.

> **Order:**
> 1000 U-clamps @ $0.85 = $850.00
> 5000 3-inch pins @ $0.27 = $1350.00
> Total order = $2200.00

9. **B** The "bill to" address on the fax is in Montrose. Eliminate answer choice (A). The "ship to" address on the fax is in Chico, so answer choice (B) is the correct response. The name of the company placing the order is Ibarra Brothers. Cross off answer choice (C). The name of the street, not the city, in the "ship to" address is De La Huerta. Eliminate answer choice (D) too.

> **Ship to:**
> Ibarra Brothers
> 430 De la Huerta Avenue
> Chico, CA 98756
> 213-555-9898

10. **D** The price for the total order of U-clamps and 3-inch pins is $2200. Get rid of answer choice (A). The price for the 3-inch pins is $1350. Eliminate answer choice (B). The number of U-clamps ordered is 1000, so cross off answer choice (C). The price of the U-clamps alone is $850. Answer choice (D) is the correct response.

Order:

1000 U-clamps @ $0.85 = **$850.00**

5000 3-inch pins @ $0.27 = $1350.00

Total order = $2200.00

PART ◆ V

Getting Ready to Take the Test

HOW TO TAKE THE PRINCETON REVIEW TOEIC PRACTICE TESTS

You should take the practice tests that come with this book only after you have finished reading the techniques, completed the drills and exercises, and review your performance on the drills thoroughly. Make sure to review all of the test-taking tips in this book before you sit down to take the practice tests.

When taking the practice test, your goal should be to approximate actual test conditions as closely as possible. To take The Princeton Review Practice Tests, you will need

- A quiet room
- A compact-disc player (preferably a Walkman or CD player that requires headphones)
- A pen or a pencil
- A watch
- Approximately two hours of uninterrupted time

It is a good idea to have extra batteries for the CD player on hand.

When you are ready to begin, remember the following:

- Adjust the volume on your compact-disc player before the actual questions begin.
- Use only the amount of time actually allotted for each section.
- Take the entire test in one sitting.
- Fill in the answer choices on the answer sheet completely, as if you were taking the real test. On the real test, answers not completely filled in will not be counted, even if they are clearly marked in your test booklet.
- Do not score the test until you have read the next couple of pages and until you have at least an hour to spend examining your results.

EVALUATING YOUR PERFORMANCE

Use the answer key that appears after the practice test to determine your score. Make sure to correct and study your performance carefully. Try to do it within 24 hours of taking the test, or you'll have a hard time remembering why you chose one answer over another. When looking at your performance on the practice test, don't just settle for counting up the number of wrong and right answers and looking up the words you didn't know. Pay special attention to all of these.

"Stupid" mistakes

We use the term *stupid mistakes* to refer to the mistakes you make on questions you *know* you should have been able to answer correctly. In other words, if the correct answer seems obvious now and you can't understand why you chose the answer you did, and you find yourself saying, "Wow, that was really stupid of me," you've run across a "stupid" mistake.

Interestingly enough, you'll find that "stupid" mistakes usually aren't stupid at all; they're more often due to simple *carelessness*, and they usually happen for one of two reasons.

Reason 1: Impatience. "Haste makes waste," the saying in English goes—you probably have a similar saying in your native language. You'll probably find that you got some questions wrong because you didn't bother to read through all of the answer choices before choosing your answer.

Reason 2: Misunderstanding the question. Sometimes even native speakers have to read a question two or three times before understanding what the question is actually asking. Why should you expect to understand everything the first time you read it? Many test takers get questions wrong just because they are answering the wrong question.

Once you figure out the real cause for any "stupid" mistakes, you know what you need to pay particular attention to the next time you take the test.

"Lucky" guesses

Sometimes the only thing more surprising than mysterious wrong answers (such as the stupid mistakes discussed above) are all those questions you answered correctly and are not sure *why*. Most students tend to attribute these right answers to plain, old-fashioned good luck. That may be true for some of them. However, that probably doesn't explain all of the questions you answered correctly, even though you didn't think you knew the answer. Chances are you were using the test-taking strategies from this book without even realizing it, the most important of which is POE.

The best way to recognize questions on which you used POE effectively is to look for questions you answered correctly but did not actually "know" the answer to. Look for your "lucky guesses." For these questions, try to remember the reasons why you chose the answers you did, and the next time you take a test, you can use those reasons to help you answer even more questions.

Other "wrong" answers

Some wrong answers are chosen due to carelessness, but some can be attributed to information you just didn't know or remember. When you look over your test, make sure that the wrong answer you chose isn't one you could have eliminated using POE. Did you pick a silly answer in the Listening Comprehension section just because you missed the statement? Did you choose an answer with poor syntax on a grammar-based question? Try to discover if you could have eliminated an answer or two before guessing.

Pacing problems

To determine if you had problems with time, ask yourself the following questions:

- Were you unable to finish any of the sections? If so, then you probably spent too much time answering one question. ETS gives you plenty of time on the TOEIC, but don't linger over questions. Choose and move on.

- Did you run out of time before getting to the last passage on the Reading section? If so, you may have spent too much time on a couple of questions. Remember, don't get bogged down on any one question! Look for structure in the passages; don't get too interested in the actual content of the passages themselves. On the other hand, it's possible that you rushed through the test and answered too carelessly.

- Did you finish any section or sections with more than one minute of the allotted time left over? If so, you need to slow down and spend more time answering the questions. There's no prize given for finishing the TOEIC early, and rushing to finish can hurt your score.

WHAT SHOULD YOU DO NOW?

If you have some time before you are scheduled to take the actual TOEIC, you can use the results of your practice test to help decide if you need any additional preparation. You can buy the *Official Test-Preparation Guide to the TOEIC* and practice with the test in that book. Just make sure you leave plenty of time to buy or order the book.

We do not recommend any test materials published by anyone other than ETS. Many of the examples in non-ETS publications contain questions that are poorly written or that just don't appear on real TOEIC exams, leading you to waste time studying things that won't help you on the test. Try to schedule your use of the materials so that you have a full-length TOEIC exam (either ours or ETS's) to take sometime in the week before the test.

THE WEEK BEFORE THE TEST

Here's a list of *dos* and *don'ts* for the week before the test:

- *Don't* try to learn any new material the week before the TOEIC. You can't learn many idioms or grammar in that amount of time. You're better off practicing the test-taking tips.

- *Do* make sure you know exactly how to get to your test location and when the test will be held. You don't want to be late, or feel rushed to get there. Getting lost is one way to really hurt your self-confidence on a day when you need to remain calm and in control. Take a practice trip to the test site so you can see how long it takes, and make sure to set your alarm correctly so you arrive at the right time.

- *Don't* study at all on the day before the test. The most helpful thing you can do is relax. At most, maybe see a movie or watch television, in English if you can, and go to sleep early.

- *Do* make sure you have ready, well in advance, everything that you need to take with you to the test.

By the time the actual test day rolls around, you won't be worrying about any minor details, and you'll be able to focus completely on the test.

THE DAY OF THE TEST

Wake up a little earlier than you have to. Give yourself time to eat a light breakfast and try to make time to do some "warm-up" questions of each type. Then make sure you have the following items with you before you leave for the test:

- Photo identification: This can be a passport, driver's license, military ID, or national ID.

- Your confirmation number or voucher

- Two to three pencils

- A positive attitude

When you're finished, go home and forget about the TOEIC. It takes several weeks for your scores to arrive. You can wait with confidence because you've mastered a skill that won't help you anywhere else in your life, the skill of taking the TOEIC. Won't it be nice to forget it?

13

The Princeton Review
TOEIC Practice Test 1

PRACTICE TEST 1

Listen to CD #1 Tracks 1–4 to take this test. When you are done with the Listening Comprehension section, do NOT take a break. Go directly to the Reading section and give yourself 75 minutes to take that section.

LISTENING COMPREHENSION

In this section of the test, you will have the chance to show how well you understand spoken English. There are four parts to this section, with special directions for each part.

PART I

Directions: For each question, you will see a picture in your test book and you will hear four statements. The statements will be spoken just one time. They will not be printed in your test book, so you must listen carefully to understand what the speaker says.

When you hear the four statements, look at the picture in your test book and choose the statement that best describes what you see in the picture. Then, on your answer sheet, find the number of the question and mark your answer.

1.

GO ON TO THE NEXT PAGE

2.

3.

GO ON TO THE NEXT PAGE

4.

Evacuation Instructions

| Listen for instructions from crew | Do not pull Emergency Brake | Remain inside train. Subway tracks are dangerous | Exit only when directed |

Priority Seating
for persons with disabilities

5.

GO ON TO THE NEXT PAGE ➤

6.

7.

GO ON TO THE NEXT PAGE ➤

8.

9.

GO ON TO THE NEXT PAGE ➤

10.

11.

GO ON TO THE NEXT PAGE ➤

12.

13.

GO ON TO THE NEXT PAGE ➡

14.

15.

GO ON TO THE NEXT PAGE ➡

16.

17.

GO ON TO THE NEXT PAGE ➤

18.

19.

GO ON TO THE NEXT PAGE

20.

GO ON TO THE NEXT PAGE ➤

PART II

Directions: In this part of the test, you will hear a question or statement spoken in English, followed by three responses, also spoken in English. The question or statement and the responses will be spoken just one time. They will not be printed in your test book, so you must listen carefully to understand what the speakers say. You are to choose the best response to each question or statement.

21. Mark your answer on your answer sheet.

22. Mark your answer on your answer sheet.

23. Mark your answer on your answer sheet.

24. Mark your answer on your answer sheet.

25. Mark your answer on your answer sheet.

26. Mark your answer on your answer sheet.

27. Mark your answer on your answer sheet.

28. Mark your answer on your answer sheet.

29. Mark your answer on your answer sheet.

30. Mark your answer on your answer sheet.

31. Mark your answer on your answer sheet.

32. Mark your answer on your answer sheet.

33. Mark your answer on your answer sheet.

34. Mark your answer on your answer sheet.

35. Mark your answer on your answer sheet.

36. Mark your answer on your answer sheet.

37. Mark your answer on your answer sheet.

38. Mark your answer on your answer sheet.

39. Mark your answer on your answer sheet.

40. Mark your answer on your answer sheet.

41. Mark your answer on your answer sheet.

42. Mark your answer on your answer sheet.

43. Mark your answer on your answer sheet.

44. Mark your answer on your answer sheet.

45. Mark your answer on your answer sheet.

46. Mark your answer on your answer sheet.

47. Mark your answer on your answer sheet.

48. Mark your answer on your answer sheet.

49. Mark your answer on your answer sheet.

50. Mark your answer on your answer sheet.

GO ON TO THE NEXT PAGE

Directions: In this part of the test, you will hear thirty short conversations between two people. The conversations will not be printed in your test book. You will hear the conversations only once, so you must listen carefully to understand what the speakers say.

In your test book, you will read a question about each conversation. The questions will be followed by four answers. You are to choose the best answer to each question and mark it on your answer sheet.

51. Why did the company team lose the softball game?
    (A) They could not see the complete picture.
    (B) The man did not play with the team.
    (C) The man went to the game and fell down.
    (D) They didn't want to play against the Tokigo Corporation.

52. What does the woman fear has happened to the ticket?
    (A) It is in the briefcase.
    (B) It has been waiting in the taxi.
    (C) It got thrown in the garbage accidentally.
    (D) It has already been found.

53. How much longer did the first man take to drive to work?
    (A) An extra 10 minutes.
    (B) An extra 3 minutes.
    (C) An extra 45 minutes.
    (D) An extra 30 minutes.

54. Why does the man want a stronger prescription?
    (A) The medication he has been taking has not cured his illness.
    (B) The current prescription makes his mouth taste bitter.
    (C) Now that he knows the facts, he wants to take a different kind of medication.
    (D) Dr. Hsu thinks he feels too bad to take the current prescription.

55. Where is the woman going in 15 minutes?
    (A) To a bus station.
    (B) To the post office.
    (C) To her job.
    (D) To a movie theater.

56. Why is the man upset?
    (A) He did not get off the bus when he was supposed to.
    (B) He did not want to go to 5th Avenue.
    (C) He wants to have a new bus stop in his neighborhood.
    (D) He cannot drive his own car.

GO ON TO THE NEXT PAGE

57. What did Linda say about the conference call?

   (A) It will be held on the West Coast.
   (B) It will have to be held on a different day.
   (C) It cannot be held on the telephone.
   (D) It will not be available on voicemail.

58. Why is the woman asking about money?

   (A) To send a check to Mr. Chekov.
   (B) To become Mr. Chekov's accountant.
   (C) To improve Bob's handwriting.
   (D) To ask Bob to check her files.

59. When will the man pick up the suit?

   (A) This morning.
   (B) Thursday morning.
   (C) Wednesday morning.
   (D) Tomorrow morning.

60. What did the newspaper say about Gentech?

   (A) That they are expanding into training.
   (B) That they are beside a train route.
   (C) That they are losing an important client.
   (D) That they are being accused of stock fraud.

61. What is the problem at the Appleton office?

   (A) Too many workers are leaving.
   (B) Too many employees are being retrained.
   (C) Too many managers are increasing wages.
   (D) Too many computers are crashing.

62. What is the man's job?

   (A) Airline pilot.
   (B) Taxi driver.
   (C) Baggage handler.
   (D) Police officer.

63. When will the man arrive at the warehouse?

   (A) In about 20 minutes.
   (B) In about one hour.
   (C) Before the end of the shift.
   (D) After the convention.

64. What should the woman do with the pen?

   (A) Show it to Mr. Aarons.
   (B) Send it to the man's room.
   (C) Bill the man for $511.
   (D) Use it to write a check for $400.

65. Why are they going to have sandwiches for lunch?

   (A) They want to eat Thai sandwiches.
   (B) They don't know where they can get pizza.
   (C) Sandwiches are lower in cholesterol.
   (D) Lenny's does not serve Chinese food.

GO ON TO THE NEXT PAGE

66. What is the woman afraid of?

   (A) That her car won't start.
   (B) That her electricity will go out.
   (C) That her train will not arrive on time.
   (D) That she will not be able to hear when she gets old.

67. What did Nancy do this weekend?

   (A) She went on a canoeing trip.
   (B) She spent it in the apartment above hers.
   (C) She bought damage insurance.
   (D) She cleaned up a mess in her apartment.

68. What does the man want to do with the lamp?

   (A) Break the switch.
   (B) Exchange it for a different model.
   (C) Throw it away.
   (D) Return it to the store.

69. Where did Frank leave his overcoat?

   (A) With another passenger.
   (B) Underneath a newspaper.
   (C) At the bus stop.
   (D) On the seat of the bus.

70. Where was the fire?

   (A) On the top floor.
   (B) In the basement.
   (C) Across the street.
   (D) A mile south.

71. Why did the man apologize to the woman?

   (A) He ordered the wrong size mattress.
   (B) He went to the wrong address.
   (C) He called her number by mistake.
   (D) He could not reach far enough.

72. How many eggs does the man want?

   (A) Three.
   (B) Two.
   (C) One.
   (D) None.

73. Where does this conversation most likely take place?

   (A) A convenience store.
   (B) A restaurant.
   (C) A bookstore.
   (D) A dry cleaner.

74. What is the man's job?

   (A) Office manager.
   (B) Bus driver.
   (C) Airline reservations employee.
   (D) Post office employee.

75. Where is this conversation most likely to take place?

   (A) A copy shop.
   (B) A music school.
   (C) A CD store.
   (D) A grocery store.

GO ON TO THE NEXT PAGE

76. Why may the people miss a deadline?

  (A) They do not have all the information they need to finish the job.
  (B) They have not yet sent out a bill for their services.
  (C) They are afraid of being audited by the government.
  (D) They do not want to have to work today.

77. Why were some e-mail messages lost?

  (A) The men were at lunch when they arrived.
  (B) The messages did not arrive on Friday.
  (C) The men could not get any service at the restaurant.
  (D) The computer system was broken for several hours.

78. Why can the woman not find the Woodley file?

  (A) Keiko has taken all the files for a drive.
  (B) Keiko has removed the active folders from the system.
  (C) Keiko has rearranged the files on the system.
  (D) Keiko will not let her use it.

79. Who owns the scarf?

  (A) The male speaker.
  (B) The female speaker.
  (C) A different woman.
  (D) The bus driver.

80. What is Jim Weislak doing right now?

  (A) Trying to fix a failing computer project.
  (B) Looking for a new position.
  (C) Running to train for a race.
  (D) Counting pages on the new website.

GO ON TO THE NEXT PAGE

Directions: In this part of the test, you will hear several short talks. Each will be spoken just one time. They will not be printed in your test book, so you must listen carefully to understand and remember what is said.

In your test book, you will read two or more questions about each short talk. The questions will be followed by four answers. You are to choose the best answer to each question and mark it on your answer sheet.

81. Where would this announcement most likely be heard?

 (A) On a subway platform.
 (B) On a ship's desk.
 (C) At an airport.
 (D) At a bus stop.

82. What is wrong with the trains?

 (A) They are not braking correctly.
 (B) They have caught on fire.
 (C) They are not running uptown.
 (D) They are being investigated.

83. Who is speaking?

 (A) A waitress.
 (B) A busboy.
 (C) A hotel concierge.
 (D) A grocery store cashier.

84. Which of the following is NOT included in the Lunch Special?

 (A) Salad.
 (B) Breadsticks.
 (C) Soft Drink.
 (D) Dessert.

85. What will be the second stop?

 (A) The Statue of Liberty.
 (B) New York City.
 (C) Ellis Island.
 (D) The Island Ferry.

86. For how long does the ferry stay in port at Ellis Island?

 (A) 2 hours.
 (B) 1 hour.
 (C) 15 minutes.
 (D) 10 minutes.

87. When should the employees respond to the invitation?

 (A) By the last day of the coming week.
 (B) By the end of the day.
 (C) By December 20th.
 (D) By 7:11.

88. What time does the party begin?

 (A) At 11 A.M.
 (B) At 7 P.M.
 (C) At 8 P.M.
 (D) At 11 P.M.

89. The party will include which of the following?

 (A) Debate.
 (B) Candy.
 (C) Drinks.
 (D) E-mail.

GO ON TO THE NEXT PAGE

90. Who is speaking?

    (A) A special correspondent.
    (B) A radio-show host.
    (C) A county commissioner.
    (D) A construction contractor.

91. Who is Jillian Jaffe?

    (A) A radio reporter.
    (B) A county commissioner.
    (C) A school principal.
    (D) A television anchor.

92. Who is the subject of a scandal?

    (A) Jillian Jaffe.
    (B) A special correspondent.
    (C) The County Commissioner.
    (D) Eva Glassberg.

93. This speech is being held at the opening of what?

    (A) A technology exhibit.
    (B) A weather experiment.
    (C) A forestry demonstration.
    (D) A photography show.

94. What is Amy Oakes' position?

    (A) Photographer.
    (B) Gallery owner.
    (C) Painter.
    (D) Actress.

95. What will Ms. Sunwoo be doing for the next few weeks?

    (A) Investigating the inventory process.
    (B) Running a marathon.
    (C) Specializing in Logistics.
    (D) Moving to San Francisco.

96. Why was Ms. Sunwoo called in?

    (A) To increase the amount of action in the office.
    (B) To introduce herself to the employees.
    (C) To improve efficiency in an ongoing process.
    (D) To close outstanding loans.

97. Where is this speech most likely to be heard?

    (A) An employee evaluation.
    (B) A corporate meeting.
    (C) A recruiting rally.
    (D) An awards luncheon.

98. Who will be leading the meetings after dinner?

    (A) Motivational speakers from the region.
    (B) Drill sergeants from boot camp.
    (C) Management employees from Arlington Technologies.
    (D) Trained teachers from the conference center.

99. How long will the conference last?

    (A) 4 days.
    (B) 5 days.
    (C) 10 days.
    (D) 2 weeks.

100. What is the purpose of the conference?

    (A) To become physically fit.
    (B) To explore technology.
    (C) To practice motivational speaking.
    (D) To learn to be a good director.

STOP the recording

READING

In this section of the test, you will have a chance to show how well you understand written English. There are three parts to this section, with special directions for each part.

PART V

Directions: Questions 101–140 are incomplete sentences. Four words or phrases, marked (A), (B), (C), (D), are given beneath each sentence. You are to choose the one word or phrase that best completes the sentence. Then, on your answer sheet, find the number of the question and mark your answer.

101. The sales manager's ------- on potential markets lasted 45 minutes.

(A) presentation
(B) present
(C) presenting
(D) presently

102. Before she left the company, Ms. Gutierrez hired a ------- replacement to fill her position.

(A) suitably
(B) suitable
(C) suite
(D) suitability

103. Because of recent budget deficits we have ------- off one-third of the workers at the Texas factory.

(A) laid
(B) laying
(C) lay
(D) lays

104. After his long battle with the regulators, our lawyer ------- to back down and settle our case for less than we were asking.

(A) rescinded
(B) reminded
(C) respected
(D) refused

105. The letter from the head of research and development ------- my boss's argument that we should change the formulation of the solvent.

(A) advance
(B) advanced
(C) advancing
(D) advantageous

106. Mr. Jones was worried ----- the slow fourth-quarter sales.

(A) at
(B) about
(C) for
(D) to

GO ON TO THE NEXT PAGE

107. ------- our team had sold the most plans in January, we received the coveted Early Bird Award.

(A) While
(B) Nevertheless
(C) Since
(D) Although

108. The new data has been ------- all the decisions of the research group.

(A) influenced
(B) influencing
(C) influences
(D) influence

109. The accountant placed his own financial gain ------- the well-being of his client.

(A) above
(B) near
(C) through
(D) beside

110. Her goal was to do ------- with the most selective laboratory team in the country.

(A) researcher
(B) researching
(C) research
(D) researched

111. The best manager in our division always allows her employees to find solutions that work for -------.

(A) their
(B) them
(C) they
(D) theirs

112. The results of the study were ------- we had expected them to be.

(A) better
(B) better than
(C) good
(D) good than

113. The CEO's speech was a huge departure ------- the norm—he predicted trouble with the new computer system.

(A) to
(B) of
(C) for
(D) from

114. The contractor waited to bill us until the project was ------- finished.

(A) completion
(B) more complete
(C) complete
(D) completely

115. One school of ------- is that a company's culture is determined from the top down.

(A) education
(B) learning
(C) thought
(D) student

116. Ms. Han was asked to supervise the changes that were to be made ------- the database.

(A) because
(B) from
(C) to
(D) though

GO ON TO THE NEXT PAGE

117. Despite our request, the judge decided to ------- the period of discovery.

(A) prolongation
(B) prolong
(C) prolonging
(D) prolonged

118. Because of Mr. Padmanthan's facility with databases, he was asked to share ------- methods of analysis with the division.

(A) him
(B) he
(C) his
(D) himself

119. She dropped her wallet as she ------- her attaché case at the front desk.

(A) opens
(B) was opening
(C) opened
(D) open

120. As a reminder, all ------ to the charity are tax-deductible.

(A) contraband
(B) contributions
(C) continuations
(D) continents

121. Until the Allies were able to learn the code, encoded messages that were intercepted sounded like ------.

(A) innocence
(B) indolence
(C) arrogance
(D) nonsense

122. A cabin that was built by the Shoshone Indians ------ still standing beside Lake Hopatcong.

(A) is
(B) are
(C) were
(D) had been

123. Crime scene investigators are now able to detect fibers that are less than one hundredth of a ------ long.

(A) milliliter
(B) milligram
(C) millimeter
(D) millisecond

124. At Comcorp, all mid-level ------ receive yearly bonuses and have access to a company car.

(A) examples
(B) executives
(C) exteriors
(D) expatriates

125. In a recent survey, 14 percent of respondents said they were ------ Republicans nor Democrats.

(A) either
(B) neither
(C) whether
(D) rather

126. The top floor of this building has a rooftop restaurant and an ------ deck.

(A) oration
(B) ovation
(C) oblation
(D) observation

GO ON TO THE NEXT PAGE

127. I would prefer to remain ------ rather than get involved in this dispute.

(A) neutral
(B) central
(C) spectral
(D) causal

128. Traffic was blocked in many directions due to the three-car ------ at the intersection.

(A) precision
(B) incision
(C) collision
(D) decision

129. You may not return goods to our store if they have been ------ in any way.

(A) damage
(B) damaged
(C) damaging
(D) damages

130. Many economists ------ that the recession will get worse before it gets better.

(A) arguing
(B) arguably
(C) argument
(D) argue

131. Last night, the union ------ management's most recent contract proposal.

(A) accept
(B) accepted
(C) accepting
(D) accepts

132. We must delay the launch of our new software, because the developers are ------ schedule.

(A) behind
(B) believe
(C) beneath
(D) become

133. Importers protested the new steel tariffs, which made foreign steel much too ------.

(A) expansive
(B) explosive
(C) expensive
(D) expedient

134. When I first met Ms. Rodriguez, we ------ business cards.

(A) executed
(B) exchanged
(C) exhausted
(D) extended

135. I'm still hungry, because food at the luncheon was ------.

(A) inedible
(B) incredible
(C) interminable
(D) impossible

136. Upon receipt of this invitation, the favor of a ------ is requested.

(A) replies
(B) reply
(C) replying
(D) replied

GO ON TO THE NEXT PAGE

137. If you encounter a problem with your computer, please consult your user's ------.

(A) manually
(B) manipulate
(C) manual
(D) manufacture

138. Over the years, we here at MC Data Corporation have worked hard to build our business ------.

(A) reputation
(B) reputable
(C) reputedly
(D) reputed

139. For safety reasons, smoking is prohibited within the vicinity of ------ liquids.

(A) compatible
(B) comparable
(C) combustible
(D) commendable

140. Due to a favorable exchange rate, foreign goods are now much more ------.

(A) predictable
(B) affordable
(C) considerable
(D) debatable

GO ON TO THE NEXT PAGE

PART VI

Directions: In **Questions 141–160,** each sentence has four words or phrases underlined. The four underlined parts of the sentence are marked (A), (B), (C), (D). You are to identify the one underlined word or phrase that should be corrected or rewritten. Then, on your answer sheet, find the number of the question and mark your answer.

141. The concierge <u>can make</u> restaurant <u>nor</u> theater reservations for <u>anyone</u> <u>staying</u> at the hotel.
    A   B   C   D

142. Mr. Grieco <u>asked her</u> his assistant to fax a document <u>to</u> the <u>head</u> office <u>in</u> Moorhead.
            A   B   C   D

143. Once <u>submitted</u>, your application will be processed and <u>you</u> should receive a response <u>of</u> our
          A   B   C

    office <u>within</u> 10 business days.
         D

144. The customer service representatives <u>had fielded</u> more than 150 calls <u>every</u> day <u>regarding</u> the
                                   A   B   C

    new name <u>of</u> the company.
           D

145. Past <u>performing</u> of <u>our</u> software product <u>does</u> not guarantee future results <u>for</u> your company.
           A   B   C   D

146. The firm <u>decided</u> to terminate the analyst's contract in an effort <u>of</u> avoid <u>being</u> associated <u>with</u>
           A   B   C   D

    the ratings scandal.

147. The lowest bid <u>on project</u> was <u>submitted</u> by a company <u>with</u> a <u>poor</u> service rating.
                  A   B   C   D

148. We <u>have received</u> many requests <u>for</u> expand <u>our</u> product line <u>to</u> include software for mobile
        A   B   C   D

    phones.

149. <u>Because of</u> the rent on the New York storage space increased, the company moved <u>all</u> <u>its</u>
        A   B   C

    records <u>to</u> New Jersey.
           D

150. <u>If</u> she comes <u>at</u> 10 we <u>will be gone</u> to the exhibit <u>together</u>.
    A   B   C   D

151. Our boss <u>invited</u> us to a party <u>at</u> <u>his</u> summer <u>housing</u> next weekend.
             A   B C   D

GO ON TO THE NEXT PAGE

152. To secure the flap, insertion the tab into the bottom hole and tug gently.
  A   B   C   D

153. I drive this building regularly, but I never knew it housed the head offices of our major
            A   B   C D

competitor.

154. Despite the upturn in the economy, we have less clients this year than we did last year
  A   B   C

at this time.
  D

155. The driver requested our cancel receipts as proof of ticket purchase before we could get
                                  A   B   C

on board the bus.
  D

156. Unless having seen the document myself, I cannot attest to its authenticity.
  A   B   C D

157. The regulation states that no open containers if developer should be left in the loading area.
  A   B   C   D

158. While it isn't the most popular e-business software application, NewHope X is gained market
            A   B   C

share all the time.
        D

159. Annalisa Roehme won company's Good Citizen award for her work with Habitat for Humanity
                        A   B C

throughout the year.
  D

160. Although it is gone from the MOMA, the exhibit can viewed at any of the five other museums
  A   B   C   D

on the 2002 tour.

GO ON TO THE NEXT PAGE ➡

PART VII

Directions: Questions 161–200 are based on a selection of reading materials, such as notices, letters, forms, newspaper and magazine articles, and advertisements. You are to choose the one best answer (A), (B), (C), or (D) to each question. Then, on your answer sheet, find the number of the question and mark your answer. Answer all questions following each reading selection on the basis of what is stated or implied in that selection.

Questions 161–162 refer to the following notice.

> In case of emergency, pull red handle toward you and down. Push glass out of frame with feet, and exit the vehicle carefully.

161. Where would this notice most likely be seen?

(A) An office building.
(B) A bus.
(C) An airport lounge.
(D) An apartment.

162. How should the glass be removed?

(A) By pushing.
(B) By pulling.
(C) By exiting.
(D) By handling.

GO ON TO THE NEXT PAGE

Questions 163–164 refer to the following program insert.

> *Please be advised that there has been a change to the seminar schedule. "Maximizing Your Publicity Dollars" with Coco Smith will now be held at 3 P.M. in Ballroom A, while "Inventory Control Methods" with Charles Bell will now be held at 1 P.M. in Ballroom C.*

163. Where would this program insert be most likely to be found?

(A) In a program for a business seminar.
(B) In a program for a musical.
(C) In a program for a graduation ceremony.
(D) In a program for a dance competition.

164. Ms. Smith is leading a seminar on which of the following topics?

(A) The methods of controlling inventory.
(B) The costs of publicizing companies or products.
(C) The process of changing schedules.
(D) The systems of running a business.

GO ON TO THE NEXT PAGE

Questions 165–167 refer to the following memo.

MEMORANDUM

TO: All Employees

FROM: Human Resources

The company-wide annual meeting will be held Monday at 1 P.M. in the conference room. Lunch will be provided. Employees are asked to sit with their department heads and bring their completed goals worksheets.

165. When should the employees fill out the goals worksheets?

(A) During lunch.
(B) On Monday at 1.
(C) Before Monday at 1.
(D) After the meeting.

166. Who will be at the meeting?

(A) The human resources department.
(B) The entire staff.
(C) The department heads.
(D) The company president.

167. What will be provided at the meeting?

(A) Resources.
(B) Bonuses.
(C) Lunch.
(D) Worksheets.

GO ON TO THE NEXT PAGE

Questions 168–169 refer to the following receipt.

```
7/12/02
1:03 P.M.

Deposit to checking
Account # 434543778609
$1256.76

Balance
$3452.45

Available balance
$2195.69
```

168. How much could be withdrawn from the account right now?

(A) About $1200.
(B) About $2200.
(C) About $3500.
(D) About $4300.

169. When was the money deposited?

(A) January 3.
(B) June 12.
(C) July 12.
(D) December 7.

GO ON TO THE NEXT PAGE

Ms. Amy Wyatt
20 Bounding Brook Drive
Winona, MN 55987
February 1, 1998

Dear Ms. Wyatt,

We regret to inform you that your claim for $3036 is denied. Under the terms of your contract, dental implants are not covered unless medically necessary. Without substantiating documents from three independent physicians and/or dentists, implants are not considered to be medically necessary.

Claims Department

Phoenix Insurance

170. Who wrote the letter?

(A) A health insurance company.
(B) An auto insurance company.
(C) A life insurance company.
(D) A property insurance company.

171. What does the author of the letter regret?

(A) That the company cannot pay for Ms. Wyatt to study to become an independent physician.
(B) That the company does not consider her contract to be valid.
(C) That the company has not filled out the paperwork for Ms. Wyatt's case correctly.
(D) That the company will not reimburse Ms. Wyatt for money she spent.

172. How can Ms. Wyatt appeal the decision?

(A) By switching to another insurance company.
(B) By obtaining documentation from three doctors or dentists.
(C) By resubmitting her claim in triplicate.
(D) By renewing her contract.

GO ON TO THE NEXT PAGE

Alec Schlitz
133 E 12th Street, Apt. 12D
Newark, NJ 08777

Dear Mr. Schlitz,

Thank you for your interest in TCB Industries. Unfortunately, we do not have any openings for people with your skills at this time. We will keep your resume on file and will contact you if any suitable positions open up.

Again, thank you for your interest in our company, and good luck in all your future endeavors.

Sincerely,

Krista Magid

Krista Magid
Hiring Manager

173. This letter is a response to which of the following?

(A) A job application and resume.
(B) A sales call.
(C) A request for a prospectus and press kit.
(D) A newspaper article.

174. What is Krista Magid's job?

(A) She audits corporate accounts.
(B) She manages temporary workers.
(C) She hires new employees.
(D) She writes press releases.

175. When will TCB Industries contact Alec Schlitz?

(A) Only if they have a job he is qualified for.
(B) Only if Krista Magid decides to quit.
(C) Only if he earns an advanced degree.
(D) Only if he sends them a resume.

GO ON TO THE NEXT PAGE

Question 176–177 refer to the following schedule.

United Artists Union Square Stadium 14
850 Broadway, New York, NY 10003

8 Mile
(R, 118 min.)

11:00am | 11:30am | 12:15pm | 1:00pm | 1:30pm | 2:00pm | 2:45pm | 3:30pm | 4:00pm | 4:30pm | 5:15pm | 6:30pm | 7:00pm | 7:45pm | 9:10pm | 9:40pm | 10:20pm | 11:00pm

Santa Clause 2
(G, 105 min.)

11:20am | 1:50pm | 4:20pm | 7:10pm | 9:30pm

Harry Potter and the Chamber of Secrets
 (PG, 161 min.)

11:00am | 11:55am | 12:15pm | 1:20pm | 2:20pm | 3:20pm | 3:40pm | 4:40pm | 5:40pm | 6:45pm | 7:05pm | 8:10pm | 9:10pm | 10:10pm | 10:30pm

Punch-Drunk Love
(R, 89 min.)

12:00pm | 2:10pm | 5:00pm | 7:30pm | 9:50pm

176. This schedule is for which type of establishment?

(A) A dance club.
(B) A movie theater.
(C) A children's museum.
(D) A parochial school.

177. Which of the shows is the longest?

(A) *8 Mile.*
(B) *Santa Clause 2.*
(C) *Harry Potter and the Chamber of Secrets.*
(D) *Punch-Drunk Love.*

GO ON TO THE NEXT PAGE

Questions **178–180** refer to the following card.

Questions 178–180 refer to the following card.

Customer Comment Card

Did someone on our staff do something exceptionally well? Were our services not up to your expectations? Please let us know by filling out this customer comment card and dropping it in the box at the Concierge Desk.

Name of staff member you would like to commend:

What did this staff member do that was so outstanding?

How could we improve the guest experience here at the Taft Hotel?

Name (optional):

Address (optional):

Telephone number (optional):

Would you like a member of our management office to contact you about your experience?

---

178. Where would this card most likely be found?

(A) A corporate dining room.
(B) A restaurant bathroom.
(C) A hotel room.
(D) An airport lounge.

179. Which of the following would be a reason someone would fill out this card?

(A) To report a robbery in a conference center.
(B) To request a company prospectus.
(C) To combine two bank accounts into one.
(D) To compliment a pleasant concierge.

180. How should this card be submitted to the management office?

(A) By sending it through the mail.
(B) By leaving it in a special box at the hotel.
(C) By faxing it in to the office.
(D) By e-mailing the comments.

GO ON TO THE NEXT PAGE

Questions 181–184 refer to the following e-mail.

From: "Doris Glossing" <dorisg@hilltop.org>

To: "Romulus Wayne" <romulusw@hilltop.org>,

"Bob Bull " <robertb@hilltop.org>, "Carolyn Stewart" <carolyns@hilltop.org>, "Maria Pisano" <mariap@hilltop.org>, "Elvin Wagner" <elvinw@hilltop.org>, "Harry Novachik" <harryn@hilltop.org>

Cc: "Pixie Wittles" <pixiew@hilltop.org>, "Fredo Chung" <fredoc@hilltop.org>

Subject: Executive Committee Meeting -- Tuesday, December 3rd

Date: Thu, 21 Nov 2002 14:09:42 -0500

Importance: Normal

November will be over before we know it, so I am sending this reminder now about the Executive Committee meeting scheduled for Tuesday, December 3rd, at 7 P.M.

If you received funds from the allocation process in September, I hope you will be prepared to report on the results of your expenditures and to provide a tentative budget for the next quarter.

As a refresher for all, and as information to those new department chairs among us, I am attaching a copy of the minutes from our last meeting.

Please let me know if there is any item you would like to have on the agenda. I look forward to seeing you at the meeting.

Doris G

Attachment: Executive Committee minutes 091302.doc

181. How much time will elapse between this email and the meeting?

(A) About a week.
(B) About a week and a half.
(C) About two and a half weeks.
(D) About a month.

182. How many people received this e-mail?

(A) 8
(B) 9
(C) 10
(D) 12

183. What is one item on the agenda of the meeting?

(A) Providing a budget for the next three months.
(B) Refreshing the minutes.
(C) Beginning the September allocation process.
(D) Choosing new department chairs.

184. What is most likely the website address of this organization?

(A) www.091302.doc
(B) www.091302.com
(C) www.hilltop.com
(D) www.hilltop.org

GO ON TO THE NEXT PAGE

Questions 185–186 refer to the following bill.

```
05/19/2001
1:57 P.M.
Your server is Janice.


1 Coke                          $1.50
1 Iced Tea                      $1.00
1 Fried Calamari                $5.00
1 Grilled Chicken Sandwich      $7.00
1 Meatloaf Special              $8.50
2 Chocolate Cake                $7.00

Total                          $30.00
Tax @ 0.0775%                   $2.33

Grand Total                    $32.33


Thank you for your business!

Janice
```

185. How many drinks did the table order?

- (A) None.
- (B) One.
- (C) Two.
- (D) Three.

186. Which of the following does the bill NOT include?

- (A) The cost of the desserts.
- (B) The tip for the server.
- (C) The sales tax.
- (D) The server's name.

GO ON TO THE NEXT PAGE

To all 3rd-floor employees:

Please be advised that we are now renting copiers from All-Copy. As of 3/12 our service contract with CopyMate will no longer be valid. If a copier breaks down, please DO NOT TRY TO FIX IT YOURSELF. Instead, follow the following procedure:

1) Call the receptionist at x3333 and let her know the number of the copier that is broken, your name, and your extension.

2) Call All-Copy at 1-888-555-1234 and give them customer code #3412-3, your name, and your extension. They will come to fix the copier within 24 hours (except on weekends).

3) Do NOT ask the receptionist to call All-Copy for you. This is not one of her duties. Do NOT call All-Copy more than once, or if the receptionist says that someone else reported the same copier broken.

If everyone follows these new procedures, we will be able to keep our copiers up and running without incurring unnecessary fees for multiple service calls.

187. Where would this notice most likely be posted?

(A) A fitness center.
(B) A business office.
(C) An airport ticket counter.
(D) A copy shop.

188. What should a person do first if a copy machine breaks?

(A) Call All-Copy.
(B) Call CopyMate.
(C) Call the receptionist.
(D) Call a 3rd-floor employee.

189. If a copier is reported broken on a Thursday, when will it be fixed?

(A) By Thursday.
(B) By Friday.
(C) By Saturday.
(D) By Monday.

GO ON TO THE NEXT PAGE

To: Robert Strand

From: Martin Hobbie

Subject: conference next month

Date: March 30, 1999

Dear Rob,

Mariana mentioned that you'll be in town for the conference next month. I hope you'll have time to visit our office on Tuesday before the conference starts. You gave us such a great reception when we were in Fargo last year that we'd like to reciprocate by taking you out to lunch. And let us know if you need a ride from the airport—someone will be happy to pick you up.

Karen Arias from our office is going to be giving a talk on Wednesday afternoon of the conference on housing starts in the Northeast, and we'll all be there. If you don't have other plans, we'd love to go out for a drink with you then, too.

Please keep in touch as soon as you know what your travel plans are so we can plan lunch.

Take care,

Martin

190. Who is the recipient of this memo?

(A) Martin Hobbie.
(B) Robert Strand.
(C) Mariana.
(D) Karen Arias.

191. What does Mr. Hobbie want Mr. Strand to do?

(A) Go to the conference in Fargo next month.
(B) Pick up Mariana from the airport.
(C) Give a talk on housing starts in the Northeast.
(D) Go to lunch with the people in Mr. Hobbie's office.

192. What is the relationship between Mr. Hobbie and Mr. Strand?

(A) They are brothers.
(B) They work in the same office.
(C) They are colleagues in different cities.
(D) They only know each other through e-mail.

GO ON TO THE NEXT PAGE

Processing Error Sends Thousands Wrong Checks

INDIANAPOLIS—A processing error in the offices of the Indiana Internal Revenue Service (IIRS) sent 5,678 taxpayers the wrong refund checks, sources revealed yesterday. The source, who declined to be named, is an employee in the Indianapolis office of the IIRS that sends out the checks. He reported that last Friday the office began getting calls from taxpayers who had received checks meant for other taxpayers. The IIRS processed 34 of these calls before they were able to search the database and discover the extent of the error.

A processing error on the part of the employees who stuff the envelopes caused each person to receive the check meant for the person whose name was ahead of his or hers on the alphabetical list, the source stated. The checks were printed with the names, addresses, and Social Security numbers of the intended recipients. Using this information, anyone could obtain personal information about the taxpayers without their knowledge.

The IIRS has not made a decision yet about how they will rectify this error. An official spokesperson for the IIRS could not be reached for comment.

193. What is the name of the source of this story?

(A) The author doesn't know the name of the source.

(B) The source does not want his name to be known.

(C) The IIRS won't reveal the name of the source.

(D) The source is the official spokesperson for the IIRS.

194. What caused the errors?

(A) The computer that printed the checks.

(B) The company that manufactures the envelopes.

(C) The taxpayers who received the refunds.

(D) The people who stuffed the checks into the envelopes.

195. How will the errors be fixed?

(A) The IIRS has not announced how they will fix the problem.

(B) The IIRS will issue a double-refund to every taxpayer.

(C) Each taxpayer will be responsible for fixing his or her own problem.

(D) Each taxpayer will be asked how he or she wants the error to be fixed.

GO ON TO THE NEXT PAGE

FOR RENT. 1 bedroom apartment, Westville Heights area. All new appliances, dishwasher, washer/dryer. Utilities included. No pets. First month plus deposit due on signing lease. $450 a month. Call 314-555-1234 after 7 P.M.

---

196. Where would this notice likely be found?

(A) A novel.
(B) A church newsletter.
(C) A questionnaire.
(D) A newspaper.

197. How much will the tenant pay for electricity per month?

(A) The cost of electricity is included in the monthly rent.
(B) The cost of electricity will vary from month to month.
(C) The cost of electricity will be approximately $450 a month.
(D) The cost of electricity is determined by the electric company.

GO ON TO THE NEXT PAGE

Questions 198–200 refer to the following letter.

July 23, 2001

Dear Ms. Andocek,

Thank you so much for taking the time to interview me on Wednesday. After discussing the post of transition team leader with you, I feel even more strongly that I am the right person for this position. I have the experience managing diverse groups of people as well as the ability to crunch the numbers and make the difficult decisions that the position requires. I was impressed by the relaxed and energized feel of the office, and would love the chance to work at EnGen.

Again, thank you for your time. I look forward to hearing from you.

Sincerely,

Anna Mott Kerr

198. What is the purpose of this letter?

(A) To thank someone for a job interview.
(B) To ask for a job application.
(C) To recommend a company's stock.
(D) To discover what made a project fail.

199. Which one of the following does Ms. Kerr NOT have experience doing?

(A) Leading different groups of people.
(B) Making decisions about complicated situations.
(C) Managing a large budget.
(D) Analyzing figures.

200. How did Ms. Mott send this letter?

(A) By mail.
(B) By e-mail.
(C) By fax.
(D) By messenger.

STOP

14

The Princeton Review TOEIC Practice Test 1: Answers and Explanations

ANSWER KEY FOR PRACTICE TEST 1

LISTENING COMPREHENSION

1. A	36. B
2. C	37. B
3. B	38. A
4. A	39. B
5. B	40. A
6. A	41. C
7. A	42. B
8. D	43. A
9. A	44. B
10. C	45. C
11. D	46. A
12. B	47. B
13. B	48. A
14. A	49. C
15. D	50. A
16. C	51. B
17. B	52. C
18. A	53. D
19. B	54. A
20. B	55. D
21. A	56. A
22. B	57. B
23. C	58. A
24. A	59. C
25. B	60. D
26. C	61. A
27. A	62. B
28. A	63. A
29. B	64. B
30. C	65. C
31. B	66. C
32. A	67. D
33. B	68. D
34. C	69. D
35. C	70. C

71. C
72. B
73. A
74. D
75. C
76. A
77. D
78. C
79. C
80. A
81. A
82. C
83. A
84. D
85. C
86. D
87. A
88. B
89. C
90. B
91. A
92. C
93. D
94. A
95. A
96. C
97. B
98. C
99. B
100. D

READING

101. A
102. B
103. A
104. D
105. B
106. B

107. C
108. B
109. A
110. C
111. B
112. B
113. D
114. D
115. C
116. C
117. B
118. C
119. C
120. B
121. D
122. A
123. C
124. B
125. B
126. D
127. A
128. C
129. B
130. D
131. B
132. A
133. C
134. B
135. A
136. B
137. C
138. A
139. C
140. B
141. B
142. A
143. C
144. A
145. A

146. B	185. C
147. A	186. B
148. B	187. B
149. A	188. C
150. C	189. B
151. D	190. B
152. B	191. D
153. A	192. C
154. B	193. B
155. A	194. D
156. A	195. A
157. C	196. D
158. C	197. A
159. A	198. A
160. D	199. C
161. B	200. A
162. A	
163. A	
164. B	
165. C	
166. B	
167. C	
168. B	
169. C	
170. A	
171. D	
172. B	
173. A	
174. C	
175. A	
176. B	
177. C	
178. C	
179. D	
180. B	
181. B	
182. A	
183. A	
184. D	

EXPLANATIONS

LISTENING COMPREHENSION

1. **A** The doors of the train are open and the train is stopped at the station. Some people are getting on and some are getting off. The answer is (A).

2. **C** The hallway is long and empty. There is no man or phone in the photo. The answer is (C).

3. **B** The car is parked near a parking meter, not driving. There is no way to know if it will get a ticket, and there is no driver in the photo. The answer is (B).

4. **A** The seat is reserved for people with disabilities. The picture shows a wheelchair, not a bicycle, and does not mention elderly people. The answer is (A).

5. **B** The room is full of office cubicles. There is no way to know if the people are working late or if they need to finish a project. "Too bright" is subjective, and cannot be determined from this photo. The answer is (B).

6. **A** The woman is handing the clerk something. The store is a bookstore, not a hamburger or clothing store. The woman on the right is wearing a coat, so it is probable that she doesn't work there. The answer is (A).

7. **A** The woman has an unhappy expression on her face as she looks at the man, so this indicates that she doesn't like what he's saying. There is no car in the photo, and no way to tell if he is telling the truth or if they are brother and sister. The answer is (A).

8. **D** The photo is of a subway entrance. There is no man, rain, or museum in the photo. The answer is (D).

9. **A** The photo shows empty seats near a baggage carousel. The baggage may already have come, and there is no way to tell if the people are waiting for their bags or not. The photo does not contain a garage. The answer is (A).

10. **C** There is no snow in the photo, and there are two men at the café, so it can't be closed. There is no way to know if it is a holiday or not, but the café is not busy. The answer is (C).

11. **D** The photo shows a taxi at a stoplight. There is no garage or snow in the photo, and there is no way to know if the taxi has run out of gas. The answer is (D).

12. **B** The woman has her wallet in her hand. There is no way to know if the man owns the store or how much money the woman has. There are signs advertising cigarettes for sale. The answer is (B).

13. **B** The cases are full of glasses, not umbrellas. There is no way to know whether the store is about to close or how you can pay in the store. The answer is (B).

14. **A**   The sign says, "Recession Special!" which means that they are having a sale. We don't know if the woman is eating papaya or not, and she is not wearing a gray shawl. The sale is for seventy cents off, not seventy percent. The answer is (A).

15. **D**   We don't know if she is about to pay, whether the doughnuts are fresh, or whether this is her breakfast, but we do know that the bakery is open. The answer is (D).

16. **C**   The photo shows a crowded market. There is no way to know what day of the week it is or what the people are buying. This does not look like a protest. The answer is (C).

17. **B**   The photo shows a lone man waiting at a bus stop, with no van, dog, or fire. The answer is (B).

18. **A**   The garbage truck is parked. There is no garage, woman, or men in the picture. The answer is (A).

19. **B**   The photo shows a woman leaning against a blackboard. She is not writing or driving anything, and there is no way to know what she is saying. The answer is (B).

20. **B**   The people are dressed casually, not for business. There are no cars in the photo, and there is no way to know if the people have seen a movie or not. The answer is (B).

21. **A**   The question asks *how soon*, and the answer tells a time in the future. The answer is (A).

22. **B**   The question asks *where*, and the answer gives directions. The answer is (B).

23. **C**   The question asks a yes/no question, and the answer gives a response. The answer is (C).

24. **A**   The question asks about a person, and the answer gives his name. The answer is (A).

25. **B**   The question asks *why*, and the answer gives a reason. The answer is (B).

26. **C**   The question asks *when*, and the answer gives a date. The answer is (C).

27. **A**   The question asks *how long*, and the answer gives a time. The answer is (A).

28. **A**   The question asks a yes/no question, and the answer responds to that topic. The answer is (A).

29. **B**   The question asks *when*, and the answer gives a time. The answer is (B).

30. **C**   The question asks *whose*, and the answer gives a name. The answer is (C).

31. **B**   The question asks *where*, and the answer gives directions. The answer is (B).

32. **A**   The question asks *who*, and the answer gives a person. The answer is (A).

33. **B**   The question is a yes/no question, and the answer responds to the topic. The answer is (B).

34. **C**   The question asks *how tall*, and the answer gives a height. The answer is (C).

35. **C**   The question is a yes/no question, and the answer stays on topic. The answer is (C).

36. **B**   The question asks *how much*, and the answer gives an amount. The answer is (B).

37. **B**   The question asks for a number, and the answer gives a number. The answer is (B).

38. **A**   The question asks for ingredients, and the answer lists them. The answer is (A).

39. **B**   The question asks *where*, and the answer gives a location. The answer is (B).

40. **A**   The question asks about a problem, and the answer names the problem. The answer is (A).

41. **C**   The question asks *when*, and the answer gives a date. The answer is (C).

42. **B**   The question asks *how many*, and the answer gives a number. The answer is (B).

43. **A**   The question is a yes/no question, and the answer stays on topic. The answer is (A).

44. **B**   The question is a yes/no question, and the answer stays on topic. The answer is (B).

45. **C**   The question asks for a name, and the answer tells it. The answer is (C).

46. **A**   The question asks *why not*, and the answer gives a reason. The answer is (A).

47. **B**   The question asks *when*, and the answer gives a date. The answer is (B).

48. **A**   The question is a yes/no question, and the answer stays on topic. The answer is (A).

49. **C**   The question is a yes/no question, and the answer stays on topic. The answer is (C).

50. **A**   The question asks *how*, and the answer gives a method. The answer is (A).

51. **B**   The team lost because they didn't have a good pitcher, and the man is a good pitcher. He says that if he had played, the team would have won. The answer is (B).

52. **C**   The woman says she hopes the ticket didn't go out with the trash. Trash is garbage, so the answer is (C).

53. **D**   The second man says it took him an extra 10 minutes to drive to work. The first man says it took him three times as long to go through the same park. This means it took him 30 extra minutes, so the answer is (D).

54. **A** The man says, "I've been taking the antibiotics she prescribed for 10 days, but I don't feel any better." The medication has not cured his illness. The answer is (A).

55. **D** The woman says she lost her wallet at the 7 P.M. show, which indicates that she was at a movie. Therefore, she must be going to a movie theater to pick up her wallet. The answer is (D).

56. **A** The man says that he "missed his stop," which means that he did not get off when he should have gotten off. The answer is (A).

57. **B** The conference call "has to be rescheduled," which means that it must be held on a different day. The answer is (B).

58. **A** The woman is asking about a "check request," which is a document submitted to ask for a check to be sent in payment to someone. This means that she is going to send a check to Mr. Chekov, so the answer is (A).

59. **C** The woman says that the man can get the suit on Wednesday morning, and he says he will come get it at 11. The answer is (C).

60. **D** The article says that they are being accused of "insider trading," which is illegal stock trades. The answer is (D).

61. **A** The man says that the Appleton office is having problems with "employee retention," or keeping employees working there. The answer is (A).

62. **B** Someone who is paid money to drive someone somewhere is most likely a taxi driver. The answer is (B).

63. **A** The man says that he is 20 minutes away from the warehouse, and will be there as soon as possible. The answer is (A).

64. **B** The man asks the woman to have it sent to his room. The answer is (B).

65. **C** They do not eat pizza because they want something lower in cholesterol, and they choose sandwiches. Therefore, sandwiches must be lower in cholesterol. The answer is (C).

66. **C** The woman says she is afraid of a delay. A delay means that her train would arrive late, so the answer is (C).

67. **D** There was a leak into Nancy's apartment that caused a mess in her kitchen. She spent the weekend cleaning it up, so the answer is (D).

68. **D** The man asks to return the lamp to the store, so the answer is (D).

69. **D** Frank put his overcoat on the seat, and forgot it there when he got off the bus. The answer is (D).

70. **C** The fire was in the building across the street. The answer is (C).

71. **C** The man dialed the woman's number, thinking it was the number of a mattress store. The answer is (C).

72. **B** The man asks for two eggs and cheese. The answer is (B).

73. **A** A convenience store sells newspapers and bottled water, so the answer is (A).

74. **D** The man is helping the woman send a package, so he must work for the post office. The answer is (D).

75. **C** The woman wants to buy a recording, so the conversation takes place in a CD store. The answer is (C).

76. **A** The client has not sent them all the information they need to finish the audit. The answer is (A).

77. **D** The system was down (or broken) for several hours and the messages were lost. The answer is (D).

78. **C** Keiko has reorganized the files on the computer system, so the woman has to ask her how they are organized now. The answer is (C).

79. **C** The two passengers figure out that it must belong to a different woman, who has already gotten off the bus. The answer is (C).

80. **A** Jim Weislak is trying to fix a computer system that isn't working. The answer is (A).

81. **A** The announcement is about trains and stations, so it must be about a train station or subway platform. The answer is (A).

82. **C** The announcement said that the trains are not running uptown between 14th Street and Grand Central Station. The answer is (C).

83. **A** *Server* is a gender-neutral term for waiter or waitress. Shelley is the server. The answer is (A).

84. **D** The Lunch Special includes salad, breadsticks, an entrée, and a soft drink, but no dessert. The answer is (D).

85. **C** The first stop is the Statue of Liberty, and the second stop is Ellis Island. The answer is (C).

86. **D** The ferry stays at Ellis Island for 10 minutes. The answer is (D).

87. **A** The speaker says the employees should respond "by the end of next week." The answer is (A).

88. **B** The party runs from 7 P.M. to 11 P.M. The answer is (B).

89. **C** Drinks will be served at the party. The answer is (C).

90. **B** The speaker is Eva Glassberg, host of the radio show *Washington News*. The answer is (B).

91. **A** Jillian Jaffe is the reporter covering the new charter school. The answer is (A).

92. **C** The County Commissioner is the subject of a scandal involving kick-backs from contractors. The answer is (C).

93. **D** This is the introduction to the opening of the photography show *Snow Days*. The answer is (D).

94. **A** Amy Oakes is the photographer of the exhibit *Snow Days*. The answer is (A).

95. **A** Ms. Sunwoo is coming to observe and make a plan for the company's inventory process. The answer is (A).

96. **C** Ms. Sunwoo is there to improve the inventory process, which happens every year. The answer is (C).

97. **B** The event is a five-day meeting for future directors from a company. The answer is (B).

98. **C** The meetings will be led by directors from Arlington Technologies. The answer is (C).

99. **B** The conference will last for five days. The answer is (B).

100. **D** The conference is held to train employees to become good directors. The answer is (D).

READING

101. **A** The possessive *manager's* indicates that we are looking for a noun. The only noun in the answer choices is *presentation*, so the answer is (A).

102. **B** The blank is between the article *a* and the noun *replacement*, so it must be an adjective. The only adjective in the answer choices is *suitable*, so the answer is (B).

103. **A** The blank is part of a verb phrase consisting of the helping verb *have* and the past participle of the verb. The only past participle in the answer choices is *laid*, so the answer must be (A).

104. **D** Since the answer choices are different words, we should put in our own word for the blank. The only words that fit here are words indicating that the lawyer made a decision, like *decided* or *decided not to*. Neither *rescinded, reminded,* nor *respected* match up with our words, so eliminate them. The only choice left is (D), *refused*, which means *decided not to*.

105. **B** The part of the sentence before the blank is the subject of the sentence, while the part after the blank is the object of the sentence. The blank must be a verb connecting the subject and object. Eliminate (C) because *advancing* is a gerund, and (D) because *advantageous* is an adjective. The subject of the sentence, *letter*, is singular, but answer choice (A), *advance*, is plural, so eliminate it. *Advanced* is singular, so the answer is (B).

106. **B** The correct idiom is *worry about*. The answer is (B).

107. **C** The word in the blank must be a word indicating the relationship between the phrase before the comma and the phrase after the comma. Since they are in agreement (selling the most and getting an award), the word must indicate agreement. Eliminate (A), (B), and (D). The answer must be (C).

108. **B** The blank is part of a verb phrase consisting of the words *has been* and the present participle of the verb. The only present participle among the answer choices is *informing*, so the answer is (B).

109. **A** A word that fits well in the blank is *ahead of*. The words *near, through,* and *beside* do not match, so eliminate them. *Above* matches, so the answer is (A).

110. **C** The phrase *to do* is followed by a noun, so eliminate answer choices (B) and (D). Answer choice (A) doesn't make sense, as you can't *do researcher*, so get rid of it. The answer is (C).

111. **B** The blank must be an object pronoun. Answer choice (A) is a possessive, so cross it off. Answer choice (C) is a subject pronoun, so eliminate it. Answer choice (D) is a possessive object, so get rid of it too. The answer is (B).

112. **B** The sentence sets up a comparison between the results and the expectation, so the comparison word *better* must be used. Eliminate answer choices (C) and (D). The idiom is *better than*, so get rid of (A), and the answer is (B).

113. **D** The idiom is *departure from*. The answer is (D).

114. **D** The blank modifies the adjective *finished*, so it must be an adverb. The only adverb among the answer choices is *completely*, so the answer is (D).

115. **C** The correct idiom is *school of thought*, so the answer is (C).

116. **C** The correct idiom is *make changes to*. The answer is (C).

117. **B** The blank is part of the infinitive form of the verb, *to prolong*. Eliminate answer choices (A), (C), and (D). (B) is the correct answer.

118. **C** The blank is a word indicating that the *methods* belong to Mr. Padmanthan. *Him* is an object pronoun, so cross off (A). *He* is a subject pronoun, so eliminate (B). *Himself* is an object pronoun, so eliminate (D) too. The answer is (C).

119. **C** In this sentence, the structure of the verbs *dropped* and *opened* should be parallel, meaning that they should be the same tense. Eliminate answer choices (A), (B), and (D). The answer is (C).

120. **B** A good word to put in the blank is *donations*. Answer choices (A), (C), and (D), aren't interchangeable with *donations*, so cross them off. *Contributions* means *donations*, so the answer is (B).

121. **D** A good word to put in the blank is *gibberish*. Eliminate answer choices (A), (B), and (C), as they don't mean *gibberish*. *Nonsense* means *gibberish*, so the answer is (D).

122. **A** The word *still* indicates that the verb needs to be in the present tense, so eliminate answer choices (C) and (D). The subject is *cabin*, so the verb needs to be singular. Get rid of (B). The answer is (A).

123. **C** The blank is describing a unit of measurement of length. The only word indicating length is *millimeter*, so eliminate (A), (B), and (D), and the answer is (C).

124. **B** A good word to put in the blank is *employees*. Answer choices (A), (C), and (D) aren't interchangeable with *employees*, so eliminate them. *Executives* can be *employees*, so the answer is (B).

125. **B** The correct idiom is *neither...nor*, so the answer is (B).

126. **D** A deck on top of a building would be for looking around at the city, so a good word to put in the blank is *lookout*. Answer choices (A), (B), and (C) can't be substituted for *lookout*, so cross them off. *Observation* can mean *lookout*, so the answer is (D).

127. **A** Since the speaker does not want to get involved, a good word to put in the blank is *unbiased*. Answer choices (B), (C), and (D) can't be substituted for *unbiased*, so eliminate them. *Neutral* can mean *unbiased*, so the answer is (A).

128. **C** A good word to put in the blank is *accident*. Answer choices (A), (B), and (D) don't mean the same as *accident*, so get rid of them. A *collision* can be an *accident*, so the answer is (C).

129. **B** The blank is part of a verb phrase consisting of the words *have been* and the past participle of the verb. The only past participle among the answer choices is *damaged*, so the answer is (B).

130. **D** The sentence is in the simple present tense, so the word that goes into the blank is a present-tense verb. The only present-tense verb among the answer choices is *argue*, so the answer is (D).

131. **B** The words *last night* indicate that the action happened in the past. The only past-tense verb among the answer choices is *accepted*, so eliminate (A), (C), and (D), and the answer is (B).

132. **A** A good word to put in the blank is *off*. Answer choices (B), (C), and (D) don't mean the same as *off*, so cross them off. *Behind* can mean *late* or *off* schedule, so the answer is (A).

133. **C** A good word to put in the blank is *costly*. Answer choices (A), (B), and (D) don't mean costly, so eliminate them. *Expensive* means *costly*, so the answer is (C).

134. **B** A good word to put in the blank is *gave each other*. Answer choices (A), (C), and (D) don't mean *gave each other*, so get rid of them. *Exchanged* can mean *gave each other*, so the answer is (B).

135. **A** A good word to put in the blank is *bad-tasting*. Answer choices (B), (C), and (D) don't mean the same as *bad-tasting*, so eliminate them. Something that is *inedible* can be *bad-tasting*, so the answer is (A).

136. **B** The blank comes after the word *a*, so the blank must be a noun. Answer choices (A), (C), and (D) are not nouns, so cross them off. *Reply* is a noun, so the answer is (B).

137. **C** The possessive *user's* indicates that the blank is a noun. The only noun in the answer choices is *manual*, so the answer is (C).

138. **A** The blank must be a noun, because it is the object of the phrase *to build our* business. The only noun among the answer choices is *reputation*, so the answer is (A).

139. **C** A good word to put in the blank is *dangerous*. Answer choices (A), (B), and (D) don't mean the same as *dangerous*, so eliminate them. Something that is *combustible* can be *dangerous*, so the answer is (C).

140. **B** A good word to put in the blank is *cheap*. Answer choices (A), (C), and (D) don't mean *cheap*, so get rid of them. Something that is *affordable* can be *cheap*, so the answer is (B).

141. **B** The sentence indicates that the concierge can make reservations for either type of entertainment, not *neither* type, so the incorrect answer is (B). *Nor* should be *or*.

142. **A** *Her* in answer choice (A) is unnecessary, because *his* is already in the non-underlined part of the sentence. The incorrect answer is (A).

143. **C** The correct idiom is *response from*, not *response of*, so answer choice (C) is incorrect.

144. **A** The sentence indicates that the calls continue to come in, so the verb in answer choice (A) should indicate that this action still continues. *Had fielded* is a completed past tense, so answer choice (A) is incorrect.

145. **A** The word that follows *past* should be a noun, not a gerund. Answer choice (A) is incorrect.

146. **B** The correct idiom is *effort to*, not *effort of*, so answer choice (B) is incorrect.

147. **A** Answer choice (A) is missing the article *the* to make it idiomatically correct: *on the project*. Answer choice (A) is incorrect.

148. **B** The word *request* can be followed by *for* and then a noun, or *to* and then a verb. In this sentence *request* is followed by a verb, so the correct idiom is *request to*. Answer choice (B) is incorrect.

149. **A** The phrase *because* of needs to be followed by a noun phrase. Answer choice (A) is incorrect.

150. **C** The sentence sets up a conditional tense, so the underlined verb in answer choice (C) should be in the future tense, not the future past tense. Answer choice (C) is incorrect.

151. **D** *Housing* isn't absolutely grammatically wrong , but the word *house* is simpler and expresses the same idea better. Answer choice (D) is incorrect.

152. **B** The word after the comma should be a verb, not a noun *(insertion)*. Answer choice (B) is incorrect.

153. **A** *Drive this building* simply makes no sense. Answer choice (A) is incorrect.

154. **B** The noun *clients* is countable, so the word *less* should be *fewer*. Answer choice (B) is incorrect.

155. **A** The word before the noun *receipts* must modify it, so the underlined word in answer choice (A) should be an adjective. *Cancel* is a verb, not an adjective, so answer choice (A) is incorrect.

156. **A** The word *unless* as part of a phrase should be followed by a subject, and it's not in this sentence. Answer choice (A) is incorrect.

157. **C** To express that the *containers* are full of *developer*, we need to use the preposition *of*, not the conjunction *if*. Answer choice (C) is incorrect.

158. **C** To indicate the present continuous tense, the verb phrase is followed by the present participle. *Gained* is the past participle, not the present participle, so answer choice (C) is incorrect.

159. **A** Answer choice (A) is missing the article *the* to make it idiomatically correct: *won the company's...award*. Answer choice (A) is incorrect.

160. **D** The verb phrase needs the word *be* to express the idea fully: *can be viewed*. Answer choice (D) is incorrect.

161. **B** The word *vehicle* indicates that the notice would not be in a building, lounge, or apartment. Eliminate answer choices (A), (C), and (D). The answer is (B).

162. **A** The passage says, "Push glass out of frame." The answer is (A).

163. **A** The passage says, "the seminar schedule," so it must be a seminar, and the topics are applicable to business. The answer is (A).

164. **B** Ms. Smith's seminar is "Maximizing Your Publicity Dollars," so it is about publicizing companies or products. The answer is (B).

165. **C** The employees are told to bring "completed goals worksheets," so this means they need to fill them out before the meeting on Monday at 1. The answer is (C).

166. **B** The memo is addressed to "All Employees," and it is a "company-wide" meeting, so the entire staff should come. The answer is (B).

167. **C** The passage says, "Lunch will be provided." The answer is (C).

168. **B** The "available balance" is $2195.69, so about $2200 could be taken out right now. The answer is (B).

169. **C** The American way of writing dates is to use the format month/day/year. So 7/12/02 is July 12, 2002. The answer is (C).

170. **A** The letter is about a dental procedure, so the insurance must be related to health, not cars, life, or property. The answer is (A).

171. **D** The passage says, "your claim for $3036 is denied," which means that they will not pay her that money. The answer is (D).

172. **B** The passage says, "Without substantiating documents from three independent physicians and/or dentists," meaning that if she had these substantiating documents, the circumstances of her claim would change. The answer is (B).

173. **A** The passage says, "We will keep your resume on file," indicating that he sent in a resume to the company. The answer is (A).

174. **C** Her title is "Hiring Manager," which means that she is in charge of hiring new employees. The answer is (C).

175. **A** The passage says, "will contact you if any suitable positions open up." The answer is (A).

176. **B** The items on the schedule are movies and movie times, so the schedule must be for a movie theater. The answer is (B).

177. **C** *8 Mile* is 118 minutes long, *Santa Clause 2* is 105 minutes long, *Harry Potter* is 161 minutes long, and *Punch-Drunk Love* is 89 minutes long. *Harry Potter* is the longest of the four movies, so the answer is (C).

178. **C** The passage says, "here at the Taft Hotel," so it would be found in a hotel. The answer is (C).

179. **D** The card is used to let the management know if employees are doing a good job or a bad job. It has nothing to do with crime, prospectii, or bank accounts. The answer is (D).

180. **B** The passage says, "dropping it in the box at the Concierge Desk," which is at the hotel. The answer is (B).

181. **B** The e-mail was sent on November 21, and the meeting is December 3. There are 12 days, or a week and a half, between the e-mail and the meeting. The answer is (B).

182. **A** Doris sent the e-mail to six people: Romulus, Bob, Carolyn, Maria, Elvin, and Harry. She copied (cc'd) Pixie and Fredo. So, eight people received the e-mail. The answer is (A).

183. **A** The passage says, "provide a tentative budget for the next quarter." A quarter is three months, so the answer is (A).

184. **D** All the people listed on the e-mail have addresses at hilltop.org, so this must be the organization's website address. The answer is (D).

185. **C** The bill lists "1 Coke" and "1 Iced Tea," which makes two drinks. The answer is (C).

186. **B** The bill lists "2 Chocolate Cake," so eliminate answer choice (A). The bill lists "Tax @ 0.0775%," so cross off answer choice (C). It also gives the server's name, Janice, so eliminate answer choice (D). The answer is (B).

187. **B** This notice would be posted where "all 3rd-floor employees" would use copy machines, which is a business office. The answer is (B).

188. **C** The passage says, "1) Call the receptionist at x3333." The answer is (C).

189. **B** The passage says, "They will come to fix the copier within 24 hours (except on weekends)." Since Thursday is not a weekend, the repair person will fix the copier within 24 hours, or by Friday. The answer is (B).

190. **B** The "To:" line of the memo heading says "Robert Strand." The answer is (B).

191. **D** The passage says, "we'd like to reciprocate by taking you out to lunch." The answer is (D).

192. **C** The warm tone of the e-mail indicates that the two men are friendly but not close. The e-mail also says that Mr. Strand was very hospitable when Mr. Hobbie was in Fargo. This indicates that they work for the same company but in different offices. The answer is (C).

193. **B** The passage says, "The source, who declined to be named," to indicate that the source does not want to be revealed. The answer is (B).

194. **D** The passage says, "A processing error on the part of the employees who stuff the envelopes." The answer is (D).

195. **A** The passage says, "The IIRS has not made a decision yet." The answer is (A).

196. **D** This notice would be run where the most potential renters would see it, which is in the "For Rent" section of a newspaper. The answer is (D).

197. **A** Electricity is a utility. The phrase "Utilities included" in the passage means that the tenant does not pay any extra money for electricity. The answer is (A).

198. **A** The passage says, "Thank you so much for taking the time to interview me." The answer is (A).

199. **C** The passage says that Ms. Kerr has experience "managing diverse groups of people," so eliminate answer choice (A). It says that she has "the ability to crunch the numbers," so get rid of answer choice (D). It also says that she can "make the difficult decisions," so cross off answer choice (B). It does not mention that she has experience managing large budgets. The answer is (C).

200. **A** In general, thank-you notes are sent either by mail or, in some situations, by e-mail. Since there are no headers indicating that this is an e-mail, it must have been sent by mail. The answer is (A).

Transcripts

1. (A) The train doors are open.
   (B) The subway car is in motion.
   (C) The people are all getting off the train.
   (D) I hope the subway car comes.

2. (A) The hallway is full.
   (B) The man is wearing a heavy coat.
   (C) The hallway is long.
   (D) There is plenty of time to call.

3. (A) The car will get a ticket.
   (B) The car is parked near a meter.
   (C) The car is driving down the street.
   (D) The driver is walking in the dark.

4. (A) This seat is reserved.
   (B) He is on a bike.
   (C) The sign is not important.
   (D) Elderly people get priority in this seat.

5. (A) The people are working late.
   (B) The room contains many cubicles.
   (C) The lights in the room are too bright.
   (D) The people need to finish a project.

6. (A) She is paying the clerk.
   (B) She is ordering a hamburger.
   (C) The store sells clothing.
   (D) They both work at the store.

7. (A) She does not like what he's saying.
   (B) He is not telling the truth.
   (C) They are washing a car.
   (D) They are brother and sister.

8. (A) He is asking for directions.
   (B) It is raining today.
   (C) This is the entrance to the museum.
   (D) You can enter the subway here.

9. (A) The seats are empty.
   (B) The baggage will come on this carousel.
   (C) They are waiting for their luggage.
   (D) No one is in the garage.

10. (A) The snow is deep.
    (B) The café is closed.
    (C) The outdoor café is not busy.
    (D) Today is a holiday.

11. (A) The taxi is parked in a garage.
    (B) The taxi is stuck in the snow.
    (C) The taxi is out of gas.
    (D) The taxi is waiting at the traffic light.

12. (A) The man behind the counter owns the store.
    (B) She has her wallet out of her purse.
    (C) They don't have any cigarettes to sell.
    (D) She does not have enough money to pay for her purchase.

13. (A) This store sells umbrellas.
    (B) The display cases are full.
    (C) They are about to close.
    (D) You can pay by cash or check only.

14. (A) The store is having a sale.
    (B) She is eating papaya.
    (C) She is wearing a gray shawl.
    (D) They are offering seventy percent off everything.

15. (A) She is about to pay.
    (B) The doughnuts are fresh.
    (C) She is buying her breakfast.
    (D) The bakery is open.

16. (A) It must be a Saturday.
    (B) They are buying presents.
    (C) The market is crowded.
    (D) They are protesting a tax increase.

17. (A) There is a van at the bus stop.
    (B) He is waiting alone.
    (C) The woman is walking her dog.
    (D) The bus stop is burning.

18. (A) The truck is parked at the curb.
    (B) There is no room in the garage.
    (C) She is leaning against the tree.
    (D) The men are unloading the truck.

19. (A) She is writing a report.
    (B) She is leaning against the board.
    (C) She is asking a question.
    (D) She is driving a car.

20. (A) They are dressed for business.
    (B) They are chatting with each other.
    (C) They are learning to drive.
    (D) They have just seen a movie.

Part II

21. (Woman) How soon can you repair my watch?
    (Man)
    (A) It will be ready next week.
    (B) I will turn off the television.
    (C) Almost two hours ago.

22. (Woman) Where is the nearest bus stop?
    (Man)
    (A) The light has turned red.
    (B) Two blocks in that direction.
    (C) I have forgotten my gloves.

23. (Man) Is your desk drawer locked?
    (Woman)
    (A) I need to purchase some pencils.
    (B) My chair is broken.
    (C) Yes, and here is the key.

24. (Man 1) Who is leading the new software project?
    (Man 2)
    (A) I believe John is in charge.
    (B) I prefer the purple shirt.
    (C) The batteries have gone dead.

25. (Woman) Why did you take a taxi to work this morning?
    (Man)
    (A) No, today is Saturday.
    (B) The subway workers are on strike.
    (C) On Fridays, we are allowed to dress casually.

26. (Woman) When did Mr. Ramirez move to Boston?
    (Man)   (A) His family lives nearby.
            (B) If you keep still, he can't hear you.
            (C) Two years ago.

27. (Man)   How long will the trip last?
    (Woman) (A) Almost three hours.
            (B) I can't run because my leg is injured.
            (C) I can sew it back together for you.

28. (Man 1) Do I need permission to buy this stock?
    (Man 2) (A) Yes, you need to ask the company's lawyers.
            (B) Yes, the building will be closed on Sunday.
            (C) Yes, tomorrow is my sister's birthday.

29. (Woman) When does your son have to go to bed?
    (Man)   (A) The sheets have blue stripes on them.
            (B) At ten o'clock.
            (C) It is too dark to see in this room.

30. (Man)   Whose office is that?
    (Woman) (A) Your computer needs to be turned off.
            (B) The floor measures 12 feet by 14 feet.
            (C) It belongs to Mrs. Alvarez.

31. (Man)   Where do I sign up for a library card?
    (Woman) (A) This book is more than 300 pages long.
            (B) Go to the office at the end of the hall.
            (C) My working visa expires in August.

32. (Man 1) Who is available to fix the printer?
    (Man 2) (A) A maintenance person will be there shortly.
            (B) I'd like to purchase a newspaper.
            (C) My uncle works for the phone company.

33. (Woman) May I borrow your stapler?
    (Man)   (A) I have to order more paper clips.
            (B) Please return it shortly.
            (C) The loan carries a 7 percent interest rate.

34. (Man)   How tall is that building?
    (Woman) (A) I am late for basketball tryouts.
            (B) Deliveries must be dropped off in the back.
            (C) I think it has 45 stories.

35. (Man)   Did you hear about Rosa's sister?
    (Woman) (A) I think the airplane is late.
            (B) It's almost five-thirty.
            (C) Is she all right?

36. (Man 1)　How much is this coupon worth?
　　(Man 2)　(A)　It expires on May 31.
　　　　　　(B)　Fifty cents.
　　　　　　(C)　That store doesn't sell batteries.

37. (Woman)　What is the town's ZIP code?
　　(Man)　(A)　I wish the temperature was warmer.
　　　　　　(B)　It is 48392.
　　　　　　(C)　Please do not run alongside the pool.

38. (Woman)　What is in this sandwich?
　　(Man)　(A)　Ham, cheese, lettuce, and tomato.
　　　　　　(B)　Either one is fine with me.
　　　　　　(C)　I like this design on the plate.

39. (Man)　Where are you going for vacation?
　　(Woman)　(A)　I am moving to a new apartment.
　　　　　　(B)　We are going to the beach.
　　　　　　(C)　I loaned my sunglasses to Jorge.

40. (Man 1)　What is the problem with your credit card?
　　(Man 2)　(A)　When I tried to make a purchase, it was rejected.
　　　　　　(B)　The bank is closed for the federal holiday.
　　　　　　(C)　Mr. Ortiz called in sick today.

41. (Woman)　When will I receive your company's prospectus?
　　(Man)　(A)　I would prefer to go alone.
　　　　　　(B)　Maria views this problem differently than I do.
　　　　　　(C)　In two to three weeks.

42. (Man)　How many people are going to the conference?
　　(Woman)　(A)　Miami is very rainy this time of year.
　　　　　　(B)　A total of 51, including the secretaries.
　　　　　　(C)　I am afraid I have misplaced my purse.

43. (Man)　Does this blouse go with this skirt?
　　(Woman)　(A)　I think they look great together.
　　　　　　(B)　Geoffrey's apartment is on the second floor.
　　　　　　(C)　My sleeves are too long.

44. (Man 1)　Has this milk gone bad?
　　(Man 2)　(A)　I don't think my supervisor likes me.
　　　　　　(B)　Yes, I don't think it smells very good.
　　　　　　(C)　No, I shouldn't eat cookies.

45. (Woman)　What is your dog's name?
　　(Man)　(A)　My brother gave it to me.
　　　　　　(B)　I wish I had some mustard.
　　　　　　(C)　We call him Sparky.

46. (Woman) Why shouldn't I buy this house?
    (Man) (A) The roof has a leak.
          (B) Please park your car around the corner.
          (C) I like the fence that you built.

47. (Man) When will the next board meeting be held?
    (Woman) (A) I don't think this book is interesting.
            (B) We will gather again in July.
            (C) Look in the closet on the top shelf.

48. (Woman) Is the elevator broken?
    (Man) (A) Yes, please take the stairs instead.
          (B) Yes, the water is unsafe for drinking.
          (C) Yes, it is an endangered species.

49. (Woman) Do you recommend this stock?
    (Man) (A) No, my grandfather is in the hospital.
          (B) No, the wheels are too close together.
          (C) No, I think it will be worth much less next year.

50. (Man 1) How can you stay in such great shape?
    (Man 2) (A) There is a gym in my building.
            (B) That circular saw is on sale at the hardware store.
            (C) The floor measures 200 square feet.

PART III

51. (Man) How did the softball game go last night? Did we win?
    (Woman) No. The Tokigo Corporation's team beat us. We didn't have a good pitcher.
    (Man) I knew I should have gone to the game. I'm a great pitcher. Now I feel like I let the company team down.

52. (Woman) The taxi is waiting downstairs. Do you have your ticket?
    (Man) I can't seem to find it. I thought it was in my briefcase, but now it's not here.
    (Woman) I hope it didn't go out with the trash!

53. (Man 1) The construction on Adams Street is blocking my route to work.
    (Man 2) Isn't it annoying? It took me an extra 10 minutes to drive through Martindale Park this morning.
    (Man 1) I wish I could say that! It took me three times as long as that to get through the park.

54. (Man)   Please tell Dr. Hsu that I've been taking the antibiotics she prescribed for 10 days, but I don't feel any better.

(Woman)   That's too bad. I'll ask her to prescribe something stronger for you, and then I'll fax the prescription to your pharmacy.

(Man)   Good. When can I go pick it up?

55. (Woman)   Hello. I was at the 7 P.M. showing of *Castaway* last night, and I think I dropped my wallet on the floor. Did anyone find it?

(Man)   Let me check. *(Pause.)* Yes, it looks like one of our employees did find a wallet last night.

(Woman)   Great. I'll be there in 15 minutes to pick it up!

56. (Man)   What stop is this?

(Woman)   6th Avenue. The bus won't stop again until 8th Avenue.

(Man)   Oh, no! I was supposed to get off at 5th Avenue.

57. (Woman)   Did you get the message from Linda Kerr?

(Man)   No, I haven't checked my voicemail yet. What did she say?

(Woman)   It looks like the conference call has to be rescheduled. The West Coast office is having problems with their telephone system and can't connect to the call.

58. (Woman)   Hi, Bob? This is Alyssa in accounting. I need to ask you about the check request you submitted yesterday.

(Man)   The one for Andrew Chekov?

(Woman)   Right. I couldn't read your handwriting. Is it for $2,400 or $2,900?

59. (Man)   How soon can I have the suit?

(Woman)   Our tailor's not in this morning, sir, but he'll be here tomorrow. You can have the suit first thing on Wednesday.

(Man)   I'll be in at 11 to get it, then.

60. (Man)   Did you read the financial section of the paper today?

(Woman)   Yes. Things don't look good for Gentech, do they?

(Man)   Not if the allegations of insider trading are true.

61. (Man)   How are things going at the Bemidji office, Lisa?

(Woman)   Just fine. We've been installing a new computer system, so that's been causing some billing delays. But everything else is running smoothly.

(Man)   That's good to hear. I was afraid the Bemidji office might be having some of the same problems with employee retention that the Appleton office is.

62. (Woman) How much will you charge to drive me to the airport?

 (Man) The flat fee is $40, plus tolls and tip, ma'am. Do you have any luggage?

 (Woman) Just this carry-on. I need to go to Terminal D to catch the shuttle to Boston.

63. (Woman) This is the dispatcher. I need you to come pick up a delivery for Allerton Gardens. How long will it take you to get back to the warehouse?

 (Man) About 20 minutes. I'm driving down the Kennedy Parkway right by the convention center.

 (Woman) Great. They need it within an hour. We'll see you in a little while.

64. (Man) Excuse me. Can you tell me how much this pen costs?

 (Woman) The Excelsior III? It's $400, sir.

 (Man) Can you have it sent to my room? My name is Aaron Daniels, and I'm in room 511.

65. (Man 1) What do you want for lunch? I was thinking about Thai food.

 (Man 2) I had Thai yesterday. How about pizza?

 (Man 1) I'm trying to cut down on cholesterol. Let's order sandwiches from Lenny's.

66. (Woman) Can you tell me what the conductor said? I couldn't hear because of the static.

 (Man) I couldn't hear either. I hope there are no station changes.

 (Woman) I know. I'm already late for work, so I hope we don't get delayed any more.

67. (Man) How was your weekend, Nancy?

 (Woman) Not too good. I was about to leave for a canoeing trip on Saturday morning, when the apartment above mine leaked dirty water into my kitchen. I spent the whole rest of the weekend cleaning up the mess.

 (Man) That's horrible! I hope your renter's insurance covers the damages.

68. (Man 1) I'd like to return this desk lamp. The switch seems to be broken, because it won't turn on.

 (Man 2) No problem, sir. Do you have your receipt?

 (Man 1) No, I don't. I threw it away as soon as I bought the lamp. Is there any way for me to return the lamp without it?

69. (Man 1) What's wrong, Frank? You look angry.

    (Man 2) I just realized I left my overcoat on the bus. It was so warm I took it off when I got on and put it on the seat next to me. Then I was reading the newspaper and lost track of time. I almost missed my stop and ran off the bus, and forgot the coat.

    (Man 1) I'm sorry. Maybe you can call the company and see if the driver has found the coat. Or maybe another passenger turned it in.

70. (Woman) Did you hear all the noise on the south side of the building? I wonder what all the sirens were about.

    (Man) Susie told me there was a fire in the building across the street. Apparently there was some sort of explosion in the boiler room.

    (Woman) I hope everyone's OK. The building was pretty old, so I bet there was a lot of damage.

71. (Man) Is this Partelli Mattresses? I'd like to order a king-size mattress.

    (Woman) You have the wrong number. This is a private residence, not a store. What number were you trying to reach?

    (Man) 288-2351. Oh, wait—I read the listing wrong. Sorry to have bothered you.

72. (Man 1) I'll have two eggs and cheese on a roll, and a black coffee.

    (Man 2) That will be $3.25. Do you want ketchup on the sandwich?

    (Man 1) No, thanks. But could I have extra salt and pepper, please?

73. (Woman) I'd like a copy of the *Tribune* and a bottle of water, please.

    (Man) $1.50, please. Would you like a bag?

    (Woman) No, thanks.

74. (Woman) How much will it cost to send this package to Eugene, Oregon?

    (Man) Let's see. *(Pause.)* It'll be $5.83 to send it first class, or $12.00 to send it priority. First class should get there in a week, and priority will be there for sure in three days.

    (Woman) It needs to be there by Thursday, so I guess I'll spend the extra money to send it priority.

75. (Woman) Excuse me, can you tell me where the classical music department is?

    (Man) Sure. It's down that aisle and to the left. Can I help you find something?

    (Woman) Yes. I'm looking for the latest release by the group Chanticleer. I think they're a singing group.

76. (Woman) When do you think you'll have the audit of the Phillips account finished?

(Man) I've got most of it done. I'm just waiting for them to fax me a few billing orders. I've already asked them to send them twice.

(Woman) Well, if they don't fax them by the end of the day today, we may miss our deadline.

77. (Man 1) Did you read the e-mail I sent you this morning?

(Man 2) No. We were having server problems, and we lost all the messages that came in or went out of the company between 7 and 10. I've spent all day trying to recover everything I lost.

(Man 1) Well don't worry about the message I sent you. I was only asking where we should have lunch on Friday.

78. (Woman) Ron, I've been looking for the summary of the Woodley case all morning, but I can't seem to find it. Do you know what directory it's in?

(Man) It used to be in the "Active" directory, but I know Keiko rearranged all the directories and subfolders on the C drive last week. You should probably call her and ask what the new organization method is.

(Woman) Thanks. I wondered why nothing looked familiar anymore. I'll give her a call right now.

79. (Man) Excuse me, is this your scarf? It was on the floor next to your seat.

(Woman) Why, no. It's not mine. It must belong to the lady who got off at the last stop.

(Man) I guess I'll give it to the driver, then. Maybe the woman will call about it.

80. (Woman) I just reviewed the new website. There were so many mistakes I stopped counting them! Who should I talk to about fixing the problems?

(Man) Jim Weislak. But he's probably not available right now. The e-commerce software they just installed crashed last night, and he's working frantically to get it back up and running.

(Woman) What a mess. I'm glad I'm not in his position right now.

PART IV

Questions 81–82 refer to the following announcement.

Attention passengers. Due to a police investigation at the 33rd Street station, no 4, 5, or 6 trains are going uptown at this time between 14th Street and Grand Central Station. If you would like to go uptown, please take the N or R to 59th Street, then transfer to the 4, 5, or 6 train going either uptown or downtown. Thank you for your patience.

Questions 83–84 refer to the following speech.

Good afternoon, folks. My name is Shelley and I'll be your server this afternoon. I'd like to suggest that you take advantage of our Lunch Special. It includes a Caesar salad, unlimited breadsticks, three choices of entrée, and a soft drink, all for the bargain price of $6.95. Our entrée choices for today are eggplant parmigiana, chicken-fried steak, and grilled salmon. I'll be back in just a minute to take your drink orders.

Questions 85–86 refer to the following announcement.

Welcome to the Liberty Island–Ellis Island Ferry. Our first stop will be Liberty Island, home of the Statue of Liberty. It will take us approximately 15 minutes to get to Liberty Island. Once we dock, you can disembark for the Statue of Liberty, or stay on the ferry for 10 minutes until we leave for our next stop. Our next stop will be Ellis Island, home of the Ellis Island Museum of Immigrants. We will stay in port at Ellis Island for 10 minutes and then return to port here in New York City. Thank you for riding the Liberty Island–Ellis Island Ferry.

Questions 87–89 refer to the following speech.

Hello everyone. I'm Kent Homburgh, Assistant Director of Human Resources. I wanted to come down to personally invite all of you to the company Holiday Party. We'll be holding it at the Grand Hyatt Hotel in Troy on December 20th. Everyone is invited to bring a spouse or date. We'll have open bar and heavy hors d'oeuvres from seven until 11. Please let Sandy at extension 2132 know if you can come by the end of next week. I'll be sending out an e-mail later today with driving directions to the Grand Hyatt.

Questions 90–92 refer to the following talk.

Welcome to "Washington News," the weekly radio show covering local news for Washington County. I'm Eva Glassberg. Today's special correspondent is Anthony Carbill, who has been covering the scandal in the County Commissioner's office. He'll be updating us on the allegations that Sandra Pinkus has been receiving kick-backs from the contractors she's chosen to work on countywide construction projects. After Anthony's report, we'll hear from Jillian Jaffe, who reports on the proposal for a new charter elementary school. Stay with us.

Questions 93–94 refer to the following speech.

Good evening. I'm so glad you could all join us to celebrate the opening of this exciting new exhibit here at Chesterfield Gallery. Artist Amy Oakes has an unflinching eye for detail and an uncanny ability to make you think and feel at the same time. This collection of photographs, entitled *Snow Days*, explores our relationship with nature within the urban context. One hour from now Amy will explain her vision for the show as a whole and how the individual pieces are integrated. In the meantime, please have some wine and enjoy the exhibit.

Questions 95–97 refer to the following speech.

Good morning. I'm glad to see that you all survived yesterday's inventory marathon. I'd like to introduce you to Jen Sunwoo, who will be working with us for the next three months. Jen is on loan to us from the San Francisco office, where her specialty is Logistics and Inventory Flow. During the next few weeks she's going to be interviewing each of you and reviewing your logs of this year's inventory process to see what we do well and what could be done better. Then she will be presenting us with an action plan to follow to improve our efficiency for next year. Please introduce yourself to Jen sometime today.

Questions 98–100 refer to the following announcement.

Welcome to Arlington Technologies' 4th annual Director Boot Camp. During the next five days you will learn everything you need to know to be a successful director with Arlington. Each day will kick off with a breakfast talk by one of the region's top motivational speakers. At 10 we'll split off into morning seminars, followed by lunch and then afternoon seminars. After dinner we'll be in small groups led by top directors at Arlington, some of whom are successful grads of earlier Director Boot camps. Tonight's program is a mixer designed to help you meet and greet your fellow directors. Don't hesitate to collect as many business cards as you can, and have a wonderful week!

15

The Princeton Review
TOEIC Practice Test 2

PRACTICE TEST 2

Listen to CD #2 Tracks 1–4 to take this test. When you are done with the Listening Comprehension section, do NOT take a break. Go directly to the Reading section and give yourself 75 minutes to take that section.

LISTENING COMPREHENSION

In this section of the test, you will have the chance to show how well you understand spoken English. There are four parts to this section, with special directions for each part.

PART I

Directions: For each question, you will see a picture in your test book and you will hear four statements. The statements will be spoken just one time. They will not be printed in your test book, so you must listen carefully to understand what the speaker says.

When you hear the four statements, look at the picture in your test book and choose the statement that best describes what you see in the picture. Then, on your answer sheet, find the number of the question and mark your answer.

1.

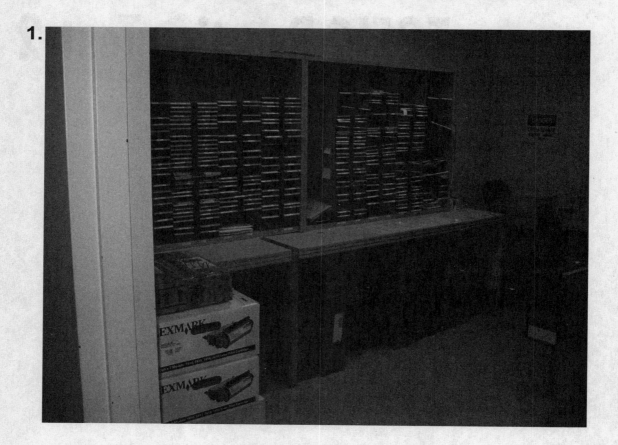

GO ON TO THE NEXT PAGE

2.

GO ON TO THE NEXT PAGE

3.

4.

GO ON TO THE NEXT PAGE ➤

5.

6.

GO ON TO THE NEXT PAGE

7.

8.

GO ON TO THE NEXT PAGE ➤

9.

10.

GO ON TO THE NEXT PAGE ➡

11.

12.

GO ON TO THE NEXT PAGE ➤

13.

GO ON TO THE NEXT PAGE ➡

14.

15.

GO ON TO THE NEXT PAGE ➤

16.

17.

GO ON TO THE NEXT PAGE ➡

18.

19.

GO ON TO THE NEXT PAGE ▶

20.

PART II

Directions: In this part of the test, you will hear a question or statement spoken in English, followed by three responses, also spoken in English. The question or statement and the responses will be spoken just one time. They will not be printed in your test book, so you must listen carefully to understand what the speakers say. You are to choose the best response to each question or statement.

21. Mark your answer on your answer sheet.

22. Mark your answer on your answer sheet.

23. Mark your answer on your answer sheet.

24. Mark your answer on your answer sheet.

25. Mark your answer on your answer sheet.

26. Mark your answer on your answer sheet.

27. Mark your answer on your answer sheet.

28. Mark your answer on your answer sheet.

29. Mark your answer on your answer sheet.

30. Mark your answer on your answer sheet.

31. Mark your answer on your answer sheet.

32. Mark your answer on your answer sheet.

33. Mark your answer on your answer sheet.

34. Mark your answer on your answer sheet.

35. Mark your answer on your answer sheet.

36. Mark your answer on your answer sheet.

37. Mark your answer on your answer sheet.

38. Mark your answer on your answer sheet.

39. Mark your answer on your answer sheet.

40. Mark your answer on your answer sheet.

41. Mark your answer on your answer sheet.

42. Mark your answer on your answer sheet.

43. Mark your answer on your answer sheet.

44. Mark your answer on your answer sheet.

45. Mark your answer on your answer sheet.

46. Mark your answer on your answer sheet.

47. Mark your answer on your answer sheet.

48. Mark your answer on your answer sheet.

49. Mark your answer on your answer sheet.

50. Mark your answer on your answer sheet.

GO ON TO THE NEXT PAGE

Directions: In this part of the test, you will hear thirty short conversations between two people. The conversations will not be printed in your test book. You will hear the conversations only once, so you must listen carefully to understand what the speakers say.

In your test book, you will read a question about each conversation. The questions will be followed by four answers. You are to choose the best answer to each question and mark it on your answer sheet.

51. Where are the people?

   (A) In an elevator.
   (B) In a store.
   (C) In a cafeteria.
   (D) In a factory.

52. Where does the second man work?

   (A) In a laundromat.
   (B) In a mail room.
   (C) In a garage.
   (D) In a supermarket.

53. What has happened to the woman?

   (A) She was robbed.
   (B) She was promoted.
   (C) She was accepted to a university.
   (D) She was fired.

54. Where are the two men?

   (A) At a press conference.
   (B) At the theater.
   (C) At the bank.
   (D) At a basketball game.

55. Why is the woman upset?

   (A) She is locked out of her office.
   (B) She wants to go on a trip.
   (C) She wasn't told something important.
   (D) She has lost a report.

56. In what year was the building's construction completed?

   (A) 1871.
   (B) 1874.
   (C) 1878.
   (D) 1941.

57. What time was the old deadline for receiving a car ride home?

   (A) 7:00 P.M.
   (B) 8:00 P.M.
   (C) 9:00 P.M.
   (D) 10:00 P.M.

58. What is the man planning to do?

   (A) He is going to make a phone call.
   (B) He is going to go for a drive.
   (C) He is going to get something to drink.
   (D) He is going to write a report.

59. Why doesn't the man have a working wristwatch?

   (A) He wants to buy a new one.
   (B) He thinks it is uncomfortable.
   (C) He thinks it is unattractive.
   (D) He is too busy to get it fixed.

GO ON TO THE NEXT PAGE

60. What has Mr. Alfieri been doing?

   (A) He won't return phone calls.
   (B) He can't decide on a final
       version of the document.
   (C) He has been learning how to
       drive a car.
   (D) He has been sleeping too
       much.

61. What happened to the print shop?

   (A) It is closed for the holidays.
   (B) It is no longer operating.
   (C) It is being renovated.
   (D) It burned down.

62. What will the first man's
grandchildren be doing in the
backyard?

   (A) Barbecuing.
   (B) Chopping wood.
   (C) Swimming.
   (D) Building a stone wall.

63. Where is the man going?

   (A) The barber shop.
   (B) The health club.
   (C) The supply closet.
   (D) The Philippines.

64. Where is this conversation taking
place?

   (A) In a department store.
   (B) In a police station.
   (C) In a car dealership.
   (D) In a parking garage.

65. Where is the woman going?

   (A) To a restaurant.
   (B) To London.
   (C) To the airport.
   (D) To the paper towel factory.

66. What is the relationship between the
two men?

   (A) Man 1 works for Man 2.
   (B) Man 2 is Man 1's lawyer.
   (C) Man 1 is Man 2's father.
   (D) Man 1 and Man 2 have just
       met.

67. What is the most likely reason the
woman called Mr. Flores?

   (A) She wants to return his
       newspaper.
   (B) She wants to work for him.
   (C) She wants to go on vacation.
   (D) She wants to go into
       advertising.

68. Based on the conversation, which of
the following is true?

   (A) Man 1 suffers from a severe
       case of hearing loss.
   (B) Man 2 is disappointed
       with the quality of work
       performed by Man 1.
   (C) The two men are not in the
       same room.
   (D) The men are making plans to
       have dinner together.

69. Where does the man work?

   (A) At a movie theater.
   (B) At a car rental office.
   (C) At a hotel.
   (D) At a restaurant.

GO ON TO THE NEXT PAGE

70. What is the man afraid might happen?

(A) The police will make them pay a fine for driving too fast.
(B) The woman will only drive for 45 minutes.
(C) Their car will break down if they drive 55 more miles.
(D) The woman will forget to sign an important document.

71. What is the problem with the woman's order?

(A) They do not have enough fruit to make the item.
(B) The item is not in stock right now.
(C) It must be handmade, so she will have to wait six months to get it.
(D) The item has been discontinued.

72. What are the men doing?

(A) Playing a round of golf.
(B) Working in a steel factory.
(C) Relaxing at the beach.
(D) Repairing a lawn mower.

73. What is the second man about to do?

(A) Sell the first man a watch.
(B) Put a bandage on the first man's foot.
(C) Give the first man a flying lesson.
(D) Repair the first man's shoes.

74. What occupation does the first man have?

(A) Barber.
(B) Policeman.
(C) Surgeon.
(D) Tailor.

75. Where are the two people?

(A) In a vegetable garden.
(B) In a jewelry store.
(C) In a restaurant.
(D) In their kitchen.

76. What happened to the man last week?

(A) He went to a haunted house.
(B) He almost lost the files on his computer.
(C) He bought a bullet-proof vest.
(D) He had a severe head cold.

77. Why has the man come to the building?

(A) He wants to buy a pack of cigarettes.
(B) He has arranged to meet his friend there.
(C) He is building a new flight of stairs.
(D) He is applying for a job as a security guard.

78. What is the woman about to do?

(A) She is going on a trip.
(B) She is going to retire.
(C) She is going to have a baby.
(D) She is going to law school.

79. What does the man think is wrong with the plant?

(A) It is not getting enough sunshine.
(B) It is too large.
(C) It is leaking on the carpet.
(D) It needs to be transplanted into a larger pot.

GO ON TO THE NEXT PAGE ➡

80. What is the woman's advice to the man?

(A) She thinks the man should buy some ties.
(B) She thinks the man should think about quitting.
(C) She thinks the man should ignore the rule.
(D) She thinks the man should complain to his supervisor.

PART IV

Directions: In this part of the test, you will hear several short talks. Each will be spoken just one time. They will not be printed in your test book, so you must listen carefully to understand and remember what is said.

In your test book, you will read two or more questions about each short talk. The questions will be followed by four answers. You are to choose the best answer to each question and mark it on your answer sheet.

---

81. The person making this announcement is most likely which of the following?

(A) A radio announcer.
(B) An airline pilot.
(C) A train conductor.
(D) A professional actor.

82. How many minutes do passengers have left to board the train?

(A) 3 minutes.
(B) 6 minutes.
(C) 7 minutes.
(D) 8 minutes.

83. A person getting off at Latrobe would get off before a passenger getting off at which of the following stops?

(A) Bensonville.
(B) Sheiner.
(C) North Caldwell.
(D) Tewkheim.

84. What is the destination of the bus?

(A) Washington, D.C.
(B) Washington State.
(C) New York City.
(D) Idaho.

85. How many stops will the bus make before it reaches its destination?

(A) Six.
(B) Two.
(C) One.
(D) None.

86. Which of the following is permitted on the bus?

(A) Smoking.
(B) Listening to loud music.
(C) Watching movies.
(D) Drinking alcohol.

GO ON TO THE NEXT PAGE

87. Who is most likely to be making this announcement?

(A) A receptionist at a small company.
(B) An executive assistant at a large corporation.
(C) An accountant at a shipping company.
(D) A lawyer at a legal firm.

88. What type of business is Fast Express?

(A) A gift-wrapping service.
(B) A telephone answering service.
(C) A shipping company.
(D) An events planner.

89. Where is this story most likely to be heard?

(A) On a television broadcast.
(B) In a business press conference.
(C) Over a public-address system.
(D) On a voicemail message.

90. How much money did the man steal?

(A) $15,000.
(B) $30,000.
(C) $32,000.
(D) $100,000.

91. Who discovered the thefts?

(A) The man's employer.
(B) The Staten Island police.
(C) Gregory Navarro.
(D) A government auditor.

92. Where would you be most likely to hear this announcement?

(A) On the subway.
(B) In a fast food restaurant.
(C) On a telephone line.
(D) In an airport waiting area.

93. Who is most likely to be speaking?

(A) A recorded voice.
(B) A live operator.
(C) A live police officer.
(D) A recorded train operator.

94. What type of organization is Overcoming Challenges?

(A) A corporation.
(B) A charity.
(C) A government agency.
(D) A fraternal organization.

95. Who is most likely to be the audience of this speech?

(A) Professional recruiters for top colleges.
(B) Professors who recruited teachers to work for Overcoming Challenges.
(C) Potential employees of Overcoming Challenges.
(D) People who have given money to Overcoming Challenges.

96. What age group of people does Overcoming Challenges help?

(A) Infants.
(B) Children.
(C) Adolescents.
(D) Elderly people.

GO ON TO THE NEXT PAGE

97. Where is Jenny Rivera planning to go to college in the fall?

(A) Rutgers University.
(B) Hunter College.
(C) Washington University.
(D) Parks College.

98. What are Dan Conlon's qualifications?

(A) He is a customer.
(B) He is a top salesman.
(C) He is a high-school teacher.
(D) He is a webmaster.

99. Instead of selling, what does Dan Conlon do?

(A) Tricks the customer with half-truths.
(B) Pressures the customer into buying.
(C) Teaches his customers about the product.
(D) Listens to lessons about sales.

100. Why would a person go to Dan Conlon's website?

(A) To get help using Dan Conlon's methods.
(B) To find customers.
(C) To meet potential dates.
(D) To learn to use Dan Conlon's software.

STOP the recording

READING

In this section of the test, you will have a chance to show how well you understand written English. There are three parts to this section, with special directions for each part.

PART V

Directions: Questions 101–140 are incomplete sentences. Four words or phrases, marked (A), (B), (C), (D), are given beneath each sentence. You are to choose the one word or phrase that best completes the sentence. Then, on your answer sheet, find the number of the question and mark your answer.

101. There were few vegetables at the supermarket because the ------ truck broke down.

(A) program
(B) profane
(C) profile
(D) produce

102. Please arrive ------, because the seminar will begin at 9 a.m. sharp.

(A) promptly
(B) prompt
(C) prompted
(D) prompting

103. Individuals should be extra ------ of investing in companies with negative earnings.

(A) cautiousness
(B) caution
(C) cautiously
(D) cautious

104. In order to obtain access to the conference room, all employees must ------ their identification cards.

(A) presentation
(B) present
(C) presented
(D) presently

105. My briefcase is locked, and I've ------ the combination.

(A) forgetful
(B) forgettably
(C) forgotten
(D) forget

106. For further detail regarding our calculations, please consult the figures in the ------ at the end of this report.

(A) table of contents
(B) title page
(C) prologue
(D) appendix

GO ON TO THE NEXT PAGE

107. During times of economic uncertainty, bond prices can become quite ------.

   (A) voluntary
   (B) volatile
   (C) voluminous
   (D) volcanic

108. Our analysis indicates that oil prices will ------ within six months and then head steadily downward.

   (A) peak
   (B) bottom
   (C) drop
   (D) disappear

109. The company's CEO was handsome and friendly, but he also possessed great business ------.

   (A) regimen
   (B) vitamin
   (C) acumen
   (D) banishment

110. Managers must learn to ------ between employees who work hard and those who do not.

   (A) differentiate
   (B) commiserate
   (C) substantiate
   (D) appreciate

111. On Tuesday, the travel ------ met to discuss changing the reimbursement process.

   (A) compassion
   (B) committee
   (C) commerce
   (D) commitment

112. In case of fire, all employees are advised to avoid the elevator and go to the ------.

   (A) doorway
   (B) freeway
   (C) stairway
   (D) highway

113. Soft-drink companies lowered their costs considerably when they shifted from steel to ------ cans.

   (A) aloof
   (B) allusion
   (C) aluminum
   (D) allude

114. My tax return was very confusing until my accountant ------ it for me.

   (A) testified
   (B) justified
   (C) nullified
   (D) clarified

115. Our spokesperson will now ------ the added benefits of the updated version of our product.

   (A) elucidate
   (B) demonstrate
   (C) abdicate
   (D) concentrate

116. The office decor is much too ------; I wish it was just a bit more exciting.

   (A) arbitrary
   (B) customary
   (C) ordinary
   (D) secondary

GO ON TO THE NEXT PAGE

117. The managing director usually
------ authority to his three closest
assistants when he goes on
vacation.

(A) delegates
(B) deletes
(C) delays
(D) deludes

118. It's ------ to attempt to launch a new
product without first conducting
extensive market research.

(A) feeble
(B) faithful
(C) futile
(D) fatal

119. Congresspeople and senators are
responsible for passing ------ and
sending it to the President for
signature.

(A) laceration
(B) legislation
(C) legalization
(D) limitation

120. Sadly, since the two sides have
not made any progress in their
negotiation, they appear to be at an
------.

(A) impression
(B) information
(C) importance
(D) impasse

121. Thanks to the company's budget
------, we will be able to give out
larger bonuses this year.

(A) surprise
(B) surplus
(C) sermon
(D) surname

122. After the stock price went below
$1.00, Mr. Stevenson was almost
------.

(A) pointless
(B) penniless
(C) pitiless
(D) populace

123. In order to be promoted, each
employee must ------ a graduate
program in business.

(A) apprehend
(B) ascend
(C) amend
(D) attend

124. Company ------ require all personnel
to wear business clothes to work.

(A) declines
(B) redlines
(C) guidelines
(D) sidelines

125. Our factories are far too outdated;
we must raise some money in order
to ------ them.

(A) plagiarize
(B) modernize
(C) exercise
(D) pulverize

126. The bulb in our ------ has burned
out, so we will have to wait until it is
replaced.

(A) projector
(B) projecting
(C) projects
(D) projected

GO ON TO THE NEXT PAGE

127. Any employees who are convicted of a felony will be ------ to the fullest extent of the law.

(A) placated
(B) implicated
(C) executed
(D) prosecuted

128. If you take the time to research your investments, you are likely to ------ from them.

(A) profits
(B) profiting
(C) profit
(D) profitably

129. I'm not convinced that your idea is the best ------ to follow at this time.

(A) strategy
(B) synergy
(C) salary
(D) secretary

130. This bold new idea represents a ------ shift in this company's business model.

(A) marginal
(B) manipulate
(C) maneuver
(D) monumental

131. I am ------ to announce that our company has finally reported a profitable quarter.

(A) please
(B) pleases
(C) pleased
(D) pleasing

132. The president and the senior vice president, who went to the same university, ------ late to the meeting.

(A) was
(B) were
(C) is
(D) to be

133. The company's accounting scandal was ------ to many of its stockholders.

(A) alarm
(B) alarmed
(C) alarms
(D) alarming

134. We are skeptical ------ the new CEO's ability to turn the company around.

(A) to
(B) of
(C) through
(D) above

135. Before we proceed any further, I would like to ------ your attention to our next chart.

(A) direct
(B) directs
(C) director
(D) direction

136. Never attempt to leave the building with computer equipment without first ------ with Security.

(A) check
(B) checks
(C) checked
(D) checking

GO ON TO THE NEXT PAGE

137. The ------ of our newspaper is
approximately 500,000.

(A) calculation
(B) circulation
(C) reciprocation
(D) incarceration

138. Could you please ------ me to the
new sales director?

(A) interject
(B) intermingle
(C) introduce
(D) introvert

139. Do you have an ------ for why we
failed to meet our sales quotas this
month?

(A) expiration
(B) explanation
(C) expedition
(D) exposition

140. Before we claim the rest of our
baggage, there is something we
need ------ at the customs desk.

(A) have declared
(B) are declaring
(C) to declare
(D) declaration

GO ON TO THE NEXT PAGE

PART VI

Directions: In **Questions 141–160,** each sentence has four words or phrases underlined. The four underlined parts of the sentence are marked (A), (B), (C), (D). You are to identify the one underlined word or phrase that should be corrected or rewritten. Then, on your answer sheet, find the number of the question and mark your answer.

141. In the case of a fire or other emergency, please go at the nearest exit.
        A   B   C   D

142. If you waited here, Mrs. Johnson will see you in just a moment.
   A   B   C   D

143. Every six months, each employee is gave a performance review by the supervisor.
   A   B   C   D

144. Please review the document and to call me if you have any questions or comments.
        A   B   C   D

145. I have sorry, but I do not have the contact information that you requested.
   A   B   C   D

146. If you refinance your home now, you are sure to earn a considerably profit.
   A   B C   D

147. Investments in government bonds can often be used to make up from losses in the stock market.
      A   B   C   D

148. This report needs to be rewritten, because assistant manager has not given his approval.
             A   B   C   D

149. For our next discussion, I would like to direct your attention over the chart on page 25.
     A   B   C   D

150. Each governing board member for the World Bank has to sell all of his stock holdings before taking office.
                     A   B   C   D

151. If you are interested, copies of my book can purchase at the counter at the front of the store.
     A   B   C   D

152. At my opinion, this applicant is not qualified to perform the duties of the job.
   A   B   C   D

GO ON TO THE NEXT PAGE

153. We have deciding not to give holiday bonuses this year until we have the opportunity to
            A   B   C   D
 re-examine the finances.

154. I can meet with you on Friday, unless the person I was supposed to meet just called to cancel
               A   B   C
 our appointment.
     D

155. We will have to discussing your proposal with the president before we can give you an
    A   B   C   D
 answer.

156. Mr. Gonzalez will not be able to meet with you today, because he already has too much
                A   B   C   D
 appointments.

157. By signing this document, you agree not to withdraw any funds when the date indicated on
    A   B   C   D
 page 45.

158. A composite list of all of the products our company offers are available on our website.
             A   B C   D

159. During the last recession, consumer preferred to save their money rather than buy expensive
   A   B   C   D
 products.

160. If you are looking for extra tax forms, you can find it at your local post office.
    A   B   C   D

GO ON TO THE NEXT PAGE

Directions: Questions 161–200 are based on a selection of reading materials, such as notices, letters, forms, newspaper and magazine articles, and advertisements. You are to choose the one best answer (A), (B), (C), or (D) to each question. Then, on your answer sheet, find the number of the question and mark your answer. Answer all questions following each reading selection on the basis of what is stated or implied in that selection.

Questions 161–162 refer to the following notice.

*Because it takes 40 minutes to prepare, please notify your server when you place your dinner order that you would like a Molten Chocolate Cake For Two for dessert.

161. Where would this notice be likely to be found?

(A) In a newspaper editorial.
(B) In a restaurant menu.
(C) In a balance statement.
(D) In a train schedule.

162. Why does the cake need to be ordered at the same time as the dinner?

(A) It takes a long time to clean up.
(B) It takes a long time to place the order.
(C) It takes a long time to make.
(D) It takes a long time to eat.

GO ON TO THE NEXT PAGE

Questions 163–165 refer to the following notice.

BUYING A HOUSE

Learn the ins and outs of buying a house at this informational seminar. This dynamic, info-packed seminar will cover mortgages, pre-qualification, dealing with real estate agents and lawyers, making a bid, inspection, closing, and much more! The seminar will be led by successful real-estate lawyer Gary Willis. There is no fee for this seminar.

Saturday, April 23
1-5 pm
Radisson North Oaks
Registration required.
314-555-1234

---

163. Where would this notice most likely be found?

(A) In a restaurant menu.
(B) In a newspaper.
(C) In a corporate newsletter.
(D) In a museum catalog.

164. Who is conducting the seminar?

(A) A professional seminar facilitator.
(B) A success coach.
(C) A real estate agent.
(D) A lawyer specializing in housing.

165. How much does it cost to attend the seminar?

(A) $100.
(B) Members of the Radisson North Oaks can attend at a reduced fee.
(C) You can find out by calling 314-555-1234.
(D) Nothing.

GO ON TO THE NEXT PAGE

Patients with allergies to any component of Agarast™ should not take Agarast™. The active ingredient in Agarast™ is isopolyformonin. The inactive ingredients are listed at the end of this leaflet.

The safety and efficacy of Agarast™ has not been established in children younger than 2 years of age.

The side effects of Agarast™ are usually mild.

The list below is NOT a complete list of side effects reported with Agarast™. Your doctor can discuss with you a more complete list of side effects. The most common side effects are listed below:

tiredness   nausea

fainting   stomach (abdominal) pain

dizziness   heartburn

headache   ulcer

fever

Less common side effects include the following:

allergic reactions, including   insomnia
swelling of the face, lips,
tongue, and/or throat   diarrhea

bad/vivid dreams   bruising

hallucinations   edema

restlessness

166. What is Agarast™?

(A) A type of medication.
(B) A type of automobile.
(C) A type of accounting procedure.
(D) A type of software.

167. Is Agarast™ safe for babies younger than 2 years old?

(A) They may have more side effects from taking it than adults will.
(B) It is mostly safe.
(C) The safety for infants has not been determined.
(D) Babies are usually allergic to isopolyformonin.

168. Which of the following side effects of Agarast™ is not listed on the notice?

(A) Bruising.
(B) Nausea.
(C) Restlessness.
(D) Stroke.

GO ON TO THE NEXT PAGE

Questions 169–171 refer to the following article.

Manufacturing Breakthrough Alters Plastic Production

Rochester, NY—A breakthrough in the manufacturing process of plastic medical supplies will revolutionize production of these parts, a spokesperson for Northland Manufacturing Company said in a press conference yesterday. Judith Lei, Northland's press director, stated that engineers at the Rochester-area Northland plant had been working on a method of putting the plastics through several different heating and cooling stages for several years. The research has finally paid off in a more streamlined, efficient process that will also produce more flexible parts that are stronger and more leak-resistant.

This new process could revolutionize the production of medical parts, and shoot Northland to the top of the industry. In fact, this process could lower the prices of certain medical parts, making them more accessible worldwide, while simultaneously increasing Northland's per-part profit. "This is a win-win situation for everyone," said Ms. Lei. "We have hopes that increased profits will allow us to focus on more research to streamline production of even more parts, thereby saving lives throughout the world."

Northland Manufacturing Company is a privately held company. A spokesperson for Northland's main competitor, IGD Industries, could not be reached for comment.

---

169. What is the main component of the new process?

(A) A press release detailing the changes.
(B) A new chemical composition of the parts.
(C) A series of hot and cold treatments of the plastic.
(D) Increasing efficiency of production.

170. What is Judith Lei's job?

(A) She represents Northland to the public.
(B) She develops new manufacturing processes for Northland.
(C) She competes against IGD Industries.
(D) She compiles industrywide research.

171. Who will benefit most from Northland's new process?

(A) Northland itself and health consumers.
(B) Northland's stockholders.
(C) IGD Industries.
(D) The worldwide medical parts industry.

GO ON TO THE NEXT PAGE

Ask about our soup of the day.

There is a $2 fee for delivery of an order totaling less than $15.

We accept cash, Visa, MasterCard, and American Express.

We do not accept personal checks.

For corporate catering accounts, please call our catering manager at 212-444-1234.

172. This notice is most likely posted on a menu from what type of restaurant?

(A) Fine dining.
(B) Sushi.
(C) Diner.
(D) Tea salon.

173. What will the catering manager do?

(A) Help set up a corporate account.
(B) Make a different soup every day.
(C) Write a personal check.
(D) Waive the fee for delivery of a small order.

GO ON TO THE NEXT PAGE

MEMO

TO: All 4th-Floor Employees

Human Resources is organizing a trip to see the musical *Chicago* at the Houston Central Amphitheater on Thursday, October 21. Tickets are discounted for our group from a regular price of $50 to our special rate of $30. Each employee may bring one guest at this special rate. We need to reserve our tickets by October 4, so please call Linda in Human Resources by the end of the day on October 3 to let her know how many tickets you need. This should be a really fun event for everyone on the 4th Floor!

174. When does an employee need to RSVP for this event?

(A) By October 3.
(B) By October 4.
(C) By October 21.
(D) Before the end of the week.

176. How much does each ticket cost at the special rate?

(A) $21.
(B) $22.
(C) $30.
(D) $50.

175. Where is the musical being staged?

(A) Chicago.
(B) Houston.
(C) Human Resources.
(D) New York.

GO ON TO THE NEXT PAGE

Questions 177–179 refer to the following notice.

Corporate Air Travel Policy

All employees are required to book work-related air travel through our travel agency, Cartright Tours. Our dedicated agent at Cartright is Angela Baumann. She can be reached by phone at 202-555-4321 or by e-mail at angela@cartrighttours.com.

Employees will be assigned the most economical air travel within the following guidelines for length of trip and number of stops:

300 miles—direct (nonstop)

301–500 miles—maximum of 1 stop

501–1000 miles—maximum of 2 stops

more than 1000 miles—maximum of 3 stops

177. How can employees book business air travel?

(A) Only through the approved agency.
(B) With any agency they choose.
(C) Only by booking online through a discount website.
(D) By any method they choose.

178. How can Angela Baumann be reached?

(A) By phone only.
(B) By fax only.
(C) By phone or fax.
(D) By phone or e-mail.

179. A trip of 745 miles could have a maximum of how many stops?

(A) Three.
(B) Two.
(C) One.
(D) None.

GO ON TO THE NEXT PAGE

IMPORTANT INFORMATION

CHECK-IN AND BOARDING REQUIREMENTS: Passengers not checked in and at the designated gate area at least 15 minutes before scheduled departure time for domestic flights (except Hawaii); 30 minutes for flights to/from Hawaii, Canada, Alaska, Mexico and the Caribbean, and 60 minutes for all other International flights may have their pre-assigned seat assignment and reserved space canceled and will not be eligible for boarding compensation. Boarding passes for all flights may be obtained at an E-Service Center airport kiosk or at any check-in position.

---

180. Where is this notice most likely to be found?

(A) On an airline ticket.
(B) On a medicine bottle.
(C) On a restaurant menu.
(D) On an instruction manual.

181. What could happen if a passenger is not checked in for a flight in time?

(A) The passenger will have to leave his or her luggage at the destination airport.
(B) The passenger will only be eligible to take a domestic flight.
(C) The passenger will be fined.
(D) The passenger will not be able to take that flight.

182. For which flights does a passenger need to be at the airport the earliest?

(A) Flights to Europe.
(B) Flights to Hawaii.
(C) Flights to Canada.
(D) Flights to California.

183. Before a passenger boards an airplane, he or she needs to do which of the following?

(A) Go to Hawaii.
(B) Claim his or her luggage.
(C) Read the information on the safety card.
(D) Check in for the flight.

GO ON TO THE NEXT PAGE

Question **184–186** refer to the following schedule.

Trailston
Hamilton
Norwalk Junction
to New York City (Penn Station)
Effective September 22, 2002

Trailston	Hamilton	Norwalk Jct.	New York
A.M.	**A.M.**	**A.M.**	**A.M.**
5:40	5:55	6:10	6:30
6:10	6:25	6:40	7:00
6:40	6:55	7:10	7:30
7:10	7:25	7:40	8:00
7:40	7:55	8:10	8:30
8:10	8:25	8:40	9:00
8:40	8:55	9:10	9:30
9:10	9:25	9:40	10:00
9:40	9:55	10:10	10:30
10:10	10:25	10:40	11:00
10:40	10:55	11:10	11:30
P.M.	**P.M.**	**P.M.**	**P.M.**
4:40	4:55	5:10	5:30
5:10	5:25	5:40	6:00
5:40	5:55	6:10	6:30
6:10	6:25	6:40	7:00
6:40	6:55	7:10	7:30
7:10	7:25	7:40	8:00
7:40	7:55	8:10	8:30
8:10	8:25	8:40	9:00
8:40	8:55	9:10	9:30

GO ON TO THE NEXT PAGE

184. This is most likely a schedule for which type of travel?

(A) Taxi.
(B) Airplane.
(C) Subway.
(D) Train.

185. To get to New York by 10 A.M., what time would you have to leave Hamilton?

(A) 8:55.
(B) 9:10.
(C) 9:25.
(D) 9:55.

186. How long does the trip from Norwalk Junction to New York take?

(A) 50 minutes.
(B) 35 minutes.
(C) 30 minutes.
(D) 20 minutes.

GO ON TO THE NEXT PAGE

LOST: BRIEFCASE

Dark brown leather briefcase lost 3/6 at the bus stop in the 1200 block of Carter Avenue.

$1000 reward for return with all contents intact. No questions asked.

Call 312-444-1234 and leave a message for Ned.

187. Who would be most likely to have found the briefcase?

(A) A person who cleans Ned's office.
(B) A person who gets on the bus where Ned does.
(C) A person who fixes Ned's car.
(D) A person who delivers Ned's mail.

188. How much will the reward be if the briefcase is returned?

(A) $1000, but only if the briefcase is returned empty.
(B) $1000, but only if the briefcase is returned with everything still in it.
(C) $1200, but only if the briefcase is returned empty.
(D) $1200, but only if the briefcase is returned with everything still in it.

GO ON TO THE NEXT PAGE

Questions 189–191 refer to the following article.

Career Corner

Ajax Industries announced a major promotion in its legal department. John Baxter will become Chief Counsel for Ajax on March 4th. Baxter was formerly lead counsel for the plastics division of Ajax, a position that will now be filled by Susana Ling-Wong.

****

Mortensen and Long, the international marketing firm, has hired Anna Hoxby to head the new Scandinavian division. Ms. Hoxby has been a marketing consultant with her own firm for the past 10 years.

---

189. This notice would be most likely to appear in which section of the newspaper?

(A) The classified ads.
(B) The business section.
(C) The stock market listings.
(D) The real estate section.

190. Who is Susana Ling-Wong replacing?

(A) John Baxter
(B) Anna Hoxby
(C) Mortensen Long
(D) Chief Counsel for Ajax Industries

191. What was Anna Hoxby's job before she was hired by Mortensen and Long?

(A) She was head of the Scandinavian division.
(B) She owned her own consulting business.
(C) She was a lawyer.
(D) She managed the plastics division.

GO ON TO THE NEXT PAGE

SPECIAL HOLIDAY HOURS

This branch will have special holiday hours this week in honor of New Year's Eve and New Year's Day.

Monday	Dec 30	9 A.M. to 5 P.M.
Tuesday	Dec 31	9 A.M. to 3 P.M.
Wednesday	Jan 1	closed
Thursday	Jan 2	9 A.M. to 5 P.M.
Friday	Jan 3	9 A.M. to 5 P.M.

---

192. On which day will the branch close early?

(A) Monday.
(B) Tuesday.
(C) Wednesday.
(D) Thursday.

193. On which day will the branch be closed entirely?

(A) The first day of December.
(B) The last day of December.
(C) The first day of January.
(D) The last day of January.

194. What is the first day on which a customer can make a transaction in January?

(A) January 1.
(B) January 2.
(C) January 3.
(D) January 4.

GO ON TO THE NEXT PAGE

E-Sheet Workshop

All employees are invited to attend a special in-house workshop on the new E-Sheet spreadsheet software. Each session will be two hours long and will focus on the basics of the software. (Advanced sessions will be conducted after the new year.) There will be three sessions to choose from: Monday, November 10, 8–10 A.M.; Tuesday, November 11, 1–3 P.M.; and Thursday, November 13, 3–5 P.M. Space is limited. To attend, please call Kim Yoshigi-Myers at extension 5432.

---

195. What will be taught at the workshop?

(A) How to use a computer program.
(B) How to fold sheets.
(C) How to use an extension cord.
(D) How to schedule a workshop.

196. When could an employee attend a workshop session?

(A) November 10 from 1–3 P.M.
(B) November 11 from 8–10 A.M.
(C) November 13 from 1–3 P.M.
(D) November 13 from 3–5 P.M.

197. How many employees can attend these workshops?

(A) A limited number.
(B) The entire staff.
(C) Only those invited by Kim Yoshigi-Myers.
(D) Only those who know how to use E-Sheet software.

GO ON TO THE NEXT PAGE

Questions 198–200 refer to the following e-mail.

To: All Employees
From: Margaret O'Hanlon
CC: Dante Burgess
Subject: Lunch Orders

This is a reminder that everyone needs to let us know when you order in lunch for delivery. When you don't let us know, the delivery person comes to reception and there's no way for Dante or me to track down the order. When you place an order, please send me (MargaretO) and Dante (DanteB) an e-mail with the subject line "Lunch" and the name of the restaurant. In the message text put your name and extension, so we can call you when the food comes.

If everyone follows this system you'll all get your food a lot faster, and Dante and I will be able to get all our work done.

Thanks!

Margaret and Dante at the Reception Desk

198. What is the problem with ordering lunch?

(A) Employees are charging lunch to the corporate account without permission.
(B) The receptionists don't know who ordered from what restaurant.
(C) Some of the restaurants do not accept e-mail orders.
(D) Extra-long lunches are decreasing employee productivity.

199. What is Margaret's job?

(A) Food-delivery person.
(B) E-mail administrator.
(C) Receptionist.
(D) Intern.

200. Who is Dante Burgess?

(A) Receptionist with Margaret O'Hanlon.
(B) E-mail administrator with Margaret O'Hanlon.
(C) President of the company.
(D) Chief Counsel for the firm.

STOP

16

The Princeton Review
TOEIC Practice Test 2:
Answers and
Explanations

ANSWER KEY FOR PRACTICE TEST 2

LISTENING COMPREHENSION

1. B	36. C
2. C	37. B
3. A	38. C
4. D	39. A
5. B	40. A
6. C	41. B
7. B	42. A
8. A	43. C
9. D	44. B
10. B	45. A
11. B	46. C
12. A	47. B
13. A	48. A
14. C	49. C
15. B	50. C
16. B	51. A
17. C	52. B
18. D	53. B
19. B	54. A
20. A	55. C
21. C	56. C
22. A	57. B
23. A	58. C
24. B	59. D
25. B	60. B
26. A	61. B
27. B	62. C
28. C	63. C
29. A	64. D
30. C	65. C
31. A	66. C
32. B	67. B
33. C	68. C
34. A	69. D
35. B	70. A

71. B	108. A
72. A	109. C
73. D	110. A
74. A	111. B
75. C	112. C
76. B	113. C
77. B	114. D
78. C	115. B
79. A	116. C
80. B	117. A
81. C	118. C
82. A	119. B
83. C	120. D
84. A	121. B
85. D	122. B
86. C	123. D
87. A	124. C
88. C	125. B
89. A	126. A
90. D	127. D
91. D	128. C
92. C	129. A
93. A	130. D
94. B	131. C
95. D	132. B
96. C	133. D
97. A	134. B
98. B	135. A
99. C	136. D
100. A	137. B
	138. C

READING

101. D	139. B
102. A	140. C
103. D	141. D
104. B	142. B
105. C	143. C
106. D	144. B
107. B	145. A
	146. D

147. C	186. D
148. C	187. B
149. D	188. B
150. A	189. B
151. C	190. A
152. A	191. B
153. A	192. B
154. B	193. C
155. B	194. B
156. D	195. A
157. D	196. D
158. C	197. A
159. B	198. B
160. D	199. C
161. B	200. A
162. C	
163. B	
164. D	
165. D	
166. A	
167. C	
168. D	
169. C	
170. A	
171. A	
172. C	
173. A	
174. A	
175. B	
176. C	
177. A	
178. D	
179. B	
180. A	
181. D	
182. A	
183. D	
184. D	
185. C	

EXPLANATIONS

LISTENING COMPREHENSION

1. **B** The photo shows empty mailboxes. There is no mail and there are no people in the photo. The answer is (B).

2. **C** The sign in the photo shows a bus route. There is no man in the photo, and the sign does not say "Do Not Enter." The answer is (C).

3. **A** The woman is getting into the open door of a taxi. She is not in the driver's seat, and there is no way for us to know whether she can drive or not. The answer is (A).

4. **D** The photo shows people in a magazine store. The store is obviously open, because there are people in it. The store does not sell fruit, only magazines. There is no way for us to know if the man is finding the magazine he wants. The answer is (D).

5. **B** The woman is removing a card from the machine. There is no way to know if her subway pass will function. She is not at a bank, and there is no telephone in the photo. The answer is (B).

6. **C** The woman is pointing at the blackboard with a piece of chalk. There is no way to know if she is explaining a marketing plan. She is the only person in the photo. The answer is (C).

7. **B** The photo shows many different varieties of flowers for sale. Showers are irrelevant to the photo, as are the ingredients of a cake. There is no door in the photo. The answer is (B).

8. **A** The only one of the answer choices that we know *must be true* is that it is not snowing. We do not know what the store is or was, why it was closed, or what the people in the photo do or do not know. The answer is (A).

9. **D** The "fasten seatbelt" sign is turned on. There is no way to tell whether the flight attendant is serving drinks, how long the flight is, or whether the airplane is about to land. The answer is (D).

10. **B** There are both men's and women's shoes in the photo. There is no program in the photo, and no woman's purse. The answer must be (B).

11. **B** The photo shows a fast food restaurant counter with people ordering and waiting for their food. There is no way to know if there are tables to eat at in the restaurant, or how long the food will take to be ready. None of the men is wearing a hat. The answer is (B).

12. **A** The man is wearing a coat and hood for the cold weather. The man is selling pineapples. There is no way to know if all the fruit will be sold or if the man has had any customers. The answer is (A).

13. **A** The woman is typing on a computer keyboard. There is no way to know what relationship the people have. They are not making copies. The answer is (A).

14. **C** They are in a pharmacy in the personal-care aisle. They are not eating lunch. There is no way to know what they want to buy or if they are brother and sister. The answer is (C).

15. **B** The man is sitting at his desk in his office, which is neat and orderly. There is no way to know if his e-mail inbox is full or if his job requires strong math skills. The answer is (B).

16. **B** The people are working together on something written in the notebook. There is no way to know if they are at a conference or if he is a consultant. They are not driving to work. The answer is (B).

17. **C** They have boarded the airplane and are sitting in their seats. They are not at the office and are not folding papers. There is no way to know if they have eaten lunch yet. The answer is (C).

18. **D** The tree is in a park. There are no people in the park. There is no indication of danger from walking. The answer is (D).

19. **B** The view from the window is of a body of water and some buildings. The window is not broken, and there is no indication of wind. There are no people in the photo. The answer is (B).

20. **A** The cars are parked on the street. There are no leaves, people, or dogs in the photo. The answer is (A).

21. **C** The question asks *what*, and the answer is specific. The answer is (C).

22. **A** The question asks *what*, and the answer gives a specific choice. The answer is (A).

23. **A** The question asks *why*, and the answer gives a reason. The answer is (A).

24. **B** The question asks a yes/no question, and the answer responds to that topic. The answer is (B).

25. **B** The question asks *who*, and the answer gives information about a person. The answer is (B).

26. **A** The question asks a yes/no question, and the answer responds to that topic. The answer is (A).

27. **B** The question asks *where*, and the answer gives a location. The answer is (B).

28. **C** The question asks *where*, and the answer gives a location. The answer is (C).

29. **A** The question asks *what*, and the answer is specific. The answer is (A).

30. **C** The question asks *where*, and the answer gives a location. The answer is (C).

31. **A** The question asks *where*, and the answer gives a location. The answer is (A).

32. **B** The question asks *what*, and the answer is specific. The answer is (B).

33. **C** The question asks a yes/no question, and the answer responds to that topic. The answer is (C).

34. **A** The question asks *how many*, and the answer gives a number. The answer is (A).

35. **B** The question asks a yes/no question, and the answer responds to that topic. The answer is (B).

36. **C** The question asks *when*, and the answer responds to that topic. The answer is (C).

37. **B** The question asks *where*, and the answer gives a location. The answer is (B).

38. **C** The question asks *why*, and the answer gives a reason. The answer is (C).

39. **A** The question asks a yes/no question, and the answer responds to that topic. The answer is (A).

40. **A** The question asks a yes/no question, and the answer responds to that topic. The answer is (A).

41. **B** The question asks *what*, and the answer is specific. The answer is (B).

42. **A** The question asks a yes/no question, and the answer responds to that topic. The answer is (A).

43. **C** The question asks about the difference between two items, and the answer gives the difference. The answer is (C).

44. **B** The question asks *what*, and the answer is specific. The answer is (B).

45. **A** The question asks *what*, and the answer gives a suggestion for how to find out the information. The answer is (A).

46. **C** The question asks *where*, and the answer gives a location. The answer is (C).

47. **B** The question asks *why*, and the answer gives a reason. The answer is (B).

48. **A** The question asks *which*, and the answer gives a specific direction. The answer is (A).

49. **C** The question asks a yes/no question, and the answer responds to that topic. The answer is (C).

50. **C** The question asks *where*, and the answer gives a location. The answer is (C).

51. **A** The conversation mentions pushing buttons and different floors, so the people must be in an elevator. The answer is (A).

52. **B** The first man is looking for a package, so he must be in a place where packages are received. Eliminate *laundromat*, *garage*, and *supermarket*, and the answer is (B), mailroom.

53. **B** The woman has a new office and more money, so she must have received a *promotion*. The answer is (B).

54. **A** The men are discussing business returns. They are not at the *theater*, at a *bank*, or at a *game*, so the answer is (A).

55. **C** The woman asks why no one told her that Jenkins would be gone for two weeks. This is *something important*, so the answer is (C).

56. **C** If the building was started in 1871 and finished seven years later, it was finished in 1878. The answer is (C).

57. **B** Staying until 9:00 P.M. is "an hour later," according to the conversation. 9:00 P.M. is an hour later than 8 P.M., so the answer is (B).

58. **C** The man says he is going to get a cup of coffee. Coffee is something to drink, so the answer is (C).

59. **D** The man says, "I can never find enough time to get to the repair shop." This means that he is too busy, so the answer is (D).

60. **B** The man says, "I wish he would make up his mind," so this means he cannot decide. The answer is (B).

61. **B** The woman says, "That place went out of business last month." The answer is (B).

62. **C** The man is "putting in a pool." You swim in a pool, so the answer is (C).

63. **C** Office supplies, such as paper clips, pens, folders, and staplers, are kept in a supply closet. The answer is (C).

64. **D** The woman is paying the man for the time she has parked her car. She must be in a parking *garage*, so the answer is (D).

65. **C** The woman says that she has "to pick up our daughter, who is flying in," which means she is going to the *airport*. The answer is (C).

66. **C** The phrase "your mother and I" is used by a father to speak to a child, and Man 1 is trying to tell Man 2 what decision to make. This indicates that Man 1 is Man 2's father. The answer is (C).

67. **B** The woman wants to talk to Mr. Flores about "the job opening that was advertised." This indicates that she wants to get the job and work for Mr. Flores. The answer is (B).

68. **C** The men are talking to each other through a "satellite feed," so they must be far away from each other. The answer is (C).

69. **D** The only place a person makes a reservation for tables and that involves eating in a *restaurant*. The answer is (D).

70. **A** A "ticket for speeding" is a fine given by the police if they catch a person driving faster than the posted limit. The man warns the woman to slow down so they don't get a ticket. The answer is (A).

71. **B** The man says the item is "backordered," and that they won't have it for another six weeks. This means that it isn't in stock. The answer is (B).

72. **A** The conversation uses the terms *drive, green, seven-iron,* and others which refer to the game of golf. The answer is (A).

73. **D** *Heels* are a part of *wingtips*, which are a type of shoe. The second man is going to repair the first man's shoes, so the answer is (D).

74. **A** The men discuss style, sideburns, and scissors, so the first man must be about to cut the second man's hair. That makes him a *barber.* The answer is (A).

75. **C** The people are talking about food, so eliminate (B), the *jewelry store.* The food is cooked, so cross off (A), the *vegetable garden.* The woman asks about the specials, which would be in a *restaurant,* not a private *kitchen,* so eliminate (D). The answer is (C).

76. **B** The man says that a virus got into his computer. A virus would cause problems with the *files on a computer,* so the answer is (B).

77. **B** The man says his "friend will be downstairs soon," which indicates that he is only waiting for him to come. The answer is (B).

78. **C** The words *due date* and *maternity leave* mean that the woman is going to have a baby. The answer is (C).

79. **A** The man asks if the leaves are "getting enough light," which means he is concerned with how much sunshine the plant receives. The answer is (A).

80. **B** The woman says, "You may want to consider getting into another line of work." This means that she thinks he should find another job and quit this one. The answer is (B).

81. **C** The announcement is about trains and stations, so the announcer must be a train conductor. The answer is (C).

82. **A** The train leaves at 6 o'clock and it is now 5:57, so there are 3 minutes until the train leaves. The answer is (A).

83. **C** Bensonville and Sheiner are stops before Latrobe, and the train does not stop at Tewkheim. The train stops at North Caldwell after it stops at Latrobe, so the answer is (C).

84. **A** The bus is going to Washington, D.C., so the answer is (A).

85. **D** The bus is a nonstop express bus, so it will not make any stops before it reaches the destination. The answer is (D).

86. **C** The driver says that smoking, listening to loud music, and drinking alcohol are not permitted, but that he will be showing a movie. The answer is (C).

87. **A** The announcement is informal and indicates that the speaker is at the reception desk, so the answer is (A).

88. **C** Fast Express takes packages that might need an address or billing label, so it must be a shipping company. The answer is (C).

89. **A** A breaking news story would be likely to be heard on a TV broadcast, not in a business press conference, PA system, or voicemail message. The answer is (A).

90. **D** He stole $100,000, so the answer is (D).

91. **D** An auditor for the Internal Revenue Service branch of the government discovered the thefts. The answer is (D).

92. **C** The announcement uses the words *call*, *hang up*, and *operator*. It must be about a telephone, so the answer is (C).

93. **A** This announcement is the message you hear when the telephone has been off the hook for a long time or you dial a number that does not exist. It is an automated, recorded message. The answer is (A).

94. **B** Overcoming Challenges does "the good work it does in inner-city schools," so it must be a charity. The answer is (B).

95. **D** The speech is being given at an awards dinner, and the audience is repeatedly thanked for its help in providing money, so the answer is (D).

96. **C** The recipients of the awards are in high school, so they are adolescents. The answer is (C).

97. **A** Jenny is planning to go to Rutgers. The answer is (A).

98. **B** Dan was the top salesman at Unified Products for ten years. The answer is (B).

99. **C** Dan focused on "teaching the customer how to use one of Unified's products." The answer is (C).

100. **A** The site will help you "as you integrate the system into your own routine." The answer is (A).

READING

101. **D** A good word to put in the blank is *vegetable*. Answer choices (A), (B), and (C) cannot be substituted for *vegetable*, so eliminate them. *Produce* includes *vegetable*, so the answer is (D).

102. **A** We are looking for a word that modifies *arrive*. Since *arrive* is a verb, the word must be an adverb. The only adverb among the answer choices is *promptly*, so the answer is (A).

103. **D** Because the missing word is part of the phrase *should be...*, we are looking for an adjective. The only adjective among the answer choices is *cautious*, so the answer is (D).

104. **B** The word we are looking for is part of the verb phrase containing the word *must* and the infinitive of the verb *to present* minus the word *to*. Therefore, the blank must be *present*, and the answer is (B).

105. **C** The word we need is part of the verb phrase containing the helping verb *have* and the past participle of the verb *forgotten*. The answer is (C).

106. **D** An appendix appears at the end of a book or document. Tables of contents, title pages, and prologues appear at the beginning. So, answer choices (A), (B), and (C) are incorrect. The answer is (D).

107. **B** A good word to put in the blank is *changeable*. Answer choices (A), (C), and (D) can't be substituted for *changeable*, so cross them off. *Volatile* can mean *changeable*, so the answer is (B).

108. **A** A good word to put in the blank is *go up*. Answer choices (B), (C), and (D) do not have meanings similar to *go up*, so get rid of them. *Peak* can be mean *go up*, so the answer is (A).

109. **C** A good word to put in the blank is *sense*. Answer choices (A), (B), and (D) do not have meanings similar to *sense*, so eliminate them. *Acumen* means *sense*, so the answer is (C).

110. **A** A good word to put in the blank is *tell the difference*. Answer choices (B), (C), and (D) do not mean *tell the difference*, so eliminate them. *Differentiate* means *tell the difference*, so the answer is (A).

111. **B** A good word to put in the blank is *group*. Answer choices (A), (C), and (D) cannot be substituted for *group*, so eliminate them. A *committee* can be a *group*, so the answer is (B).

112. **C** A good word to put in the blank is *stairs*. Answer choices (A), (B), and (D) do not mean the same as *stairs*, so cross them off. *Stairway* means *stairs*, so the answer is (C).

113. **C** You may not know exactly what to put in the blank, but you know it has to be some material other than steel. Answer choices (A), (B), and (D) are not materials, so eliminate them. *Aluminum* is another material, so the answer is (C).

114. **D** A good word to put in the blank is *explained*. Answer choices (A), (B), and (C) do not mean the same as *explained*, so eliminate them. *Clarified* means *explained*, so the answer is (D).

115. **B** A good word to put in the blank is *show*. Answer choices (A), (C), and (D) do not mean *show*, so get rid of them. *Demonstrate* means *show*, so the answer is (B).

116. **C** A good word to put in the blank is *boring*. Answer choices (A), (B), and (D) cannot be substituted for *boring*, so eliminate them. *Ordinary* can mean *boring*, so the answer is (C).

117. **A** A good word to put in the blank is *gives*. Answer choices (B), (C), and (D) do not match *gives*, so cross them off. *Delegates* means *gives*, so the answer is (A).

118. **C** A good word to put in the blank is *useless*. Answer choices (A), (B), and (D) do not mean *useless*, so eliminate them. *Futile* means *useless*, so the answer is (C).

119. **B** A good word to put in the blank is *a law*. Answer choices (A), (C), and (D) are not the same as *a law*, so get rid of them. *Legislation* means *a law*, so the answer is (B).

120. **D** A good word to put in the blank is *standstill*. Answer choices (A), (B), and (C) do not mean *standstill*, so eliminate them. *Impasse* means *standstill*, so the answer is (D).

121. **B** A good word to put in the blank is *excess*. Answer choices (A), (C), and (D) do not mean the same as *excess*, so eliminate them. *Surplus* means *excess*, so the answer is (B).

122. **B** A good word to put in the blank is *bankrupt*. Answer choices (A), (C), and (D) are not the same as *bankrupt*, so cross them off. *Penniless* means *bankrupt*, so the answer is (B).

123. **D** A good word to put in the blank is *go to*. Answer choices (A), (B), and (C) do not mean *go to*, so eliminate them. *Attend* means *go to*, so the answer is (D).

124. **C** A good word to put in the blank is *rules*. Answer choices (A), (B), and (D) do not mean *rules*, so get rid of them. *Guidelines* can be *rules*, so the answer is (C).

125. **B** A good word to put in the blank is *update*. Answer choices (A), (C), and (D) do not match *update*, so eliminate them. *Modernize* means *update*, so the answer is (B).

126. **A** The blank must be filled with a noun, so eliminate answer choices (B), (C) and (D). The answer is (A).

127. **D** A good word to put in the blank is *punished*. Answer choices (A), (B), and (C) do not mean the same as *punished*, so eliminate them. *Prosecuted* can mean *punished*, so the answer is (D).

128. **C** The word in the blank is part of the infinitive form of the verb *to profit*. The answer is (C).

129. **A** A good word to put in the blank is *plan*. Answer choices (B), (C), and (D) do not mean the same as *plan*, so cross them off. A *strategy* can be a *plan*, so the answer is (A).

130. **D** A good word to put in the blank is *large*. Answer choices (A), (B), and (C) do not mean the same as *large*, so eliminate them. *Monumental* means *large*, so the answer is (D).

131. **C** The blank is part of the verb phrase *is pleased*, which uses the present-tense verb *is* plus the past participle of the verb. *Pleased* is the only past participle. Answer choices (A) and (B) are present-tense verbs, and answer choice (D) is a gerund. Eliminate them, and the answer is (C).

132. **B** The subject of the sentence is *the president and the senior vice president*, which is a plural subject. Therefore, the verb must be plural, and the only plural verb among the answer choices is (B).

133. **D** The blank is part of the present-tense verb phrase *is alarming*, which contains the verb *is* followed by the present participle. Answer choices (A) and (C) are present-tense verbs, and answer choice (B) is a past-tense verb. Only choice (D) is a gerund.

134. **B** The correct idiom is *skeptical of*, so the answer is (B).

135. **A** The blank is part of the infinitive of the verb *to direct*. The answer is (A).

136. **D** The blank is part of a phrase with no subject, so it can't be a present- or past-tense verb. Answer choices (A) and (B) are present-tense verbs, and answer choice (C) is a past-tense verb. Answer choice (D), a gerund, is the answer.

137. **B** A good word to put in the blank is *distribution*. Answer choices (A), (C), and (D) do not mean *distribution*, so cross them off. *Circulation* can mean *distribution*, so the answer is (B).

138. **C** A good word to put in the blank is *show*. Answer choices (A), (B), and (D) do not match show, so eliminate them. *Introduce* means *show*, so the answer is (C).

139. **B** A good word to put in the blank is *reason*. Answer choices (A), (C), and (D) cannot be substituted for *reason*, so get rid of them. An *explanation* can be a *reason*, so the answer is (B).

140. **C** The correct idiomatic verb construction to follow the word *need* is the infinitive. Answer choices (A) and (B) are verb phrases that are not the infinitive. Answer choice (D) is a noun, not a verb. Answer choice (C) is the infinitive, *to declare*. Answer choice (C) is correct.

141. **D** The correct idiom is *go to*, not *go at*. Answer choice (D) is incorrect.

142. **B** The sentence is in present/future tense, so the past-tense verb *waited* in answer choice (B) is wrong.

143. **C** The underlined word in answer choice (C) needs to be the past participle of the verb *to go* along with the verb *is*. It should be *given a*, not *gave a*. The incorrect answer is (C).

144. **B** The word *to* in answer choice (B) is unnecessary.

145. **A** The correct idiom is *I am sorry*, not *I have sorry*. The incorrect answer is (A).

146. **D** The word in answer choice (D) modifies the noun *profit*, so it must be an adjective. *Considerably* is an adverb, so (D) is incorrect.

147. **C**   The correct idiom is *make up for*, not *make up from*. Answer choice (C) is incorrect.

148. **C**   Answer choice (C) needs to include the word *the* to refer clearly to the *assistant*. Answer choice (C) is incorrect.

149. **D**   The correct idiom is *direct attention to*, not *direct attention over*. The answer is (D).

150. **A**   The correct idiom is *each...of*, not *each...for*, so the incorrect answer is (A).

151. **C**   This sentence is written in passive construction, because the books cannot buy themselves. They need to be bought by someone else. Therefore, answer choice (C) is incorrect. It should say *can be purchased* instead of *can purchase*.

152. **A**   The correct idiom is *in my opinion*, not *at my opinion*. The incorrect answer is (A).

153. **A**   The combination of *have* and the present participle form of the verb is incorrect. Answer choice (A) should be *are deciding* (acceptable but not great) or *have decided* (good). Answer choice (A) is incorrect.

154. **B**   The word in answer choice (B) needs to indicate a causal relationship between the second phrase and the first. *Unless* indicates that the phrases do not go together. The phrases do go together, though, so answer choice (B) is incorrect.

155. **B**   Answer choice (B) is part of the infinitive form of the verb with *to*. It should be *discuss*, not *discussing*. Answer choice (B) is incorrect.

156. **D**   Appointments are countable, so the word *much* should really be *many*. The incorrect answer is (D).

157. **D**   The word *when* gives the wrong time idea; it says that no funds will be withdrawn only on that day. The intended meaning is that no funds should be withdrawn *until* that day, so answer choice (D) is incorrect.

158. **C**   *List* is singular, so the verb should be singular, not plural. Answer choice (C) is incorrect.

159. **B**   The word in answer choice (B) is referred to by the pronoun *their*, so it must be plural. *Consumer* isn't plural, so answer choice (B) must be incorrect.

160. **D**   *Tax forms* are plural, so the pronoun in answer choice (D) should be *them*, not *it*. Answer choice (D) is incorrect.

161. **B**   The passage uses the words *server* and *order* and talks about chocolate cake, so it must be in a menu. The answer is (B).

162. **C**   The passage says that the cake "takes 40 minutes to prepare." *Prepare* means *make*, so the answer is (C).

163. **B** This notice is of interest to the general public, so it would most likely be in a newspaper. It has nothing to do with food, so it wouldn't be in a menu. It is not related to any particular company, so it wouldn't be in a corporate newsletter. It has nothing to do with a museum. The answer is (B).

164. **D** The seminar is conducted, according to the passage, "by successful real-estate lawyer Gary Willis." A real-estate lawyer is a lawyer specializing in housing issues, so the answer is (D).

165. **D** The passage says, "There is no fee for this seminar." This means the seminar is free, so the answer is (D).

166. **A** The passage uses the words *patient*, *doctors*, and *side effects*, so Agarast™ must be something medical. Answer choices (B), (C), and (D) have nothing to do with medicine, so the answer must be (A).

167. **C** The passage says, "The safety and efficacy of Agarast™ has not been established in children younger than 2 years of age." This means that they do not know if it is safe. The passage does not mention greater side effects for children or anything about greater allergies to isopolyformonin in babies. The answer is (C).

168. **D** The passage mentions *bruising*, *nausea*, and *restlessness*. The answer is (D).

169. **C** The breakthrough involves "putting the plastics through several different heating and cooling stages." The answer is (C).

170. **A** Ms. Lei is a *company spokesperson*, which means that she represents the company to the press and public. The answer is (A).

171. **A** The passage says that "this process could lower the prices of certain medical parts, making them more accessible worldwide, while simultaneously increasing Northland's per-part profit." This means that health consumers will be able to get the parts more often but Northland will also benefit by making more money. Eliminate answer choice (B) because Northland is privately held, so it has no stockholders. Cross off answer choice (C) because IGD is Northland's competitor. Eliminate answer choice (D) because this will help Northland more than it will help the whole industry. The answer is (A).

172. **C** Sushi restaurants and tea salons would not have "soup of the day," so cross off answer choices (B) and (D). A fine dining restaurant would not offer delivery or corporate catering accounts, so eliminate answer choice (A). The answer is (C).

173. **A** The passage says, "For corporate catering accounts, please call our catering manager." The answer is (A).

174. **A** The passage says, "please call Linda in Human Resources by the end of the day on October 3 to let her know how many tickets you need." The answer is (A).

175. **B** The name of the musical is "Chicago," but it is being staged at the Houston Central Amphitheater. The answer is (B).

176. **C** The passage says that tickets are being discounted "to our special rate of $30." The answer is (C).

177. **A** The passage says, "All employees are required to book work-related air travel through our travel agency." This means they can only use the approved agency, and the answer is (A).

178. **D** The passage gives Angela Baumann's phone number and e-mail address, so she may be reached by both these methods. The answer is (D).

179. **B** A trip of 745 miles would fall into the "501–1000 miles—maximum of 2 stops" category, so the answer is (B).

180. **A** This passage is about air travel, so it would not be found on a medicine bottle, restaurant menu, or instruction manual, but it would be found on an airline ticket. The answer is (A).

181. **D** The passage states that if passengers are not checked in on time they "may have their pre-assigned seat assignment and reserved space canceled." This means they will not be able to take the flight. The answer is (D).

182. **A** The passage says that passengers need to be checked in one hour ahead of the flight for International flights. Flights to Europe are International flights. Passengers only have to be checked in 30 minutes before the flight for flights to Hawaii or Canada, and 15 minutes before the flight for flights within the rest of the United States (including California). The answer is (A).

183. **D** The passage states that passengers must be checked in for their flights within a certain amount of time or they will not be allowed to board. This means that they must check in before they can board. They can only claim luggage or read the safety card after they board. They do not have to go to Hawaii. The answer is (D).

184. **D** Taxis do not run on schedules, so eliminate answer choice (A). Airplanes do not run this many flights along the same route per day, so eliminate answer choice (B). Subways do not run this infrequently or on such strict schedules, so eliminate answer choice (C). The answer is (D).

185. **C** The train that arrives in New York at 10:00 A.M. leaves Hamilton at 9:25 A.M. The answer is (C).

186. **D** The train leaves Norwalk Junction at 6:10 P.M. and reaches New York at 6:30 P.M., so the trip takes 20 minutes. The answer is (D).

187. **B** The briefcase was lost at the bus stop, so a person who spends time at that bus stop would be most likely to have found the briefcase. The answer is (B).

188. **B** The passage says the reward will be for $1000 if the briefcase is returned "with all contents intact." So everything must still be in it. The answer is (B).

189. **B** This notice is not an advertisement, so it would not be in the classified ads. Eliminate answer choice (A). It is not a stock market listing, so get rid of answer choice (C). It is not a real estate listing or article, so cross off answer choice (D). It is business news, so it would be in the business section, and the answer is (B).

190. **A** Ms. Ling-Wong will be "lead counsel for the plastics division of Ajax," and John Baxter used to be in that position. This means that she will be replacing him. The answer is (A).

191. **B** The passage says that Ms. Hoxby "has been a marketing consultant with her own firm," which means she owned her own consulting business. The answer is (B).

192. **B** The branch will close at 3:00 P.M. on Tuesday, December 31. The answer is (B).

193. **C** The branch will be closed on January 1, which is the first day of January. The answer is (C).

194. **B** The first day of January is January 1, but the branch is closed that day. The next day is January 2, so the first day to make a transaction in January is the 2nd. The answer is (B).

195. **A** The workshop will teach the basics of how to use E-Sheet software, which is a computer program. The answer is (A).

196. **D** The session on November 10 is from 8–10 A.M., so cross off answer choice (A). The session on November 11 is from 1–3 P.M., so eliminate answer choice (B). The session on November 13 is from 3–5 P.M., so eliminate answer choice (C) too. The answer is (D).

197. **A** The passage says, "Space is limited," so not everyone can attend the workshops. The answer is (A).

198. **B** This e-mail asks employees to let the receptionists know who ordered from what restaurant so the receptionists don't have to waste time trying to figure it out. The passage doesn't say anything about corporate accounts or extra-long lunches, so eliminate answer choices (A) and (D). There is nothing about e-mail orders to the restaurants, so cross off answer choice (C). The answer is (B).

199. **C** Margaret repeatedly says that she works at the reception desk, which means that she is a receptionist. The passage discusses food-delivery people, but this is not Margaret's job. Eliminate answer choice (A). The passage is an e-mail, but this does not mean that Margaret is an administrator of the e-mail system. Get rid of answer choice (B). She is not an intern, so cross off answer choice (D). The answer is (C).

200. **A** The passage is signed "Margaret and Dante at the Reception Desk," which means that Dante works with Margaret as a receptionist. The answer is (A).

Transcripts

1. (A) There is too much mail to fit in the mailboxes.
   (B) The mailboxes are not full.
   (C) They are eating lunch.
   (D) He is sorting mail.

2. (A) The sign says, "Do Not Enter."
   (B) He is reading the sign.
   (C) The sign shows the route the bus travels.
   (D) He is signing a letter.

3. (A) She is getting into the taxi.
   (B) She is driving the taxi.
   (C) The taxi will not stop.
   (D) She does not know how to drive.

4. (A) The store sells apples as well as citrus fruits.
   (B) The store is closed.
   (C) He cannot find the magazine he wants.
   (D) There are many magazines in the shop.

5. (A) Her subway pass will not function.
   (B) She is buying something from the machine.
   (C) The bank branch is closed.
   (D) The telephone is broken.

6. (A) She is explaining a new marketing plan.
   (B) They haven't brought any slides.
   (C) She is pointing at the board.
   (D) He is playing the triangle.

7. (A) Showers are predicted for today.
   (B) There are many different varieties for sale.
   (C) You need flour and eggs to make a cake.
   (D) There is no exit from this door.

8. (A) It is not snowing today.
   (B) The store is an antiques shop.
   (C) They do not know what the signs mean.
   (D) The restaurant was closed by the health department.

9. (A) The flight will be five hours long.
   (B) The flight attendant is serving drinks.
   (C) The airplane is about to land.
   (D) The "fasten seatbelt" light is turned on.

10. (A) The shoes are all for women.
    (B) Men can buy footwear here.
    (C) They are trying to choose a program.
    (D) She does not want to lose her purse.

11. (A) You cannot eat here.
    (B) They are ordering food.
    (C) It will come in 30 minutes or less.
    (D) The man is wearing a hat.

12. (A) He is dressed for cold weather.
    (B) The fruit will not all be sold today.
    (C) He is not selling pineapples.
    (D) The man has not had any customers today.

13. (A) She is using a computer.
    (B) He is her typing tutor.
    (C) They are making copies of documents.
    (D) She is his assistant.

14. (A) They both want to buy shampoo.
    (B) They are brother and sister.
    (C) They are in a pharmacy.
    (D) They are eating lunch.

15. (A) His e-mail inbox is full.
    (B) He is sitting in his office.
    (C) He has a messy office.
    (D) His job requires strong math skills.

16. (A) The conference is full.
    (B) They are working together.
    (C) He is a consultant.
    (D) They are driving to work.

17. (A) They are at the office.
    (B) They are folding papers.
    (C) They have boarded the aircraft.
    (D) They have already eaten lunch.

18. (A) The park is full of people.
    (B) Please watch your step.
    (C) They are riding bicycles.
    (D) The tree is in a park.

19. (A) The window is broken.
    (B) The window looks out on the water.
    (C) They are trying to open the window.
    (D) The wind is blowing.

20. (A) Cars are parked along the street.
    (B) The leaves are falling from the trees.
    (C) They have taken off their coats.
    (D) His dog is on a leash.

PART II

21. (Woman) What did Mr. Patel call you about?
    (Man)   (A) I will return to the office later this afternoon.
             (B) That phone number is disconnected.
             (C) I can't tell you, because it's a secret.

22. (Man)   What color rug would you like to buy?
    (Woman) (A) I would prefer one with a blue and red design.
             (B) I can't seem to stop coughing.
             (C) I'll see you tomorrow morning.

23. (Man1)   Why isn't the report ready yet?
    (Man 2) (A) The file was erased from my computer.
             (B) This window needs to be cleaned.
             (C) Our lunch meeting has been cancelled.

24. (Man)   Did the clerk order more office supplies?
    (Woman) (A) Yes, I would like another slice of cake.
             (B) Yes, they are now stored in the closet.
             (C) Yes, we sit next to each other.

25. (Woman) Who won the election?
    (Man)   (A) My grandfather was a Republican all his life.
             (B) The current senator was defeated by the challenger.
             (C) This window faces north.

26. (Man)   Would you like to play ice hockey with me?
    (Woman)   (A) I'm sorry, but I don't know how to skate.
               (B) That horse has won many races.
               (C) Don't be too over-confident.

27. (Man 1)   Where do you keep the bread?
    (Man 2)   (A) I am worried that my car will break down.
               (B) In the corner, next to the vegetables.
               (C) No, it is purple.

28. (Woman)   Where should I mail these documents?
    (Man)   (A) The printer needs a new ink cartridge.
               (B) Women should make as much money as men do.
               (C) To the office in Buenos Aires.

29. (Woman)   What did you think of the movie?
    (Man)   (A) I thought it was very entertaining.
               (B) Your shoes look very stylish.
               (C) I forgot to shave this morning.

30. (Man)   Where did you buy those cookies?
    (Woman)   (A) This hotel suite is too expensive.
               (B) $2.50 for a dozen.
               (C) At the bakery at the end of the block.

31. (Man)   Where did Ms. Yamagachi grow up?
    (Woman)   (A) In San Francisco.
               (B) In 1962.
               (C) Tomatoes and corn.

32. (Man 1)   Can you tell me what is wrong with this cellular phone?
    (Man 2)   (A) The ice cream has melted.
               (B) The antenna is broken.
               (C) The printer is out of paper.

33. (Man)   Do you have the key to the hotel room?
    (Woman)   (A) I need to stop soon and buy some gasoline.
               (B) We need more towels.
               (C) I left it with the clerk at the front desk.

34. (Man)   How many miles is it from Jacksonville to Atlanta?
    (Woman)   (A) Almost 350.
               (B) It's a quarter past four.
               (C) 865-7309.

35. (Woman)   Have you eaten dinner yet?
    (Man)   (A) My father left the oven on.
               (B) It was delicious.
               (C) I can't decide which scarf to purchase.

36. (Man)   When does the next plane to Caracas leave?
    (Woman)   (A) You are making too much noise.
               (B) Please step into the elevator.
               (C) All of today's flights are canceled.

37. (Man 1)   Where are the cleaning supplies kept?
    (Man 2)   (A)   This carpet is very dirty.
                 (B)   In the closet next to the copy machine.
                 (C)   Your pictures will be ready tomorrow morning.

38. (Man)   Why are you going to Dallas this weekend?
    (Woman)   (A)   I need another coin for the parking meter.
                 (B)   The printer is out of paper.
                 (C)   I'm giving a seminar on niche marketing.

39. (Woman)   Do you have any ideas for our new marketing campaign?
    (Man)   (A)   I think we should get a famous athlete to endorse our product.
                 (B)   Green peppers are on sale.
                 (C)   My portfolio has gained five percent so far this year.

40. (Man)   Have you seen the plans for the new office building yet?
    (Woman)   (A)   No, I am meeting with the architect on Thursday.
                 (B)   No, I don't subscribe to cable television.
                 (C)   No, I need to contact my travel agent.

41. (Woman)   What is the best service offered by the health club?
    (Man)   (A)   There is too much lettuce on this sandwich.
                 (B)   Each member is assigned to a personal fitness instructor.
                 (C)   My doctor's appointment is on Wednesday.

42. (Man)   Have you seen Mr. Chen recently?
    (Woman)   (A)   He is at a lunch meeting until 2 P.M.
                 (B)   This restaurant doesn't allow dogs.
                 (C)   His brother taught me how to play tennis.

43. (Man)   What is the difference between an alligator and a crocodile?
    (Woman)   (A)   My sister is allergic to bee stings.
                 (B)   I am afraid of spiders.
                 (C)   One has a sharper nose and grayer skin.

44. (Man 1)   What are you drinking?
    (Man 2)   (A)   Sure, I am very thirsty.
                 (B)   This is a glass of ginger ale.
                 (C)   Your life vest is located under your seat.

45. (Woman)   What does this word mean?
    (Man)   (A)   I'll look for a dictionary.
                 (B)   You should always be nice to your elders.
                 (C)   The average value is 9.26.

46. (Woman)　Where is the best place to have my dress altered?
(Man)
(A)　I would prefer these shoes if they were brown.
(B)　One of the basement pipes has a leak.
(C)　My tailor on Fifth Street does very good work.

47. (Man 1)　Why will Ms. Ortega be out of the office next week?
(Man 2)
(A)　She went to the supply room to get some paper clips.
(B)　She is traveling to see her grandson.
(C)　She will not be happy if you are late again.

48. (Woman)　Which direction does this window face?
(Man)
(A)　We are looking west, toward the sunset.
(B)　You look a little bit tired this morning.
(C)　I think shaving is unpleasant.

49. (Woman)　May I leave the office early today?
(Man)
(A)　Tomorrow is the first day of spring.
(B)　It is supposed to be very cold tonight.
(C)　That's fine, as long as your work is done.

50. (Man)　Where is the company barbecue this year?
(Woman)
(A)　The butcher's window is at the back of the supermarket.
(B)　I got a haircut last Thursday.
(C)　We are going to the Crossett Lake campground.

PART III

51. (Woman)　Since your arms are full of shopping bags, I'd be happy to push the button for you.
(Man)　Thank you, that's very nice. 15th floor, please.
(Woman)　That's an interesting coincidence. I work on the 15th floor as well.

52. (Man 1)　Have you seen a package for me? It was sent more than a week ago, but I haven't received it yet.
(Man 2)　I haven't seen it, sir, but I'll be sure to ask the others here to look out for it. Who is it from?
(Man 1)　It was sent by a consulting firm that we hired to do some market research in Madrid.

53. (Man) So, how does it feel to have your new corner office?

(Woman) It's been a dream for a long time, and I can't believe it has come true. The extra money has also been useful, since my oldest daughter is about to start college in the fall.

(Man) Really? Where does she want to go?

54. (Man 1) In conclusion, ladies and gentlemen, I'm disappointed to report that MondoCorp will lose money this quarter. I will now take your questions.

(Man 2) Can you tell us what you plan to do in order to reverse this trend and turn a profit?

(Man 1) After I meet with the board of directors on Thursday, I will be able to answer that question.

55. (Woman) Have you seen Jenkins? I've just learned some new information that he needs to include in the report he's working on.

(Man) He is on vacation, and he won't be back in the office for another two weeks.

(Woman) This is very frustrating. Why didn't anyone tell me that he would be gone for so long?

56. (Man) Do you know when this building was built?

(Woman) Andrew Carnegie first commissioned the project in 1871, but the building wasn't actually finished for another seven years.

(Man) It's amazing how some architectural styles never change.

57. (Man 1) The company policy regarding company cars has changed. From now on, if you want a ride home, you must work until 9:00 P.M.

(Man 2) Making us stay an hour later is completely unfair. My supervisor often keeps me late during the week, but there's never enough work to keep me until 9:00.

(Man 1) I'm sorry, but the managing director's decision is final.

58. (Man) When is the meeting going to start?

(Woman) I'm not sure, but I don't think it will begin for another half an hour. Ms. Chung called to say that she is delayed in traffic.

(Man) OK. I'm going to go downstairs for a cup of coffee.

59. (Man)   Have you got the correct time? It looks as though my watch has stopped again.

    (Woman)   Why don't you get that thing repaired? You've already missed three meetings this month.

    (Man)   I'd like to, but I can never find enough time to get to the repair shop.

60. (Woman)   Mr. Alfieri called to say that he has more suggestions for amending the licensing agreement.

    (Man)   Again? I wish he would make up his mind; all these changes are becoming tiresome.

    (Woman)   I know what you mean. It's hard to remember what the initial agreement looked like.

61. (Man)   In order to get this presentation ready, we'll have to send these documents to our usual print shop.

    (Woman)   Didn't you hear? That place went out of business last month.

    (Man)   Oh, well. I guess we'll have to look elsewhere. Do you have any suggestions?

62. (Man 1)   I can't host the company barbecue this year, because we are having some work done on our backyard.

    (Man 2)   I like your yard the way it is. Why are you changing it?

    (Man 1)   Now that our grandchildren are getting older, we're taking out the stone wall and putting in a pool.

63. (Man)   I need to go get some paper clips and some pens.

    (Woman)   As long as you're going there anyway, could you get me a box of manila folders and a stapler?

    (Man)   Sure. Come to think of it, I should also order my desk calendar for next year.

64. (Woman)   I'm here to pick up my beige Cadillac, please. Here's my ticket.

    (Man)   It says here that you arrived here this morning, so that's a total of 14 hours. That will be $22.50, please.

    (Woman)   Let me get my purse. Do you have change for a fifty?

65. (Man)   In order to celebrate the successful launch of the Peppy paper towel campaign, we're all going out to eat. Do you want to come along?

(Woman)   I can't. My husband and I have to pick up our daughter, who is flying in from London.

(Man)   That's great. I hope I get to visit there again soon.

66. (Man 1)   Your mother and I think you should reconsider your decision to go to art school.

(Man 2)   Why? I've told you a number of times that I don't want to be a lawyer.

(Man 1)   Yes, but we think trying to make a career as an illustrator is a far riskier proposition.

67. (Woman)   Hello? May I please speak to Mr. Flores? I need to talk to him about the job opening that was advertised in the local newspaper.

(Man)   Mr. Flores will be traveling for another three days. May I take a message for him?

(Woman)   That's OK. I'll call back at the end of the week.

68. (Man 1)   Could you please repeat that last comment? There was a glitch in the satellite feed, and we didn't hear what you just said.

(Man 2)   I was merely commenting that the work you and your team did was quite helpful, and we would be happy to hire you again at a later date.

(Man 1)   I'm glad you are satisfied with our work.

69. (Woman)   Hello. I'd like to make a reservation for tomorrow night at 8. There will be five of us.

(Man)   I'm sorry, ma'am, but we're completely booked for 8 o'clock. We can seat a table of five at 7 or at 10.

(Woman)   Hmmm. Well, I guess we'll come in at 7, then. We don't want to eat too late in the day.

70. (Man)   Rhonda, did you notice the sign back there? It says the speed limit is down to 45 miles per hour.

(Woman)   Uh oh! I didn't see it at all. I'd better slow down—I'm going 55.

(Man)   I'm glad I mentioned it, then. We don't want to get a ticket for speeding.

71. (Man)   Good evening. Lakeside Casuals. This is John. How can I help you?

    (Woman)   I'd like to order a few things. Let's start with item number 1345-78V5. The lady's raincoat, size large, in periwinkle.

    (Man)   I'm sorry, but we're backordered on that item. It won't be available for another six weeks. We do have that item in raspberry and sunshine in size large, if you'd rather not wait.

72. (Man 1)   That was a wonderful drive. You probably have no more than 150 yards to the green.

    (Man 2)   Thanks. I've been taking a lot of lessons lately, and they appear to be paying off. I think I'll use the seven-iron.

    (Man 1)   Sounds good to me. Be careful, though, since there's a lot of sand along the right side of the fairway.

73. (Man 1)   I'd like you to replace the heels on these wingtips please.

    (Man 2)   OK. That will cost $11.00. If you'd like, I'll be sure to shine them when I'm finished.

    (Man 1)   I'd appreciate that. It seems as though I can never find the time to do it myself.

74. (Man 1)   Welcome back, Mr. Rogers. Would you like the same style as last time?

    (Man 2)   Actually, I'd like a different look this month. Could you make it a lot shorter on top and leave my sideburns a little longer?

    (Man 1)   Very well. Keep your head still please; these scissors are extremely sharp.

75. (Woman)   Everything here looks really good. What are your specials today?

    (Man)   We have our usual soup and salad combination. The soup choices are tomato bisque and cream of mushroom.

    (Woman)   Those are my two favorites. It will be very difficult to make a choice.

76. (Man)   A virus found its way into our system last week, and it nearly destroyed all of last quarter's inventory records.

    (Woman)   That's awful. Did you update your protection software?

    (Man)   I hope so. I certainly don't want to go through another scary situation like that again.

77. (Woman) Excuse me, sir, but there is no smoking allowed in this building.

(Man) But I'll only be here for a minute. My friend will be downstairs soon, and we'll be on our way out to lunch in no time.

(Woman) I'm sorry, but that doesn't matter. If you'd like to smoke, kindly take your cigarette out on the patio.

78. (Man) I guess the due date is almost here. When is your last day at the office?

(Woman) I'll work through the end of next week, and then I'll be on maternity leave for most of the summer.

(Man) We sure will miss you around here. Have you picked out any names yet?

79. (Woman) It doesn't look as though these plants have been watered for a long time.

(Man) I came around with the watering can just two days ago. Are you sure the leaves are getting enough light?

(Woman) Maybe that's the answer. Can you help me move this plant closer to the window?

80. (Woman) As of January 1, our new dress code will require all men to wear ties at the office.

(Man) That's unfair. This job is already very difficult, and now I'll have to dress in clothing that is far less comfortable.

(Woman) I'm sorry to hear that. You may want to consider getting into another line of work.

Part IV

Questions 81–83 refer to the following announcement.

Attention passengers: The 6 o'clock local to Newbury is boarding on Track 8. The time is now 5:57. All aboard the 6 o'clock local to Newbury, making stops in Edgemont, Parkhurst, Sheiner, Bensonville, North Bensonville, Latrobe, Archburg, Huntington, North Caldwell, Petry, and Newbury. All aboard the 6 o'clock local to Newbury.

Questions 84–86 refer to the following announcement.

Good morning ladies and gentlemen. This is the 7:05 nonstop express bus to Washington, D.C. My name is Randolph, and I'll be your driver. I'd like to remind everyone that this is a "no smoking" bus. In addition, it is against federal law for anyone to drink alcoholic beverages or use illegal substances on this bus. If you're going to listen to a personal radio, please use headphones and make sure the volume is low enough that your neighbor can't hear it. I'll be showing the movie *Like Mike* on the video screens you see in front of you in just a few minutes. So sit back, relax, and let me do the driving.

Questions 87–88 refer to the following announcement.

Hello, everyone. It's 4:50, and Fast Express will be here in 10 minutes. If you have any packages to go out, please bring them to the reception desk right now so the FastEx man can take them. If you need a billing or address label I've got them here at the reception desk. Have a great night!

Questions 89–91 refer to the following story.

And now, a breaking news story. A local man has been charged with embezzlement. Gregory Navarro, 32, of Bay Ridge, has been charged with embezzling over $100,000 from his employer, As-Co Fasteners of Staten Island. Mr. Navarro allegedly altered the computer billing system to take a small percentage of each transaction and deposit it in his own personal bank account. The fraud may have been going on since 1996, sources say. The fraud was only uncovered when an IRS tax auditor discovered the discrepancy in the billing and deposit records. If convicted, Mr. Navarro could serve 15 to 30 years in a federal prison.

Questions 92–93 refer to the following announcement.

If you'd like to make a call, please hang up and try again. If you need help, hang up and then dial your operator.

Questions 94–97 refer to the following speech.

Good evening. My name is Whitney Anderson, and I'm the Executive Director of Overcoming Challenges. I'd like to welcome you all to this year's Overcoming Challenges Awards Dinner. As you all know, Overcoming Challenges could not do all the good work it does in inner-city schools without your support. Each one of you makes an enormous difference in the lives of these kids. And that's why tonight I'm so proud to honor two graduates of the Overcoming Challenges Decisionmakers Program. Your generous support has enabled us to provide these honorees with full four-year scholarships to college. Please welcome Jenny Rivera and Dylan Tran.

Jenny is a senior at Gordon Parks High school in Jersey City. In the past two years she has brought her grade-point average up from a 68 percent to a 92 percent. In addition, she is secretary of her class, sings in the school choir, and plays on the tennis team. She will be attending Rutgers University in the fall and is planning to major in Business Administration.

Dylan is a senior at George Washington High School in the Bronx. Last year he was arrested for breaking and entering, but in the past 16 months he has earned straight A's, joined the chess team and Olympics of the Mind, and works 10 hours a week at a copy shop. He will be attending Hunter College in the fall and plans to major in Criminal Justice.

Questions 98–100 refer to the following announcement.

In the next half hour you'll be hearing the secrets of Dan Conlon's No-Sell System. Dan Conlon was the top producer ten years in a row for Unified Products, but claims he never learned how to sell a single product. Instead, he focused on learning what the customer needed and then teaching the customer how to use one of Unified's products to fill that need. In this informative lesson you'll hear from Dan himself just how to use his system to create a situation in which no one feels awkward or pressured, but the customer is eager to buy your product. Then, once you've listened to the system, you'll be able to receive free online support at www.danconlon.com as you integrate the system into your own routine.

17

How to Score
Your Test

How to Score Your Test

Compared to taking the TOEIC, scoring the TOEIC is simple. Just count the number of answers you got right in each section, and write them in the box labeled "raw score" for each section in the chart below.

Test Sections	Raw Score	Converted Score Range
Listening Comprehension		
Reading		
Total Score Range		

Then convert your raw score to the corresponding "converted score range." ETS conducts "certain statistical procedures" to determine how to convert the raw scores for each section to the converted scores. They don't reveal what these calculations are, and they claim that they are different for every TOEIC they administer.

Each raw score corresponds to a converted score *range,* not a definite score. That means that there's a lot of "wiggle" room. In other words, you could answer the same number of questions right in each section on two different days and end up with different scores. Or you could answer different numbers of questions right and get the same score.

You can only use the converted score ranges to tell you *approximately* how well you're doing. So don't worry about a few points. Instead try to improve in the areas in which you have the most trouble.

Score Conversion Table			
Listening Comprehension		Reading Comprehension	
Raw Score Range	Converted Score Range	Raw Score Range	Converted Score Range
96–100	470–495	96–100	440–495
91–95	460–495	91–95	410–455
86–90	430–480	86–90	390–425
81–85	400–450	81–85	360–400
76–80	380–420	76–80	330–370
71–75	350–390	71–75	300–345
66–70	320–360	66–70	270–315
61–65	290–335	61–65	250–290
56–60	260–305	56–60	220–260
51–55	230–275	51–55	190–235
46–50	200–245	46–50	160–205
41–45	170–215	41–45	130–175
36–40	140–185	36–40	110–150
31–35	110–165	31–35	80–120
26–30	80–125	26–30	50–95
21–25	50–95	21–25	20–65
16–20	30–65	16–20	10–40
11–15	10–35	11–15	5–10
6–10	5–10	6–10	5
1–5	5	1–5	5
0	5	0	5

Now add the lowest number in your converted score range for the Listening Comprehension section to the lowest number in your converted score range for the Reading section. This gives you the low end of the range of your final score. Then add the highest number in your converted score range for the Listening Comprehension section to the highest number in your converted score range for the Reading Comprehension section. This gives you the high end of the range of your final score.

For example, someone who got 65 questions right in the Listening Comprehension section and 82 questions right in the Reading section would end up with a final score range of 650–735.

Test Sections	Raw Score	Converted Score Range
Listening Comprehension	65	290–335
Reading	82	360–400
Total Score Range		650–735

Appendix 1:
Idiom List

IDIOMS

There are two types of idioms you should learn to do well on the TOEIC. One is the true idiom, an expression that is specific to a language and that cannot be understood by understanding the individual words that make it up. The other kind of idiom is a phrase containing a preposition. There is no logic to the way prepositions appear (in any language, but especially English), so these phrases can only be learned by use. In this sense they are idioms as well.

Please take the time to read through these two lists. They are not exhaustive, but they contain a good number of the idioms that could appear on the TOEIC. If you have the time and want to study them seriously, the best way is probably to make flash cards out of them. The act of writing the idioms onto cards will help you remember them. Then you can study the cards whenever you have a spare minute.

True Idiom List

True idioms are words or phrases that do not translate literally. For example, "break down" does not mean to break something in a downward motion, but to lose control. Luckily, idioms occur infrequently on current TOEIC exams, but you should still review them. Make a list of those you have trouble with and practice using them.

break down—a collapse of physical and/or mental health; failing to work
When she heard that her pet iguana had escaped, Mary Lou *broke down* and cried in front of the whole class.
After their car *broke down*, Marty and James had to walk five miles to the nearest service station.

break in—to enter forcibly. With an item of clothing, it can mean to wear in and make comfortable
The thief *broke into* the museum and stole all the artwork.
I finally *broke in* those shoes—but not before they gave me some terrible blisters.

breakthrough—a sudden achievement or understanding
The new vaccine represented a significant *breakthrough* in the battle against the virus.

break up—to separate or collapse; to divide and disperse
In 1969, the Beatles officially *broke up* after playing together as a band for more than a decade.

clear away—to free from something
When all this trouble *clears away*, he'll be able to go back to school.
If you *clear away* the dishes, I'll wash them.

clear out—to leave a place, usually quickly
The fire marshal ordered the people to *clear out* of their homes due to the possibility that the brush fires would spread.

come about—to happen
The train wreck *came about* as a result of the engineer's negligence.

come across—to find or meet by chance
We *came across* my grandmother's old diary while cleaning out the attic.

come down with—to get sick
When she *came down with* a terrible case of laryngitis, Kathy Lou Kelly wasn't able to perform at the benefit concert.

come up with—to produce something or have an idea
It was Juan who *came up with* the scheme to trick Mrs. Huxtable.

come from—to derive or originate from
The English language *comes from* many sources, such as Greek and Latin.

come of—result from
"Nothing good will *come of* that sort of behavior," my mother always said.

come out—to disclose
The news finally *came out*—cholesterol is not as bad for you as scientists originally believed.

come through with—to do what is needed
The union finally *came through with* an offer to negotiate rather than strike.

come to—to regain consciousness; add up to
After Dorothy *came to*, she saw that she was in her own bed in Kansas.
That dress and those shoes will *come to* about $100 dollars.

come to terms with—to understand or absorb mentally
She had trouble *coming to terms with* her dog's death—it seemed so sudden.

do without—to get along without
During the drought, residents had to *do without* long, luxurious showers.

drop in/drop by—to visit casually and sometimes unexpectedly
After the movie, we'll *drop in* and see if Margie is home.
On your way to the dorm, *drop by* the library to see if the book is on reserve.

fall back on—to turn to for help
Fortunately for John, after he lost all his spending money, he had some savings to *fall back on*.

fall behind—to fail to keep up with
Mark had *fallen behind* so badly in his studies, it seemed he'd never be able to finish all his work and pass his courses.

fall for—be taken in by; duped
I can't believe that John *fell for* that trick—it was so obvious.

fill in—to substitute for
Mary Jones will *fill in* for Patty Smith during the race, as Patty is too ill to come today.

fit in—to make time for; to conform
The doctor will *fit* you *in* at about three o'clock for an appointment with her.
Teenagers often try to *fit in* with their friends by wearing the same style clothes and listening to the same music.

give away—make a gift of
The store was *giving away* a new scarf with every purchase in order to bring in more customers.

give in—to surrender
In Hesse's *Siddhartha*, the main character's father finally *gives in* and allows his son to leave home.

give up—to stop; to yield to; to part with
I finally *gave up* smoking after years of hearing all the health warnings.
Nellie wouldn't sign the legal papers yet—she wasn't sure if she wanted to *give up* her right to a trial.

go along with—to agree to
The president would *go along with* the decision to hire more people if the department could bring in more revenue.

go down—when referring to food this means it can be swallowed and digested
Ice cream was the only food that would *go down* easily after her operation.

go far—to succeed
Laura would *go far* with her hard work and intelligence.

go on—to proceed with; to happen
"I don't want to *go on* a diet again in my lifetime!" exclaimed Bob.
The speaker *went on* for almost three hours before stopping.

go through with—to do
Few people thought that the mayor would *go through with* his plans to close all the city's homeless shelters.

go under—to fail
Due to the poor economy, ten businesses have *gone under* in our town in the last year.

go up—be erected
The building *went up* in a few months and soon there were tenants in the apartments.

hang on—to hold on to; to wait or persevere
Indiana Jones managed to grab onto the cliff and *hang on* for dear life.
The receptionist told me to *hang on* while she consulted her appointment book.

hang around—to loiter
On a hot summer day, the kids like to just *hang around* at the beach.

hang up—to end a telephone conversation by putting the receiver down
Police tell you to just *hang up* if you get an obscene phone call.

heat up—to increase in pressure
The debate *heated up* significantly when Congressman Smithers mentioned plans for rezoning in the area.

keep in touch with—to stay in communication with
Please *keep in touch with* us after you move to France.

kill off—to put to death
The use of that pesticide will *kill off* ants as well as fleas.

lay aside—to give up or set aside
The mayor warned the students to *lay aside* their angry feelings toward the rival school on the day of the big soccer game.
Jan *laid aside* some money for just such an emergency.

lay off—to terminate someone's employment
The Brindley Corporation had to *lay off* ten percent of its employees due to decreased sales.

laid up—sick in bed or out of the action
Mr. Rodriquez was *laid up* for several weeks with a terrible flu.

leave out—to omit
"Don't *leave out* Aunt Mary from the wedding invitations!"

leave up to—to allow to decide
"I'll *leave* your punishment *up to* you," Principal Skinner told the kids.

live up to—to fulfill
We expect that Jim will *live up to* our plans to become the first member of the family to attend college.

live down—to bear the embarrassment
He'll never *live down* the shame of forgetting all his lines in the class play.

move on—to go in another direction
"It's time for you to *move on*," Susan told her friend, who wanted to quit her job as an editor.

off limits—restricted
That area is *off limits* to cars, due to efforts in our community to cut down on pollution.

on the mark—exactly right
"Boy, were you *on the mark* about Irene—you were the only one who thought that she'd play so well in that concert."

overkill—excess
You really didn't *need* to prepare fifteen pages for that report—it was *overkill*.

over with—finished
I was so relieved to be *over with* the TOEIC after six months of study.

pass by—to overlook
Marie was upset that the committee *passed* her *by* and chose a different finalist.

pass through—to go through
To get to New England by car from that town, it is necessary to *pass through* New York.

pass up—to refuse
We couldn't believe that Jose would *pass up* an opportunity to travel all around the country for free.

pour in—to arrive in a large amount
Cards and letters came *pouring in* to offer help and money after the news report about that young girl's need for an operation.

pull out—to take out
The United States *pulled* its last troops *out* of Vietnam in 1973, although soldiers had been leaving for years.

pull off—to accomplish something in spite of problems
Jake could hardly believe that Amanda could *pull off* that deal after she'd made such a big mistake.

pushover—someone who is easily taken advantage of
That Mrs. Jones is a real *pushover*—she always lets you hand in papers late if you ask.

put down—to insult; to suppress
I can't believe the way John *puts down* his mother when she's standing right there.
The leaders *put down* a rebellion in their country by appeasing the different groups.

put up with—to allow or go along with
New Yorkers *put up with* plenty of noise and crowds.

run by—to tell someone about
Maria asked her accountant to *run* those figures *by* her one more time before she signed the contract.

send back—to return
President Clinton vetoed the bill and *sent* it *back* to Congress for changes.

sign in—to sign your name to enter a place
Visitors must *sign in* at the front desk before going into the main auditorium.

speak out—to state publicly
Jones was afraid to *speak out* when he saw his boss stealing supplies—he didn't want to get in trouble.

speak up—to speak more loudly; to state publicly
"Please *speak up*—the rest of the group cannot hear you," Ms. Montgomery told Peter.
Activists argue that we all have the responsibility to *speak up* wherever we see injustice, or no change will ever take place.

speed up—to increase one's speed
I have been practicing my reading comprehension with the hope that I will *speed up* and finish more passages in the time allotted.

step in—to intervene
The Town Board was forced to *step in* and put a stop to the development in the area when it was judged to be unsafe.

stick to—to persist
"*Stick to* your morals and you'll do a good job," my grandfather always advised.

stick around—to stay
I think I'll *stick around*—there's no reason to head home yet.

stop by—to make a brief visit
Could you *stop by* the grocery store on your way home from work and pick up a loaf of bread?

stop up—to clog or prevent from moving
The grease and hair *stopped up* the sink and Jan had to call a plumber to fix it.
Traffic was *stopped up* for miles due to that horrible five-car accident.

think better of—to change your mind
Mark had considered dropping out of school to work, but a discussion with his parents made him *think better of it*, and he decided to stay in school.

think nothing of—to do without care
Some people in that town *think nothing of* throwing all their garbage into the river—don't they know the long-term effects?

think over—to consider
Every time Steven writes a paper he has to *think over* his topic for a few days before he even begins to write.

think through—to consider all the effects
"You obviously did not *think through* what would happen to you if you pulled that fire alarm," Principal Skinner told Marie.

tied up—busy; unavailable for use
Mr. Jones cannot come to the meeting this afternoon—he'll be *tied up* downtown until 7:00 P.M.
Since most of their money was *tied up* in long-term investments, Jan and Mark couldn't spend any of it.

turn down—to refuse; to lower
The Smiths were *turned down* for a loan because of their poor credit history.
The volume on the speakers was *turned down* because it was so late at night.

turnoff—something that disgusts a person
"Guys who only talk about themselves are such a *turnoff!*" the magazine article proclaimed.

turn over—transfer
By law, attorneys must *turn over* evidence to the court so that both sides may have a chance to review it.

turn to—to go to for guidance or inspiration
Many teenagers *turn to* their friends and family to help them decide where to attend college.

turn up—to find or uncover
It's always a good idea to browse the shelves in a library when you are doing a research paper—you never know what you may *turn up*.

up against—confronted with
In spite of being *up against* strong opposition from the larger British forces, the United States won the Revolutionary War.

up to date—current
Her clothes are always so stylish and *up to date*—she must read all the fashion magazines.

wake up—to rouse from sleep or inactivity
The young Americans of the 1960s sent a *wake up* call to the country to get involved and work for change.
Young children may *wake up* at any time in the middle of the night.

PREPOSITION IDIOM LIST

The meanings of these phrases are obvious, as they follow the dictionary definitions of the words. Therefore we have not included definitions of the words. Instead, we have provided sentences illustrating the proper use of these idioms.

able to, ability to
I am no longer *able to* run 10 miles as fast as I used to.
Sloths have the *ability* to sleep while hanging from their toes.

accede to
Once defeated, the military dictator had to *accede to* NATO's demands.

access to
After the home team lost, reporters were not given *access to* the coach's office.

according to
According to the etiquette expert, it is very rude to stick out your pinkie as you drink tea.

account for
The Brazilian rain forest *accounts for* 40 percent of all species of tree frog.

accuse of
I *accused* my little brother *of* stealing my favorite football jersey.

acquaint with
When I moved to London, I had to *acquaint myself* with English social customs.

agree with
I don't *agree with* your viewpoint.

allow for
When you budget your money, you should *allow for* emergency expenses.

amount to
When the trial was canceled, all the lawyer's preparation *amounted to* nothing.

appear to
The natives of this island don't *appear to* be very friendly.

apply to
Traffic laws don't *apply to* international diplomats.

argue over
The newly married couple didn't *argue over* money very often.

as [adjective] as
Your cat isn't *as* friendly as my cat is.

associate with
My mommy told me never to *associate with* people I don't know.

assure that
I *assure* you *that* my sister is the ideal person for this job.

at a disadvantage
Our desperate financial situation put us *at a disadvantage* while we were negotiating.

attempt to
I will *attempt to* write my B-school essays after I finish dinner.

attend to, attention to
New parents must *attend to* their child's cries.
The book editor was known for her *attention to* detail.

attest to
I can *attest to* the fact that John has never been to Indonesia.

attribute to
Many clever quotes are *attributed to* Oscar Wilde.

available to
Before you make a decision, be sure you know all the options that are *available to you*.

based on
The award-wining movie was *based on* a book that virtually no one read.

because of
Because of her broken leg, she was unable to ski for two months.

believe to be
These artifacts are *believed to be* remnants of the Ming dynasty.

between [A] and [B]
There are 14 rest stops on the highway *between* Baltimore *and* Washington, DC.

call for
Desperate times *call for* desperate measures.

choice of
Given the *choice of* liver or ice cream, I would select the latter.

choose to [verb]
Many people *choose to* attend business school after they have worked for only two years.

choose from [nouns]
Qualified candidates can *choose from* hundreds of accredited programs.

claim to
My uncle *claims to* have eaten 200 hot dogs in half an hour.

collaborate with
The actor *collaborated with* two ghost writers on his autobiography.

conclude that

After years of research, the scientist *concluded that* baked beans do not cause baldness.

consequence of

Bankruptcy is usually a *consequence of* poor money management.

consider

Dr. Melnitz is *considered* the world's foremost authority on medieval manuscripts.

consist of

The heart *consists of* four chambers that pump blood throughout the body.

consistent with

Her new findings are *consistent with* contemporary theories.

continue to

If you *continue to* make noise back there, I'll turn this car around and we'll go home.

contrast with

His low-key speaking style *contrasted with* his partner's more passionate oratory.

contribute to

Would you care to *contribute* your time *to* the church's tutoring program?

convert to

The alchemist Rumpelstiltskin could *convert* lead *to* gold.

cost of [something]

The *cost of* sending your child to college has tripled in the last decade.

cost to [someone]

After the war, the *cost to* the surviving inhabitants of the small village was devastating.

credit with

Dr. Jonas Salk is *credited with* the discovery of the polio vaccine.

date from

This ancient parchment *dates from* the second century.

deal with

I'll *deal with* that problem later.

debate over

My parents always *debate over* which movie the family will see.

decide to (not decide on)

After a lot of deep thought, Latisha *decided to* take the job offer in Moscow.

defend against
The small start-up *defended itself* against the hostile takeover.

define as
Perjury is *defined as* the act of lying while under oath.

delighted by
The woman was *delighted by* her daughter's impending solo flight.

demonstrate that
This evidence will *demonstrate that* dogs can do algebra.

depend on
Whether I go to the ballgame *depends on* the weather.

depict as
In recent textbooks, Columbus has been *depicted as* a genocidal maniac.

descend from
On the Fourth of July, lots of firecrackers *descend from* the sky.

different from
The customs of the countries in Asia are *different from* ours.

difficult to
It is *difficult to* determine whether mice can sing to each other.

distinguish [A] from [B]
Can you *distinguish* indigo *from* violet?

draw on
Surgeons *draw on* years of experience when they try new procedures.

due to
The company's shortfall was *due to* lessening global demand for its products.

[in an] effort to
In an effort to end the war, the general called for a cease-fire.

either...or
I will *either* read the paper *or* go to the movies.

enamored with
When my family met my new girlfriend, everyone was *enamored with* her.

encourage to
Recent college graduates are *encouraged to* work for five years before applying to business school.

-er than
My biceps are strong*er than* your biceps.

estimate to be
The estate of Count von Hammerbanger is *estimated to be* in the billions.

expose to
Parents are worried that television *exposed* their children *to* too much violence.

extend to
I *extended* my arm *to* the dog and let it lick my palm.

extent of
No one knows the *extent of* the queen's fortune.

fear that
I *fear that* robots will take over the world in 2013.

fluctuations in
There have been many *fluctuations in* the new company's growth pattern.

forbid to (not forbid from)
Native South Koreans are *forbidden to* attend gambling casinos within Korea.

force to
My parents *forced* me *to* attend military school, even though I didn't want to go.

frequency of
The *frequency of* electrical fires on the subway is truly alarming.

from [A] to [B]
Every house *from* Allentown *to* Bethlehem lost power during the blackout.

hypothesize that
Some nutritionists *hypothesize that* too many dairy products can cause cancer.

in contrast to
In contrast to my opponent, I believe that town funds should be used to build a new library.

in danger of
People who ignore speed limits put themselves *in danger of* causing an accident.

in order to
You have to break a few eggs *in order to* make an omelet.

in violation of
By mistreating the prisoners, the general was *in violation of* the rules laid out by the Geneva Convention.

inclined to (also disinclined to)
Young children who watch television are *inclined to* become very lazy adults.

infected with
People who are *infected with* the Ebola virus must be isolated from other patients.

instead of
Today I will eat a salad *instead of* my usual meal of meat and potatoes.

introduce to
My mother almost fainted when she was *introduced to* Frank Sinatra.

isolate from
People who are infected with the Ebola virus must be *isolated from* other patients.

just as ... so too
Just as my family managed to learn English, *so too* will many other immigrants who are new to America.

less than
On average, college students have *less* money *than* their parents do.

likely to (also unlikely to)
Whenever I eat Brussels sprouts, I'm *likely to* get sick.

liken to
The clerk *likened* the man's complaints *to* the barking of a small dog.

mistake for
My brother is often *mistaken for* Robin Williams.

model after
The Rotunda at the University of Virginia is *modeled after* the Pantheon in Rome.

more than
The Chinese eat *more* rice *than* any other people do.

move away from
The police officer told the intruder to *move away from* the door.

native to
Koala bears are *native to* Australia.

a native of
The famous opera singer is a *native of* Italy.

neither ... nor
Neither rain *nor* sleet shall keep me from the swift completion of my appointed rounds.

not [A] but [B]
The opposite of love is *not* hate *but* indifference.

not only but also
My sister is *not only* brilliant *but also* quite charming.

not so much ... as
The reason for the soaring stock market is *not so much* ignorance *as* it is optimism.

on account of
On account of the brutal winter, the farmer's corn production suffered greatly.

opportunity for [noun]
Before I take this job, tell me my *opportunity for* advancement.

opportunity to [verb]
I'd like to take this *opportunity to* thank all the little people who made this award possible.

opposed to
Pacifists are *opposed to* any form of fighting or aggression.

opposite of
The *opposite of* love is not hate but indifference.

permit to
Children are not *permitted to* attend an R-rated movie without a parent.

persuade to
I finally *persuaded* my parents *to* let me attend the rock concert.

predisposed to
Baby turtles are *predisposed to* fend for themselves early in life.

pressure to
The United Nations was *pressured to* impose sanctions on the country.

prevent from
Safety latches *prevent* small children *from* playing with cleaning products.

prized by
Rhinoceros horn is *prized by* some cultures as a potent aphrodisiac.

prohibit from
In New York City, smokers are *prohibited from* smoking inside any public building.

protect against
Chemical treatment can help *protect* your car *against* rust and corrosion.

provide with
The technical college *provides* each new student *with* a brand new computer.

question whether
I'm beginning to *question whether* saltines have any nutritional value.

range from [A] to [B]
Scores on the TOEIC *range from* 10 to 990.

rather than
I'd *rather* swim in the ocean *than* sit on the beach.

regard as
In Asian cities, waving crazily for a taxicab is *regarded as* a rude gesture.

replace with
The five-star restaurant *replaced* its homemade desserts *with* frozen ones.

required of
What exactly is *required of* the applicants for this job?

require to
Grandma always *requires* us *to* remove our shoes before we come in the house.

responsibility to (verb)
I have the *responsibility to* care for my dog.

responsible for (noun)
I am *responsible for* my dog's welfare.

result from
Success usually *results from* hard work.

result in
Hard work usually *results in* success.

rule that (subjunctive)
The principal has *ruled that* all students can call her by her first name, Maria.

the same as
Your hat is *the same as* mine.

see as
The dictator *saw* the uprising *as* a threat to his authority.

send to
I *sent* a birthday card *to* my grandmother.

sense of
Dogs have an acute *sense of* smell.

so [adjective] as to [verb]
Her debts are *so* extreme *as to* threaten the future of the company.

so ... that
His debts are *so* extreme *that* the company may soon go bankrupt.

spend on
I *spend* more than $10,000 a year *on* eating out.

subject to
Members of Congress are *subject to* the same laws as are ordinary Americans.

substitute [A] for [B]
In an effort to lower my cholesterol, I *substituted* margarine *for* butter in my diet.

suffer from
I *suffer from* the heartbreak of psoriasis.

superior to
My grandfather's spaghetti sauce is *superior to* that store-bought brand.

supplant by
After the massive cutbacks at the plant, my uncle was *supplanted by* a large robot.

suspicious of
I'm *suspicious of* people who don't shake hands firmly.

target at
The shoe company *targeted* its advertising *at* high school-aged kids.

the -er, the -er
The bigg*er* they are, *the* hard*er* they fall.

the use of
The use of atomic weapons in World War II was condemned by many nations.

the way to [verb] is to [verb]
The way to deal with my father-in-law *is to* nod enthusiastically at everything he says.

think of ... as
I've grown to *think of* my best friend *as* the brother I never had.

threaten to
After ten hours of negotiations, both parties *threatened to* walk out of the room.

train to
I *trained* my puppy *to* bring me the newspaper every morning.

transmit to
The submarine *transmitted* the coded message *to* all the ships in the area.

try to (not try and)
If you *try to* hold your breath for more than a minute, your face will turn blue.

type of
This is the *type of* situation that I usually try to avoid.

use as
My wife hates it when I *use* the lamp *as* a hat stand.

view as
The dictator *viewed* the uprising *as* a threat to his authority.

vote for
Rather than *vote for* the Democrat or Republican, I voted for the Libertarian.

willing to (also unwilling to)
Most teachers are *willing to* meet with their students after school and give extra help.

worry about
Economists *worry* too much *about* America's trade deficit.

PLAY LIST FOR AUDIO CDs

CD #1		
Track	Content	Time
	Test 1	
1	Part I	00:10:00
2	Part II	00:11:00
3	Part III	00:13:00
4	Part IV	00:10:00
	Drills	
5	Voice Emphasis Drill	00:05:00
6	Photographs Example	00:00:20
7	Photographs Drill	00:05:00
8	Question & Response Example	00:00:30
9	Question & Response Drill	00:05:00

CD #2		
Track	Content	Time
	Test 2	
1	Part I	00:09:00
2	Part II	00:11:00
3	Part III	00:13:00
4	Part IV	00:10:00
	Drills	
5	Short Conversations Example	00:00:45
6	Short Conversations Example	00:06:00
7	Short Talks Example	00:05:00
8	Short Talks Drill	00:01:00

ABOUT THE AUTHORS

ELIZABETH ROLLINS has been teaching and researching standardized tests for The Princeton Review since 1995. She lives with her family in New York City.

NOTES

NOTES

More expert advice from  The Princeton Review

Give yourself the best chances for getting into the business school of your choice with The Princeton Review. We can help you get higher test scores, make the most informed choices, and make the most of your experience once you get there. We can also help you make the career move that will let you use your skills and education to their best advantage.

Available at Bookstores Everywhere.

www.PrincetonReview.com